VEGETABLE GARDEN
Almanac & Planner

GREEN WAGON BOOK

Written and edited by Stephen Albert

Cover design: Nada Orlić
Illustrations: Dušan Pavlić
Interior design: Ljiljana Pavkov

Green Wagon Books
#615 8930 Sonoma Highway
Kenwood, California, 95452

Disclaimer:
The information in this book is true and complete to the best of our knowledge. Great care has been taken to be as accurate as possible. All information is made without guarantee on the part of the author or publisher. This book is for educational purposes only. It is not a substitute for the advice of a health care professional. The author and publisher disclaim any liability in connection with any errors or omissions or for the use of this information. Neither the author nor the publisher can be held responsible for claims arising for the mistaken identity of plants or their appropriate use. The author and publisher do not assume responsibility for any sickness or death, or other harmful effects resulting from eating or using any plant described in this book. There are thousands of varieties of vegetables, fruits, and herbs; we have not addressed all of them. As well, many plants have similar appearances. Use full caution when harvesting and eating plants you are unfamiliar with. The author and publisher cannot be held responsible for not including all of the food plant varieties available.

VEGETABLE GARDEN

Almanac & Planner

A SEASONAL MONTH-BY-MONTH GARDENER'S GUIDE

STEPHEN ALBERT

Table of Contents

Introduction

Welcome to the Vegetable Garden Almanac and Planner.

This book is a month-by-month region-by-region guide to growing vegetables in the home garden. It will give you a substantial chronological list of things to do—when to plant indoors and outdoors, when to water and feed your crops, what pests and diseases you might expect and how to deal with them, and when to harvest your crops and how to store them.

You can use this book as a handy quick reference to help you do what needs to be done and when. If you are an experienced vegetable gardener you can refer to the suggestions and tasks listed as helpful reminders. If you are new to vegetable gardening, you can use this book as a learning tool, a primer of what to do and when to do it.

This guide is a year-round reference. You can pick this book up any month of the year and find timely suggestions for your region of the country and your garden. While this book is geared to gardeners in the United States and Canada and references the United States Department of Agriculture Hardiness Zones similar zones exist throughout the world (see Appendix 3, pages 171-180 for regions and corresponding hardiness zones); you can use this book anywhere in the world.

How to Use This Book

Months and Seasons:

This book is divided into 12 chapters one for each month of the year. The 12 monthly chapters—January through December—in turn, reference the four seasons of the year—Winter, Spring, Summer, and Autumn. Because each of the four seasons last about 3 months in most parts of the country each season can be divided into early, mid-, and late and matched with its corresponding month of the year. When you turn to a chapter by month you will find the season that corresponds:

- January = mid-winter
- February = late winter

- March = early spring
- April = mid-spring
- May = late spring
- June = early summer
- July = mid-summer
- August = late summer
- September = early autumn
- October = mid-autumn
- November = late autumn
- December = early winter

At the start of each chapter there will be a list of seasonal topics for that month and season—planting, harvest, and maintenance suggestions with page number.

Hardiness Zones:

Within each chapter, planting, harvest, and maintenance topics and suggestions are grouped mainly by hardiness zone. Hardiness is a term commonly used to describe a plant's ability to tolerate and survive low temperatures. The U.S. Department of Agriculture has divided the United States and Canada into 12 zones. Zone 1 has very cold winter temperatures and Zone 12 is tropical year round. See Appendix 3 pages 171-180 to determine which hardiness zone you live in. You also can learn which zone you live in by calling a local garden center or nursery or the Cooperative Extension Service nearest you.

Here's how the USDA zones are mostly defined in the continental United States:

- USDA Zones 3, 4, 5, 6 are the most northern and coldest winter regions of the continental United States (zones 1 and 2 are in far northern Canada and Alaska). The northern parts of the Rocky Mountains, northern Plains and Midwest States and the northern regions of the Northeast and into Canada fall into zones 3 and 4; the southern range of these regions—the lower Midwest and southern Plains—fall into zones 5 and 6. Temperature lows in the coldest areas of Zone 3 can drop as low as -40°F (-40°C). For reference, Eastern Europe is largely Zone 5 and Zone 6.

- USDA Zone 7 includes coastal parts of the Northeast, Mid-Atlantic region, and eastern inland sections of the Northwest. Zone 7 is also found in other parts of the country. Temperature lows in the coldest of these regions can drop to 0°F in winter. Some southern regions of Europe are in Zone 7.

- USDA Zone 8 includes the Mid-South, coastal Pacific Northwest states and parts of Northern California. Much of the United Kingdom, France and parts of Spain are in Zone 8. The western regions of Germany are in Zone 8. Winter temperature lows in Zone 8 fall to about 10°F.

- USDA Zones 9 and 10 include the Gulf Coast and parts of the South Atlantic states, the Pacific Southwest—mainly Southern California, and parts of the Desert states. Winter lows in Zone 9 can drop to about 20°F and in Zone 10 to 30°F on occasion. In Europe, the southern parts of Spain and France, Italy, and regions of countries bordering the Mediterranean Sea are in Zones 9 and 10.

- USDA Zone 11 is found in just a few places in the continental United States—mostly in far southern Florida and California. Hawaii is in Zone 12 as are parts of central and southern Mexico.

Zone-ratings are not exclusive to the geographical regions described above. Elevation can sometimes factor into zone designations. High elevations in southern regions may experience winter cold that will put a specific location into a hardiness zone commonly found much farther north.

Here's a quick reference chart listing the USDA Hardiness Zones and the average low temperatures each winter in each zone. Also listed are a few select cities for each zone (see Appendix 3, pages 171-180 for a city or town near you).

Zone	From	To	Select cities and towns in this zone
2	-50°F	-40°F	Fairbanks
3	-40°F	-30F	Edmonton, Prince Albert
4	-30°F	-20°F	Anchorage, Butte, Calgary, Fargo, Eau Claire, Fargo, Grafton , Minneapolis, Sioux Falls
5	-20°F	-10°F	Albuquerque, Bangor, Bennington, Cheyenne, Chicago, Denver, Des Moines, Indianapolis, Lincoln
6	-10°F	-0°F	Buffalo, Boise, Boston, Cincinnati, Detroit, Knoxville, Parkersburg, Salt Lake City, Scranton, Topeka
7	0°F	10°F	Atlanta, Baltimore, Bridgeport, Dover, Little Rock, Louisville, Reno, Richmond, Tulsa, Tupelo
8	10°F	20°F	Charleston, Charlotte, Eugene, Jacksonville, Mobile, New Orleans, Seattle
9	20°F	30°F	Corpus Christi, Houston, Las Vegas, Phoenix, San Antonio, Tampa
10	30°F	40°F	Los Angeles, San Diego
11a	40°F	50°F	Hilo, Miami

Frost Dates and Growing Season:

Also important to know as you plan your vegetable garden year is the length of the growing season. The growing season each year falls between the last frost in spring and the first frost in autumn. The last and first frost dates do not fall on the same calendar date each year (nature can be fickle)—so to plan the garden year, gardeners commonly use the average date of the last frost in spring and first frost in autumn. The average dates are based on historical temperature averages—usually the average dates over the past 10 years.

Almost without exception, these averages can be used to plan the growing season—its start, middle, and end—though, again, the exact dates will vary from year to year. (See Appendix 3 for the average first and last frost dates and the average length of the growing season near where you live; these averages are given in the same chart as hardiness zones.)

All of the above said, in most regions of the United States the average date of the last frost in spring usually comes at the mid-point of late spring; for the great majority of locations this is just before or after mid-May. A few weeks after the last frost, after night time temperatures have moderated, early summer begins. And in most regions, the average date of the first frost in autumn comes in mid-autumn—usually between Halloween and Thanksgiving. And a few weeks after the first frost, as frost and freezing weather become more common, winter begins.

Finally, Experience!

Gardening is not an exact science. Many factors are at work in a garden besides temperature—the direction of the sun, the amount of sun and shade over the course of the day, moisture and humidity, slope and elevation, soil type, day length and anything else that impacts plants in the garden. Keep in mind: no two gardens are the same; the vegetable garden across the fence from you may exist in a slightly different microclimate; it may warm in spring a few days earlier or later than your garden; it may cool down in autumn a few days earlier or later than your garden. Here's a suggestion: learn from your experience. As you garden each month and garden through the year take notes; keep a garden diary or journal that you can refer back to next year. Over the course of a few years you will begin to see patterns. (There are some helpful worksheets to do this at the end of this book.) Those patterns can be used with some predictability.

The suggestions in this book are based on experience. You can use them with a good sense of predictability to grow your vegetable garden.

Get-Started Worksheet:

Now to start using this book, fill in this worksheet. You can use the answers to these simple questions to pinpoint the growing information you need in the monthly chapters that follow. If you need help completing this worksheet, turn to Appendix 3, pages 171-180.

Location of my garden:

Hardiness zone:

Last average frost date in spring:

First average frost date in autumn:

Number of days in the growing days:

(The number of days between the last and first frost on average.)

An important note: the natural growing season can be lengthened by using season extending devices such as cloches, row covers, polyethylene/plastic hoop tunnels, and cold frames before the last frost in spring and after the first frost in autumn. How to use these devices is explained month-by-month.

January

Mid-Winter

Getting Ready for the Season

January is the coldest month of the year in the northern hemisphere. This is the month to get seed catalogs and begin planning the spring garden. Beware of false spring days. Check with the weather service or local cooperative extension or Appendix 3 in this book, pages 171-180 for your area's average last frost date–the last expected frost and the start of the outdoor sowing season; plan ahead now for indoor seed starting and planting out.

Where the weather is cold and the ground frozen, plan your garden and spring planting. Where the weather is mild—parts of the South, Southwest, and California—the new garden season can get underway early in the year. Begin preparing planting beds. Spread aged compost and manure across beds then fork or spade these amendments under. In mild-winter regions where the weather is not wet, seedlings or starts of broccoli, Brussels sprouts, cabbage, and cauliflower can be set in the garden and seeds of beets, carrots, celery, fava beans, kale, kohlrabi, lettuce, mustard, snow peas, radishes, shallots, and turnips can be sown.

PLANNING THE VEGETABLE GARDEN

Garden size. Your garden should be big enough to grow what you will eat or what you plan to store or give away. Don't make your garden any bigger–a garden too big will lead to a waste of food and time. Use a list of the crops that you want to bring to the table and the number of servings you have in mind for the season to decide on the number of seeds and plants to plant. (See Appendix 2, pages 166-167, for suggestions.)

Plan the garden layout; make a map. Use graph paper to plan and map your garden. Let squares on the graph represent square feet in the garden. As you design the garden, place perennial vegetables that remain several years in the garden–such as asparagus, horseradish, rhubarb, and artichokes–at one end of the garden in dedicated planting beds. Next place annual crops that will grow in the garden the whole season (10 to 20 or more weeks)–parsnips, carrots, onions, tomatoes, peppers, melons,

and winter squash. Finally, place crops that will be in the garden for just part of a season (about 6 to 10 weeks)—mostly root and leaf crops; these crops are often planted in the same spot more than once in succession over the course of a growing season. Place tall-growing crops, like pole beans, and vining tomatoes to the north of shorter crops; that way the taller crops will not shade the shorter crops. In your plan, give space to each crop according to the crops size at maturity—that is breadth or square feet required for each plant to reach maturity (see Appendix 2, pages 166-167, for crop size at maturity). Your garden plan/map should note important details such as shade from nearby buildings or trees, windy or breezy areas, and extra wet or dry spots in the garden. You can use trace paper set over your map to plot succession crops and crop rotations. Your trace paper overlays can help you plan early, midseason, and late plantings–the rows and beds.

Garden calendar. Keep a vegetable garden calendar to record when you start seeds indoors, the dates when you sow seeds or set out transplants in the garden. Note when you expect to harvest each crop. A large calendar with extra space each day for record keeping is ideal. Keep the calendar in the garden shed or next to the door that leads to the garden. Take a couple of minutes after each visit to the garden to jot down what you've attended to. Make notes on how your crops are growing. Note when you feed and water plants. Note when pests or diseases appear. Note when harvest comes and how long it lasts. The few minutes you take each day to mark your calendar will pay off late in the season, at harvest time, and as you plan the next growing season.

Tracking the season. Here are some important items to keep track of over the course of the garden season:

- **Seed sown and transplants planted:** Keep a record of the vegetables and varieties you plant and when. Note the planting beds or rows where each crop is planted on your garden map. Your record can include where and when you bought seeds and starts and how much they cost. You may also want to include planting bed preparation: soil tilling or digging, amendments and fertilizer added, and mulching.

- **Expected harvest times:** Count ahead the days to maturity for each crop and note on the calendar the anticipated harvest time for each crop sown. This will help you harvest your crops at the peak of maturity, tenderness, and flavor.

- **Watering and rainfall:** Note irrigation and rainfall so that you don't over or under water. Keep track of rainfall–note the extent of storms and the number of inches of rain that falls on the garden.

- **Fertilizing and weeding:** Note the type of fertilizer used and the amount. Note which weeds grew in the garden and when. How did you get rid of them?

- **Pest and disease control:** Note pests and diseases found in the garden, when they arrive, and how you dealt with them. Many pests and diseases are seasonal; a calendar can help you anticipate future problems.

- **Weather and temperature.** Note the weather and temperature regularly. These notes may help answer questions that come up later in the season. A cold spell after planting in spring, for example, can delay the harvest by weeks later in the season.

- **Harvest:** Note which crops performed well and which didn't. How much did each crop produce–the yield? Note the amounts used for canning and freezing–the pints and quarts yield. Note varieties to plant again in coming seasons.

- **Crop placement and rotation:** Use your garden map alongside your calendar to plan ahead. Planning succession crops throughout the season–which crops are short-staying and which are long-staying–will help you get the most out of your garden. (See the list of short-stayers and long-stayers later in this chapter, page 14.)

- **Soil records:** Note the soil pH in differing areas around the garden. Keep track of soil amendments you've added to planting beds. Was compost or manure added to the garden? Were cover crops planted? Note soil temperature each week, especially in late winter and spring.

- **Frost and freeze dates and season extension efforts:** When did the cold weather begin and end? When did you use plastic hoop tunnels or row covers to protect the crops? When did you plant in the plastic hoop tunnel or cold frame?

- **Garden cleanup:** When did crops come out of the garden and what extra effort was made to end the season or prepare for next season.

PLANNING THE SEASON CROP-BY-CROP

You can plan the growing season using the number of frost-free days in your region—that is the time between the last frost in spring and the first frost in autumn. Choose crops that will grow to maturity between the last frost in spring and the first frost in autumn. If you want to grow outside of the natural season plan to use season extending devices such as row covers, polyethylene/plastic hoop tunnels, and a cold frame. There will be several varieties to choose from after you decide which vegetables you want to grow; some varieties will be ready early in the season, some mid-season, and some later. Some vegetables are easily grown from seed sown directly in the garden; others are best started indoors where the temperature is controlled and later transplanted to the garden when outdoor temperatures are favorable.

Cool-season crops (do best when the temperature is about 55° to 70°F):

- Beets
- Broccoli
- Brussels sprouts
- Cabbage
- Carrots
- Cauliflower
- Celery
- Chinese cabbage
- Collards
- Endive, Escarole
- Garlic
- Kale
- Kohlrabi
- Leeks
- Lettuce
- Mustard
- Onions
- Parsnips
- Peas
- Radishes
- Rutabaga
- Shallots
- Spinach
- Swiss chard
- Turnips

Warm-season crops (do best when the temperature is about 65° to 80°F):

- Beans, snap
- Beans, lima
- Beans, shell (dry)
- Corn
- Cucumber
- Eggplant
- Melons
- New Zealand spinach
- Okra
- Peppers
- Potatoes
- Pumpkins
- Squash, summer
- Squash, winter
- Sunflowers
- Sweet potatoes
- Tomatillos
- Tomatoes
- Watermelons
- Zucchini

Vegetable for beginners: These crops are relatively easy to grow. They are good choices for beginning gardeners:

- Beets
- Beans
- Broccoli
- Brussels sprouts
- Cabbage
- Carrots
- Collards
- Corn
- Cucumbers
- Kale
- Kohlrabi
- Lettuce
- Onions
- Melons
- Peas
- Peppers
- Potatoes
- Pumpkins
- Rutabagas
- Summer squash
- Tomatoes
- Turnips

Short- and Long-Stay Vegetables

Vegetables that are in the garden 5 weeks or less:

- Garden cress
- Mustard
- Radishes

Vegetables that are in the garden 5 to 10 weeks:

- Bush beans
- Beets
- Carrots
- Sweet corn
- Corn salad
- Cucumber
- Dandelion
- Lettuce
- Onions sets
- Early peas
- Spinach
- Bush squash
- Swiss chard
- Turnips

Vegetables that are in the garden 10-15 weeks:

- Bush beans
- Bush and pole lima beans
- Broccoli
- Carrots, fall and winter

- Cauliflower
- Sweet corn, late varieties
- Endive and escarole
- Kale
- Kohlrabi
- Lettuce, Romaine
- Muskmelons
- Okra
- Parsley
- Peas, midseason and later
- Pumpkins
- Rutabaga
- Turnips
- Watermelons

Vegetables that are in the garden 15 to 20 or more weeks:

- Brussels sprouts
- Cabbage, fall and winter
- Cauliflower, fall and winter
- Celery
- Celeriac
- Eggplant
- Horseradish
- Leeks
- New Zealand spinach
- Onions, from seed
- Parsnips
- Peppers
- Potatoes
- Rutabaga
- Salsify
- Swiss chard
- Tomatoes

Vegetable plant families:

When planning your garden, keep in mind that members of the same plant family often have the same growing condition requirements—sun, nutrients, and water. Planting these crops close together at the same time of the year can make caring for your garden easier. Here are plant family members:

- **Cabbage family** (*Brassica/crucifer*): arugula, bok choy, broccoli, Brussels sprouts, cabbage, cauliflower, collards, daikon, garden cress, horseradish, kale, kohlrabi, mizuna, mustard, radish, rutabaga, tatsoi, turnip; all of these crops grow best in cool spring or autumn weather.

- **Bean family** (legume): garden peas and beans including kidney bean, navy bean, pinto bean, lima bean, adzuki bean, mung bean, scarlett runner bean, broad bean, lentil, peanut and also chickpea, cowpea, black-eyed pea and cover crops such as vetch and lupines; these crops generally prefer warm to very warm summer weather.

- **Tomato family** (*Solanaceae*): eggplant, pepper, potato, tomatillo, tomato; these crops demand warm to very warm summer weather.

- **Onion family** (*Allium*): chives, garlic, leek, onion, scallion, shallot; these crops prefer cool spring or autumn weather when they get started in the garden and warm summer weather at harvest time.
- **Carrot family** (*Apiaceae*): carrot, celeriac, celery, chervil, cilantro, dill, fennel, parsley, parsnip; these crops prefer cool to warm spring and autumn weather.

WHEN TO PLANT YOUR SPRING GARDEN

This chart will help you determine when to plant each crop directly in the garden this spring. It uses the middle of each month as a marker. If the date of your average last frost varies by a week or two in either direction then simply adjust the planting dates by a week or two. To learn more about the average last and first frost dates where you live see Appendix 3: Frost Dates and Growing Season on pages 171-180 at the end of this book.

When to plant:

Vegetables	If Last Frost in Spring Feb. 15	If Last Frost in Spring March 15	If Last Frost in Spring April 15	If Last Frost in Spring May 15
Arugula	Feb. 1—Mar. 1	Mar. 1—15	Apr. 1—May 1	May 15—June 1
Asparagus	——	Feb. 1—Mar. 10	Apr. 15—May 1	May 15—June 1
Asian greens	Feb. 1—Mar. 1	Mar. 1—15	Apr. 1—May 1	May 15—June 1
Beans - Lima	Mar. 1—May. 1	Apr. 1—15	May 15—June 1	May 15—June 15
Beans - snap	Mar. 1—May 1	Mar. 15—30	May 1—June 1	May 15—June 1
Beet	Jan. 20—Apr. 1	Mar. 1—15	Apr. 15—May 1	May 15—June 1
Broccoli	Jan. 15—Feb. 15	Feb. 15—Mar. 1	Mar. 15—Apr. 15	May 1—15
Brussels sprouts	Jan. 15—Feb. 15	Feb. 15—Mar. 1	Mar. 15—Apr. 15	May 1—15
Cabbage	Jan. 1—Feb. 25	Feb. 15—Mar. 1	Mar. 15—Apr. 15	May 1—15
Cardoon	Jan. 1—Feb. 1	Feb. 15—Mar. 1	Mar. 15—Apr. 15	May 1—15
Carrot	Feb. 1—Mar. 1	Mar. 1—15	Apr. 15—May 1	May 1—June 1
Cauliflower	Jan. 1—Feb. 1	Feb. 15—Mar. 1	Mar. 15—Apr. 15	May 1—15
Celery plants	Jan. 1—Feb. 1	Feb. 15—Mar. 1	Mar. 15—Apr. 15	May 1—15
Chinese cabbage	Jan. 1—Feb. 1	Feb. 15—Mar. 1	Mar. 15—Apr. 15	May 1—15
Chives	Jan. 1—Feb. 1	Feb. 15—Mar. 1	Mar. 15—Apr. 15	May 1—15
Claytonia	Jan. 1—Feb. 25	Feb. 15—Mar. 1	Mar. 15—Apr. 15	May 1—15
Collards	Jan. 1—Feb. 1	Feb. 15—Mar. 1	Mar. 15—Apr. 15	May 1—15
Corn	Feb. 15—Mar. 1	Mar. 15—Apr. 1	Apr. 15—May 15	May 15—June 15
Cress	Feb. 1—Mar. 1	Mar. 1—15	Apr. 1—May 1	May 15—June 1
Cucumber	Mar. 1—15	Apr. 1—15	May 1—June1	May 15—June 1
Dandelion	Jan. 1—Feb. 1	Feb. 1—Mar. 15	——	——
Eggplant plants	Mar. 1—15	Apr. 1—15	May 1—June 1	June 1—15
Endive/Escarole	Feb. 1—Mar. 1	Mar. 1—15	Apr. 1—May 1	May 15—June 1
Florence fennel	Feb. 1—Mar. 1	Mar. 1—15	Apr. 1—May 1	May 15—June 1

15

Vegetables	If Last Frost in Spring Feb. 15	If Last Frost in Spring March 15	If Last Frost in Spring April 15	If Last Frost in Spring May 15
Garlic	Jan. 1—Feb. 1	Feb. 15—Mar. 1	Mar. 15—Apr. 15	May 1—15
Horseradish	——	Mar. 15—Apr. 1	Apr. 15—May 1	May 15—June 1
Jerusalem artichoke	Jan. 1—Feb. 1	Feb. 15—Mar. 1	Mar. 15—Apr. 15	May 1—June 1
Kale	Jan. 1—Feb. 1	Feb. 15—Mar. 1	Mar. 15—Apr. 15	May 1—June 1
Kohlrabi	Feb. 1—Mar. 1	Mar. 1—15	Apr. 1—May 1	May 15—June 1
Leek	Jan. 1—Feb. 1	Feb. 15—Mar. 1	Mar. 15—Apr. 15	May 1—15
Lettuce	Feb. 1—Mar. 1	Mar. 1—15	Apr. 1—May 1	May 15—June1
Mâche	Feb. 1—Mar. 1	Mar. 1—15	Apr. 1—May 1	May 15—June 1
Muskmelon	Mar. 1—15	Apr. 1—15	May 1—June 1	June 1—15
Mustard	Feb. 1—Mar. 1	Mar. 1—15	Apr. 1—May 1	May 15—June 1
Okra	Feb. 1—Mar. 1	Mar. 15—30	May 1—15	——
Onion plants	Jan. 1—Feb. 1	Feb. 15—Mar. 1	Mar. 15—Apr. 15	May 1—15
Onion seeds	Feb. 1—Mar. 1	Mar. 1—15	Apr. 1—May 1	May 15—June1
Onion sets	Jan. 1—Feb. 1	Feb. 15—Mar. 1	Mar. 15—Apr. 15	May 1—15
Parsley	Feb. 1—Mar. 1	Mar. 1—15	Apr. 1—May 1	May 15—June 1
Parsnip	Feb. 1—Mar. 1	Mar. 1—15	Apr. 1—May 1	May 15—June 1
Peas	Jan. 1—Feb. 1	Feb. 15—Mar. 1	Mar. 15—Apr. 15	May 1—June 1
Pepper plants	Mar. 1—15	Apr. 1—15	May 1—June 1	——
Potato	Jan. 1—Feb. 1	Feb. 15—Mar. 1	May 1—June 1	May 1—June 1
Pumpkin	Mar. 1—15	Apr. 1—15	May 1—June 1	——
Radish	Jan. 1—Feb. 1	Feb. 15—Mar. 1	Mar. 15—Apr. 15	May 1—15
Rhubarb plants	——	——	Apr. 1—May 1	May 1—June 1
Rutabaga	Mar. 1—Mar. 15	Apr. 1—15	May 1—June 1	June 1—15
Salsify	Feb. 1—Mar. 1	Mar. 1—15	Apr. 15—May 1	May 1—June 1
Scallions	Jan. 1—Feb. 1	Feb. 15—Mar. 1	Mar. 15—Apr. 15	May 1—15
Shallots	Jan. 1—Feb. 1	Feb. 15—Mar. 1	Mar. 15—Apr. 15	May 1—15
Sorrel	Jan. 1—Feb. 1	Mar. 1—Apr. 1	Apr. 1—15	May 1—15
Spinach	Feb. 1—Mar. 1	Mar. 1—15	Mar. 15—Apr. 15	May 1—15
Squashes	Mar. 1—15	Apr. 1—15	May 1—June 1	June 1—15
Sweet potato	Mar. 1—15	Apr. 1—15	May 1—June 1	——
Swiss chard	Jan. 1—Feb. 1	Feb. 15—Mar. 1	Mar. 15—Apr. 15	May 1—15
Tomatillo plants	Mar. 1—15	Apr. 1—15	May 1—June 1	——
Tomato plants	Mar. 1—15	Apr. 1—15	May 1—June 1	June 15—30
Turnips	Mar. 1—15	Apr. 1—15	May 1—June 1	June 1—15
Watermelon	Mar. 1—15	Apr. 1—15	May 1—June 1	June 1—15

ABOUT SEEDS

Shop seed catalogs. Winter is the time to look through seed catalogs for crops to plant this coming spring. Look for seeds that will do well in your region and also seeds that are disease and pest resistant. Look for seeds that you can start early in the season—vegetable varieties that are cold tolerant. Look also for varieties that can withstand hot weather if you live in a hot summer region. Make a list of crops you want to grow. Seed catalogs usually list days to maturity and size at maturity; this information will be helpful when you map out your season and garden.

Vegetable varieties suggested in this book. You will find many specific vegetable varieties listed in Appendix 5, pages 186-197. Nearly all of the suggested varieties recommended here will be easy to find at a nearby garden center, nursery, or online. Nearly all of the varieties suggested in this book are tried-and-true standards. Some are heirlooms that have been grown by vegetable gardeners for generation. Others are relatively new hybrids that have proven to be winners in the garden.

Which crops to grow? When planning your crops for the coming year, plan a mix of varieties that you have grown before and at least one or two varieties that you have never grown. If you are beginner, take another look at easy-to-grow crops for beginners listed earlier in this chapter. Consider varieties that are good for freezing or canning if you want to put up vegetables at the end of the season. If specific pests or diseases are common in your area, choose pest or disease resistant varieties.

Growing from seed or starts. Plants started by a grower are more expensive than seed. If you want to save money, grow from seed. Buy started plants if you don't have the time or inclination to grow from seed. Buy started plants if you don't have the room to start seed indoors.

Growing from seed schedule. In most parts of the country, most seeds can be started in the garden from March through June; if you want a head start on the season plan to sow indoors 6 to 8 weeks before the last frost. In hot summer regions where drought and mid-summer heat are extreme (most of Florida and Texas and the Southwest) you will want to start seed of hardy cool-season crops directly in the garden between December and March; that means starting seed indoors even earlier.

Buying seeds that grow where you live. When buying seed packets check out where the seeds were grown. If they come from a regional seed grower somewhere near where you live you can be assured the seed will grow well in your garden. If they come from far away, do a bit of research to make sure they grow well in all parts of the country. Seed packets that have the All-America Selections (AAS) shield are seed varieties that have been evaluated in test gardens all over the country; they should grow just fine in your garden.

Seed packet knowledge. A seed packet or plant label should give you basic growing information. Look for the following:

- Days to maturity: how many days from seed sowing to harvest.
- Best soil temperature for germination.
- Days to germination and sprouting.
- Best temperature range for growing.
- Best soil type for growing and soil pH.
- Size of plant at maturity—height and breadth.
- Pest and disease resistance.
- Heat, cold, and drought resistance.
- Flavor and use fresh, frozen, or canned.

Check seed packet for days to maturity or harvest and soil temperature needed for germination and growing.

Open-pollinated, hybrid, and heirloom plants. Seed catalogs and packets commonly note if the plant is OP or F1. OP stands for open-pollinated and F1 is short for F1 hybrid. There are, for example, both OP and F1 tomatoes. What's the difference? Open-pollinated plants are genetically stable meaning that the seed from an open-pollinated plant will grow nearly identical or "true" to its parent. When you grow from OP seed you can save seed from that plant at the end of the season and plant it next year to get a plant almost identical to the one grown this year. F1 hybrid plants are bred by plant scientists to have desirable qualities—size, color, yield, disease resistance. But F1 hybrids are genetically unstable and the seed saved from a hybrid will not grow true to its parent—it often grows to be much inferior. So if you want to grow hybrids, you must buy newly bred seed each season; you can't save hybrid seed. Heirloom varieties are open-pollinated plants that have usually been grown for many generations by gardeners who save the seed and pass it on to friends and the next generation.

Seed viability. Seeds more than a year or two old may not germinate well or at all, particularly if they have not been stored properly. Some seeds, even after a year of proper storage, may not produce the number of plants you expect or need. To test seed for germination viability, place two paper towels on top of each other and moisten them with warm water. Next place 10 or 20 seeds in the middle of the towels. Fold the towels over from the four corners to the center. Place the towels in a jar or large drinking glass with about 1 inch of water in the bottom–enough to keep the towels moist without submerging the seeds. Cover the glass with a clear plastic bag and set it in a warm place. After the average number of days to germination, unwrap the towel and count the number of seeds that have germinated. If none have sprouted re-wrap the towel and replace it in the glass and wait several more days. If seeds have sprouted, count the number of sprouts and divide by the total number of seeds on the towel—that will be the germination percentage rate. That will give you a good estimate of the germination rate for that batch of seeds and the success you can expect when you sow in the garden.

Seed life

Here is a short guide to how long vegetable seeds are viable:

- **1-2 years:** carrots, celeriac, celery, corn, leeks, onions, parsley, parsnip, scallions, shallots
- **3-4 years:** beans, beets, broccoli, Brussels sprouts, cabbage, collards, eggplant, kale, lettuce, peas, peppers, pumpkins, squash, tomatoes
- **5-6 years:** cucumbers, melons, radishes, spinach

PLANTING ZONE-BY-ZONE: Mid-Winter / January

Slow and No Growth Period: No plant growth will occur outdoors during the days when there is less than 10 hours of sunlight. This period occurs over several weeks during early, mid- and late winter depending upon where you live. Plants and seeds in the garden during this period will sit idle; plants will resume growth when there are more than 10 hours of sunlight during the day. During the no growth period, protect crops from freezing temperatures by covering them with straw or protecting them under a plastic hoop tunnel or cold frame. When hours of sunlight each day grow to more than 10 hours, plants will resume their growth towards maturity

Beginning with the warmest regions first, here is a seed starting and planting guide for mid-winter—January. Note: it is safe to plant or do any of the tasks listed for regions cooler than yours.

USDA Zone 10: No frost regions

- Sow cool-season vegetable seeds in a cold frame or plastic tunnel.
- Start warm-season vegetable seeds indoors; start seeds of tomatoes, peppers, and eggplants indoors.
- Direct seed greens, beets, carrots, and peas in the garden.
- Set out transplants of onions, potatoes, cabbage and broccoli.
- Plant edible flowers such as pansies and violas in the garden and containers.

USDA Zone 9: Low frost regions

- Sow cool-season seeds indoors in pots and flats or outdoors by mid-month. Cool-season crops include beets, carrots, cabbage family members, lettuce, peas, and spinach. Expect slow growing while the days are still short.
- Sow indoors tomato, pepper, and eggplant seeds by mid-month. Late in the month start indoors melons, cucumber, and squash seed.
- Purchase and prepare seed potatoes; cut into pieces if large and dust with sulfur and pre-sprout in preparation for planting.

USDA Zone 7-8: some freezing possible and frost likely

- Plan seed orders and get seeds ordered right away.
- Start seeds of cabbage, hardy lettuces, and onions indoors under bright lights. When plants are about 4 inches tall set them out in the garden under cloches or plastic milk jugs and harden them off.
- Harden-off cool-season transplants including cabbage and broccoli started indoors last month.
- Set out transplants of broccoli, cabbage, spinach and lettuce.
- Outdoors late in the month, sow seeds of arugula bok choy, fennel, carrot, radishes, spinach, beets, turnips, peas.
- Plant outdoors dill, parsley, cilantro, and chervil from seed or transplants.
- Shop for asparagus crowns, artichokes, rhubarb, and strawberry roots; plant them when the soil is workable.
- Plant in the garden asparagus crowns and strawberry roots.
- Set seed potatoes in a bright spot indoors to encourage sprouting.
- Clean out the cold frame and get ready for early spring seed starting.
- Collect plastic milk jugs to use as cloches.
- Be prepared to protect plants from freeze and frost with straw mulch, fleece row covers, or plastic hoop tunnels.
- Sow winter cover crops late this month if you don't need planting beds for early crops.

- Remove winter weeds and plant debris from garden.
- Cut back dried asparagus fronds if not done last autumn.
- Weed and fertilize asparagus and strawberry beds.
- Top dress vacant garden beds with aged compost and manure to prepare them for planting.
- Water plants in the garden as needed if winter is dry.

USDA Zone 5-6: freezing temperatures likely; snow possible

- Order seeds for cool-season crops: broccoli, cabbage, cauliflower, spinach, celery, lettuce, parsley, and peas.
- Get seed-starting supplies and equipment together.
- Mid-month start indoors seeds of broccoli, Brussels sprouts, cabbage, cauliflower, leeks, and onions indoors.
- Outdoors under cover direct seed: arugula, cabbage, carrots, chard, kale, lettuce, mâche, parsnips, and hardy herbs including oregano, marjoram, and thyme.
- Prepare the cold frame. Mound straw or leaves around the outside of the cold frame to help it begin holding solar heat.

USDA Zone 3-4: very cold region: snow and ice likely

- Begin seed ordering from catalogs.
- Check viability of old seeds by sprouting a few of each kind in folded damp paper towels enclosed in a plastic bag.
- Get seed-starting supplies and equipment together.
- Grow herbs indoors
- Grow micro-greens and sprouts.

MID-WINTER GARDEN CHECKLIST

- Make a garden plan for the coming season; note garden dimensions and planting beds.

- Review garden notes from last season and update planting map.
- Create your new garden map and planting schedule.
- Plan crop rotations and successions for the upcoming season.
- Inventory old seeds and order new seeds for the coming year.
- Check viability of stored seeds.
- Clean and organize seed starting supplies.
- Check supplies of fertilizers and organic sprays; replace any that are outdated.
- Get soil tested if not done last autumn.
- Renew mulch in areas where it is thinning.
- Prepare planting beds if weather permits.
- Keep an eye on the weather and forecasts; protect plants with row covers if temperatures will be below 28°F.
- Water plants well before freezing temperatures occur; make sure plants are mulched to protect them from cold.
- Ventilate cold frame when daytime temperatures warm to 60°F or warmer.
- Organize, clean, and sharpen garden tools.

MID-WINTER THINGS TO DO

Check stored onions, potatoes, garlic and winter squashes to make sure all are intact and viable. Dispose of any stored crops that are soft or starting to rot. The green tops of onions that have sprouted while in storage can be used in the kitchen as you would scallions or green onions.

Order seeds. Make sure you have the seeds you need for the coming season. Make sure you have enough seeds for succession plantings. Purchase or order seeds now.

Asparagus crowns. The bare-root asparagus roots or crowns for sale at the garden center or nursery are usually one year old, but some growers sell two-year-old crowns. Older crowns mature more quickly. Asparagus crowns are either male or female; male plants produce thicker spears; female spear produce more spears, but the spears are thinner.

Disinfect used seed-starting containers by washing them with a 10 percent bleach solution (1 part bleach to 9 parts water).

Herbs to start indoors. Basil, chives, cilantro, dill, and oregano can be started indoors in January. You can grow these herbs in a sunny window in small containers. After the last frost, herbs started indoors can be transplanted to the garden or into larger pots for the patio.

Mealybugs. If you are growing herbs or other plants indoors keep an eye out for mealybugs. Mealybugs are very small soft, oval insects that are usually covered with a white or gray waxy fluff. A mealybug is about 1/10 of an inch long. They are usually found in colonies often along stems or at the base of leaves. Mealybugs suck the juices from plants and leave behind excrement called honeydew. Honeydew excreted by mealybugs supports the growth of sooty mold fungus. Spray infested plants with stiff stream of water or soapy water, or spray with insecticidal soap.

HARVEST BY ZONE:
Mid-Winter / January

Most crops coming to harvest in January were planted late last summer or in autumn. They overwintered in the garden or were grown under cover.

- **USDA Zones 7-10:** arugula, Asian greens, beets, broccoli, Brussels sprouts, cabbage, carrots, cauliflower, celery, chervil, chives, cilantro, collards, fennel , green onions, Jerusalem artichokes, kale, leeks, lettuce, mâche, mustard, parsley, parsnips, peas, potatoes, radicchio, radishes, sorrel, spinach, strawberries, Swiss chard, thyme, turnips.

- **USDA Zones 4-6:** arugula, beets greens, broccoli, Brussels sprouts, cabbage, chicory, Chinese cabbage, carrots, chives, garlic, Jerusalem artichokes, kale, leeks, mâche, parsnips, radicchio, spinach, Swiss chard, baby turnips.

- **Crops in storage:** beets, cabbage, carrots, celeriac, garlic, kohlrabi, onions, parsnips, potatoes, rutabaga, sweet potatoes, turnips, and winter squash. Inspect stored vegetables and fruits and discard any that show signs of decay.

February

Late Winter

Early Start

February is a busy month for the vegetable gardener. In many regions, indoor and outdoor sowing and planting will begin. Gardeners in warm regions already have seed in the ground. In cold regions, where there is snow on the ground, February is still the time for making plans and preparing for spring. Here are some things you can do this month to get your garden growing:

Plan and design. Plan the spring and summer garden on paper. Sketch a base plan. Keep in mind that vegetables require at least 6 hours of sun each day to thrive. Be sure to locate your garden near a water source. Consider the location of house, garage, shed, fences, walls, and large trees that will cast shadows across the garden. Map where the snow melts first, these will be good spots for planting early crops. Consider the sunlight, water, and nutrient needs of each crop and crop family. Plan to plant crops with similar needs or crops from the same plant family close together. (See the list of plant families on page 14—in January.) If you've grown a vegetable garden before consider growing at least one crop that you've never grown before. Consult garden books and seed catalogs for suggestions.

Consider your time and effort. If your time and space is limited, choose just five or six vegetables to grow this year. You'll get the most for your money and effort from tomatoes, snap beans, carrots, and greens such as lettuce and chard.

Indoor seed sowing in cold regions. Check seed packets to determine the number of days from seed sowing to germination and sprouting. Sow cool-weather spring corps first: beets, cabbage, kale, broccoli, celeriac, leaf lettuce, bulb onions, parsley, radish, spinach, and turnips. These crops are called "hardy" because they go into the garden early in the season when the weather is still chilly— in the 40s and 50sF. You can start these crops 6 to 8 weeks before you transplant them into the garden; that means they can start indoors while outdoor temperatures are still in the 20s and 30sF.

At the end of the month, sow indoors the seeds of tender warm-weather summer-harvest vegetables such as eggplants, peppers, and tomatoes. These crops require 10 to 12 weeks or more indoors before they are transplanted into the garden. (These crops are called "tender" because they cannot withstand chilly temperatures like cold-tolerant "hardy" vegetables.)

Sow seeds in small containers or seed starting trays that have individual cells. Fill each cell with commercial seed-starting mix. Set seed-starting containers under bright fluorescent lights (shop lights will work) or grow lights which mimic sunlight.

Time indoor seed sowing so that 4- to 6-week-old plants can be transplanted into the garden when outdoor temperatures are right for that crop.

Start seed in the cold frame or plastic hoop tunnel in mild-winter regions. Sow cool-weather spring crops in the cold frame or under a plastic hoop tunnel: beets, broccoli, cabbage, cauliflower, celery, lettuce and salad greens, onions, and parsley. Make sure that the soil in the seedbed is not overly nitrogen rich; this will cause succulent, leggy growth when early season plants are better strong and stocky. Warm-season crops such as peppers and tomatoes can be started indoors this month. Time the indoor sowing of warm-season crops with the average date of the last frost in spring in mind; warm-season crops can go into the garden in the week or two after the last frost.

WHERE TO START CROPS –INDOORS AND OUT

Vegetables best started indoors:
- Broccoli
- Brussels sprouts
- Cabbage
- Cauliflower
- Eggplants
- Leeks
- Melons
- Onions
- Peppers
- Squash
- Tomatoes

Vegetables to direct sow in the garden:
- Beans
- Beets
- Carrots
- Chard
- Collards
- Corn
- Cucumbers
- Dill

- Kale
- Lettuce
- Melons
- Mustard
- Okra
- Onion sets
- Peas
- Potatoes, seed
- Radishes
- Rutabagas
- Spinach
- Squash
- Turnips
- Watermelon

Vegetables to buy as young plants:
- Broccoli
- Brussels sprouts
- Cabbage
- Cauliflower
- Celery
- Chives
- Cucumbers
- Tomatoes
- Eggplant
- Leeks
- Melons
- Onions
- Parsley
- Peppers
- Squashes

OUTDOOR PLANTING PREPARATION

Improving the soil in your garden. Add organic matter to planting beds several weeks in advance of planting if possible—several months in advance is even better. Add aged compost, well-rotted manure, chopped leaves, dry grass clipping, and decomposing vegetation to improve soil texture and enhance soil nutrients. Once organic materials are in the soil earthworms, soil microorganisms, bacteria, and fungi will begin eating their way through the material turning it into humus—the fully decomposed dark-colored organic matter which is rich in nitrogen and phosphorus and other elements essential for plant growth.

Sweet and sour soil. Alkaline soil is called sweet and acid soil is called sour. Vegetables grow best in soil that is neither sweet nor sour but soil that is close to neutral. Soil acidity and alkalinity are measured on the pH scale with 1 being most acid and 14 being most alkaline; vegetables grow best when the pH is 6.5—almost in the middle. If your soil pH is low or too acid, add lime (ground limestone) to the soil. If the soil is too alkaline, add sulfur. Before you add either lime or sulfur have the soil tested by a professional soil testing lab and ask for specific instructions on the amount of lime or sulfur to add. (Adding aged compost to either acidic or alkaline soil will help neutralize the pH.)

Fertilizer and compost nutrients. Aged compost contains all of the nutrients plants need. Aged compost is the most natural of plant foods since it is made from decomposed organic matter. If aged compost is not available, use an organic fertilizer. One tablespoon of 10-10-10 organic fertilizer is equal to about two handfuls of aged compost. Aged compost both feeds the soil and improves soil texture and moisture holding capability. Fertilizers simply feed plants.

Measuring soil temperature. Soil temperature should be about 65°F at 4 inches below the soil surface for seeds and seedlings to get a good growing start. (Some seeds can germinate in cooler soil.) There are two ways to determine if the soil is sufficiently warm for planting; first, is to simply take a handful of planting bed soil in your hand—if it feels chilly, it is; second, you can use a soil thermometer or a basic thermometer to take the soil's temperature. A soil thermometer will have a probe you can thrust into the soil. If you use a small basic thermometer, place it in a hole about 4 inches deep, mark the spot with a small stake or irrigation flag, cover the thermometer and then come back in about 15 minutes to take the reading.

Pre-warm the soil before planting. Most vegetable seeds and seedlings require the soil to be 65° to 75°F for germination and early growth. Black or clear plastic sheeting can be used to pre-warm the soil ahead of the growing season. Pull the plastic tight over the soil to eliminate as much air as possible; this will allow solar heat to be transferred directly to the soil. Plastic sheeting heated by solar energy can raise soil temperature by as much as 16°F on a cloudless day. Two weeks or more of pre-warming the soil is enough to get seeds and transplants started.

Planting through plastic sheeting. Once the soil has warmed, you can cut an X-slit in the plastic and sow seed or set transplants. Plastic can stay in place for the whole season in most regions—only in extremely hot regions might the plastic make the soil too hot for plant growth. Plastic sheeting across planting beds through the season will protect vining crops such as melons that creep across the garden from soil-borne pests and diseases.

Other ways to pre-warm the soil:

- **Floating row covers, plastic hoop tunnels, and cold frames** can be set over planting beds to pre-warm the soil. Solar heat accumulates under the cover and warms the soil.

- **Mounded or raised wide rows** running east and west will collect solar heat. Soil in beds at least 6 inches high will collect solar heat that hits the side of the bed.

- **V-shaped trenches** for sowing seed or setting transplants can be dug in advance of planting. Mound the soil to the north side of the trench then allow the soil beneath to warm over the course of a couple of weeks before backfilling the trench once the soil has warmed.

- **Hills or mounds** can be made for crops planted in clusters. Make small mounds for beans. Make larger, wider mounds for corn, melons, sweet potatoes, cucumbers, and squashes. These crops will do best on mounds 6 to 8 inches high and 3 feet wide.

Basic seed starting supplies: tray, cell containers, individual containers, seed starting mix or soil, and plant labels.

INDOOR SEED STARTING

Advantages to starting seed indoors. Vegetables started indoors will be just as tasty as those started outdoors. When you start seed indoors you get a jump start on the growing season; that means cool-season spring crops like members of the cabbage family won't run out of cool weather as summer approaches. It also means warm-season fruiting crops such as tomatoes and peppers will be ready mid-summer, not late summer. Starting 4, 8, or 12 weeks early indoors adds those weeks to the growing season.

Time to start seed indoors. Eight to twelve weeks before the last frost in spring is the time to start most vegetable seeds indoors. Start celery, leeks, and onions 12 to 14 weeks before the outdoor growing season. Start cantaloupes, watermelons, cucumbers, and squashes indoors between 12 and 8 weeks before the last frost. Tomatoes, peppers, and eggplants should be started indoors 8 weeks before you set them in the garden—about two weeks after the last frost. Keep in mind, that the last frost in spring does not fall on the same day every year, it is all but impossible to know exactly when indoor started seedlings will be transplanted to the garden; if cold weather persists these crops can be potted up to the next largest container as they wait for mild outdoor weather.

Seed starting timing. Here are a few things to keep in mind whether you start seeds indoors or outdoors:

- Know the average date of the last frost in spring. The natural growing season starts after the last frost; plants don't need protection during the natural growing season.

- Know which vegetables are best started indoors and which are best started outdoors.

- Check seed packets for number of days to germination; soil temperature required for germination; outside temperature for seed sowing or transplanting, and number of days to maturity.

- Determine the date to sow or transplant out each crop counting backward or forward from the last frost date. Most cool-season seed can be sown outdoors before the last frost; most warm-season crops must be sown or transplanted out after the last frost date.

Indoor seed starting cool-season crops. Cool-season crops can be started indoors while the weather outside is still too cold for growing. Then they can be set in the garden when the weather moderates and come to harvest before outdoor temperatures climb to the mid-70sF in late spring or early summer. Cool-season crops that are easy to start indoors from seed are broccoli, Brussels sprouts, cabbage, cauliflower, kale, leeks, lettuce, and spinach.

Indoor seed starting warm-season crops. Start warm-season crops indoors 6 to 8 weeks before the last spring frost. Set them in the garden after temperatures average 65°F or greater each day. Warm-season crops are fruiting crops including beans, cucumbers, eggplants, melons, okra, peppers, tomatoes, and squashes.

Indoor seed starting supplies. Here's a list of indoor seed starting supplies you will need:

- **Containers:** flats or individual containers at least 3 to 4 inches deep.
- **Seed-starting and potting mixes:** commercial seed-starting mix, peat moss, fine compost, perlite, and milled sphagnum moss will work for seed starting. Later you will need a commercial potting mix or a homemade mix: 1 part garden soil, 1 part perlite or builders' sand; 1 part fine compost.
- **Lights:** adjustable up and down fluorescent shop lights will do to keep plants growing.
- **Electric heating mat** with thermostat to place under containers.
- **Capillary mats** placed under containers will wick-up moisture to the seeds and seedlings.
- **Fertilizer:** half-strength fertilizer to get seedlings growing; use fish or seaweed fertilizer or compost tea.

Seed starting containers. Make sure all containers—pots, cell packs, and trays—have drainage holes. Seed-starting containers should be at least 2 to 3 inches deep to allow for early root development. Use compressed peat pellets or biodegradable pots if you don't want to disturb roots at transplanting. Clean used pots and flats with a 10 percent bleach solution—one part bleach to 10 parts water.

Bio-degradable pots for seed starting. Snap beans, lima beans, cucumbers, eggplant, melons, tomatoes, and squash are often started in bio-degradable peat or paper pots that can be planted whole into the garden (that way you won't disturb their roots at transplanting).

Seed-starting mix. Use a sterile, soilless seed-starting mix. This will guard against damping off, a soil disease that can strike young seedlings. A homemade soilless seed-starting mix is 2 parts peat moss to 1 part vermiculite or perlite.

Light for seedlings. Fluorescent tubes will provide the light seedlings need. Suspend lights 2 to 3 inches above young seedlings. Be sure the light can be raised as seedlings grow tall. Give seedlings 10 to 12 hours of light each day; use an automatic timer. If you don't have artificial light for seedlings, place them in a bright, southern facing window. To keep seedlings growing straight, attach a sheet of aluminum foil to a piece of cardboard and place the foil on the room side of the seedlings so that light hits the foil and reflects back on the seedlings. This will keep seedlings from becoming leggy.

Warm soil for seed germination. The optimal soil temperature to germinate most vegetable seeds is 70°F. Use an electric heating mat with a thermostat to warm the soil. You can also place seed trays on top of a radiator or refrigerator.

How to start seed in flats or pots. Most seeds can be started in flats or small individual pots. Here's how to get started:

- Fill the flat or pot with pre-moistened potting soil; moisten the mix by placing it in a large bucket and adding water until the mix is just moist—not wet.
- Level the potting mix in the flat or pot with a small piece of wood.
- Lightly sprinkle the seed over the soil being careful to not sow seed too thickly. Press the seed into the surface of the mix with a flat board or the palm of your hand; the seed should make good contact with the soil to speed germination.
- Sprinkle additional soil over the top of the seed; the seed should be covered to a depth of two to

four times the diameter of the seed; about a quarter of an inch for small seed.

- Place the flat or pot inside a clear plastic bag and tie the bag shut.

- Label the bag with the name of the vegetable and variety.

- Put the bag in a warm, bright spot—not direct sunlight—until the seeds sprout. Seeds should emerge in about 10 to 14 days on average. If seeds have not emerged after three weeks, you may need to replant.

- Once seeds sprout, remove the flat from the plastic bag and place it in a sunny sport or under adjustable grow lamp or fluorescent shop light.

Caring for new seedlings. Water newly sprouted seedlings from the bottom; place seed container in a tray or saucer and add just enough water to be soaked up through the soil in an hour; water in the tray after that can be drained. Keep the seedlings in a warm spot and out of drafts until they are well established in about three to four weeks. Once seedlings are established and seed leaves have dropped and two sets of true leaves have formed, the seedlings can be potted up into small 4-inch pots.

Feeding young seedlings. Use a dilute solution of fish emulsion to feed young seedlings; seed-starting mixes do not contain nutrients.

Grow strong seedlings. To ensure seedlings grow strong, place a small fan near the seedlings; a light breeze will help stems grow strong against the breeze. An alternative is to lightly brush the tops of the seedlings with your hand or with dowel or ruler. This gentle exercise will keep seedlings from being spindly and weak.

Damping off is a fungal disease that causes seedlings to die before or shortly after they emerge from the soil. Damping off is caused by several species of fungi that enter seed or plant openings most commonly when the soil is damp and cool. The fungi cause stems and roots to rot and collapse killing the plant. Seedlings that do not die become stunted. To avoid damping off use fresh, sterile seed starting mix and avoid overwatering—allow the soil to just dry between watering. Good air circulation around plants, not sowing seeds too close, plenty of light, and bottom watering are good ways to prevent damping off. When damping off occurs in the garden, add plenty of aged compost to the soil to encourage good drainage and rotate crops.

How to transplant a seedling and potting up. When a seedling has a pair of true leaves—leaves that emerge from between the original cotyledon or seed leaves (cotyledons are fleshy and don't look much like true leaves)—it is time for pricking out and potting up—which simply means transplanting the seedling to the next largest pot. Most indoor started vegetables are potted up once or twice while they wait for the chill of winter to leave the garden. Use a small flat wooden plant stick or kitchen knife to lift each seedling from its seed-starting container (gardeners call this pricking out). Hold the seedling by a leaf and ease the knife down into the soil. Lift the seedling up keeping as much soil around the roots as possible. Set the seedling into its new container and firm the soil around the roots (gardeners call this potting up). Water lightly and set the seedling out of direct light for a day or two until it becomes established.

Hardening off seedlings. The process of gradually acclimatizing seedlings to outdoor weather is called hardening-off. Plants are exposed to increasing amounts of outdoor weather and temperatures over a period of days until they can withstand outdoor nighttime low temperatures and bright sunlight without suffering. Here's how to harden off seedlings: expose the seedlings to outside conditions 90 minutes the first day and an additional 90 minutes each day after. After about 10 days you can leave the seedlings out overnight as long as temperatures do not dip below 50°F. If cold weather sets in, extend the hardening-off period.

EXTENDING THE NATURAL GROWING SEASON EARLY

Setting seedlings in the garden. Do not transplant seedlings into the garden if the weather is too cold, rainy, or windy. Wait for the weather to settle. Young transplants can't tolerate weather stress when they go into the garden. The ideal soil and air temperature for transplanting most vegetables into the garden is between 60°F and 70°F. When you set a seedling in the garden, give it a nutrient boost: use a seaweed concentrate or fish emulsion diluted to half strength.

Growing season. The natural growing season is the time of year when plants grow without protection from cold or heat. Most vegetables can grow without protection when outdoor temperatures are between 42°F and 86°F; when temperatures are lower or higher vegetables will stop growing and if the temperatures become extreme can suffer stress or death. Commonly the growing season is the time between the last frost in spring and the first frost in autumn.

Temperatures for outdoor planting and sowing. Don't rush sowing and planting outdoors. Check the soil temperature before getting started. Use a soil thermometer to take the soil temperature. When the soil temperature averages 41F for three days you can begin sowing and planting cool-weather vegetables such as fava beans, broccoli, lettuce, early peas and turnips. Here are minimum soil temperatures for sowing many vegetables:

- **41°F or warmer:** arugula, broccoli, Brussels sprouts, cabbage, cauliflower, collards, Asian greens, Chinese cabbage, fava beans, kale, kohlrabi, lettuce, mustard, peas, arugula, radish, turnips, lettuce, pea, radish, rutabaga, and turnip,
- **45°F or warmer:** beets, carrots, leek, onion, parsnip, beet, carrot, leek, onions, parsnip, Swiss chard.
- **50°F or warmer:** bush beans, pole beans, celery, corn, spinach
- **60°F or warmer:** sweet, corn, cucumber, squash, tomato, zucchini
- **65°F:** eggplant, pepper, okra.

Season extension. Season extension is the term used for growing plants outside of their natural growing season. Season extension usually requires protecting plants from temperatures too cold for growing—and sometimes temperatures too warm. Most vegetables cannot withstand a hard freeze (temperatures below 28°F)—a hard freeze is also called a killing freeze. Some plants cannot withstand frost—temperatures

just below 32°F. Vegetable gardeners extend the season by protecting plants under a cold frame, plastic hoop tunnel, cloches, or row covers. These are called season extending devices.

Cold frame and polyethylene/plastic hoop tunnel growing. A cold frame or a plastic hoop tunnel can protect vegetables from cold temperatures. A cold frame is a season-extending device so is a plastic hoop tunnel. You can grow vegetables in a cold frame or plastic hoop tunnel in containers or directly in the soil or seedbed under the frame or hoop tunnel. The temperature inside a cold frame or plastic hoop tunnel is usually 10 to 20 degrees warmer than the outside temperature. This is usually enough to start seed or plants several weeks in advance of the growing season. (Keep this in mind when the weather warms; be sure to open or ventilate a cold frame or plastic hoop tunnel when the outside temperature rises above 50°F. Remember the temperature inside will be 10 to 20 degrees warmer.) Cool-weather crops easily started in a cold frame or plastic hoop tunnel include beets, broccoli, cabbage, cauliflower, celery, lettuce and salad greens, onions, and parsley. Warm-weather crops can be started in a cold frame where the temperature stays warmer than 60°F.

Cold frames. A cold frame is a sturdy, open-bottomed box with a glass or plastic lid that lets the sunshine in but keeps the cold out. Sunlight trapped in the closed box heats the air and soil inside allowing plants to thrive. Cool-weather vegetables can begin growing in a cold frame several weeks before they can grow outside. You can also use a cold frame to harden off vegetable seedlings started in the house or greenhouse. In summer, you can remove the lid of the cold frame and use the frame to start seeds that can later be transplanted into the garden. You can buy a cold frame or make your own. Some commercial cold frames are made of thick translucent plastic. You can make a cold frame from lumber, cement blocks, or bricks. You can even fashion a cold frame from bales of hay.

How to make a cold frame. A cold frame is an open-bottomed box with a clear lid. Here's how to make a simple cold frame: construct the frame with

2 × 8 inch or 2 × 10 inch or 2 × 12 inch boards cut to size to form a box. Cut the side boards on a diagonal so that the front (southward-facing side) of the frame is lower than the back. Nails or screws and metal fasteners can be used to hold the sides together. Hinge the clear lid of the frame to the back. The lid can be made from an old window sash or framed Plexiglas or clear plastic sheeting. Set the corners of the frame slightly below grade on bricks to prevent the frame from settling. Fill in around the base of the frame with soil to keep cold air out. You can build a higher-sided cold frame by adding framed tiers atop a framed box or an existing raised-bed frame.

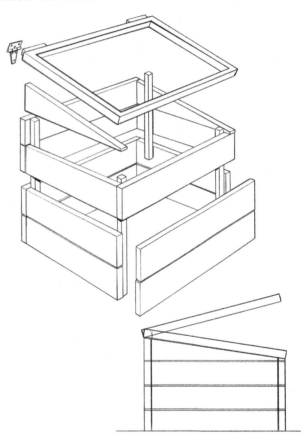

A simple cold frame construction plan.

Siting a cold frame. Site the frame where it will get full sun all day. Place the higher back side of the frame to the north and the lower front side to the south. That will insure the maximum amount of light reaches the floor of the frame throughout the day. Site the frame out of a prevailing wind. If possible,

place the frame next to the south facing wall of a building or fence where extra sunlight and heat will be reflected into the frame.

Ventilating a cold frame. Your frame must be well ventilated—especially on warm days when temperatures top 50°F (the temperature inside the frame will be about 10 to 20 degrees warmer). You can ventilate the frame by simply propping a stick or block under the sash. There are ways to make opening and closing the sash even easier: an automatic solar-powered frame opener attached to a thermostat can raise the top when the inside temperature inside reaches above 70°F. When days or nights are cold, keep the cold frame closed.

Cold frame in very cold regions. In very cold winter regions, cold frames can be fitted with insulated sides and set atop insulated foundations to retain more heat. A wooden, cement block, or solid cement cold frame can be insulated easily with the addition of 2 or more inches of Styrofoam around the inside of the frame and with a layer of 1½ inches on the bottom under the growing bed. Insulating foam can be easily cut and glued or tacked to the inside of the frame. As well foam shutters or mats can be placed atop the frame's clear lid at night. Insulation can increase night air temperature inside the frame by 8°F or even more. A double-paned glass or plastic top or a sash fitted with an under-layer of 4 to 6 mil plastic sheeting will provide additional insulation of up to 6°F.

Hot beds. A hot bed is an artificially heated cold frame. You can turn your cold frame into a hot bed by placing electric heating cables under the soil. A hot bed is useful for growing seeds in containers—much like you would grow seeds indoors or in a greenhouse. Place the heating cables about 3 inches or more below the soil surface and protect them by laying hardware cloth over the cables before covering them again with at least 6 inches of soil—especially if you plan to grow seeds directly in the soil and not in flats or pots.

Plastic (polyethylene) hoop tunnels. A plastic hoop tunnel is very similar to a cold frame. Generally, plastic hoop tunnels are a bit easier to assemble and to move around. A simple plastic hoop tunnel is made by placing sturdy, heavy gauge wire hoops over a planting bed and then draping clear plastic sheeting over the hoops. Wire hoops should be made of # 10 gauge galvanized steel and be about 54 inches long; this will allow each side of the hoop to be pushed at least 6 inches into the soil. Your plastic hoop tunnel should be about 16-18 inches tall at the center-top of the hoop. Choose polyethylene or plastic sheeting at least 4 millimeters thick, 6-8 mils thick in very cold winter regions. Tuck the sheeting into the soil or hold it down with garden pegs, boards, bricks, or stones. Like a cold frame, a plastic hoop tunnel must be ventilated when temperatures warm much above 60°F.

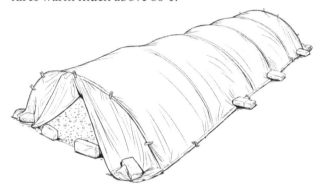

Plastic (polyethylene) hoop tunnels can be attached to a raised bed or anchored in the soil with stakes or staples.

Other season extenders include. Here a few other ways to extend the season: cloches—glass or plastic jugs that can be set over the top of individual plants; hot caps—paper or wax paper cones that can be set over plants like a cloche; a product called Wall-O-Water a sort of plastic teepee with channeled walls that are filled with water and set around plants; and floating row covers or plant blankets made of spun polyester that is simply set lightly on the top of plants.

PLANTING ZONE-BY-ZONE: Late Winter / February

Beginning with the warmest regions first, here is a seed starting and planting guide for late-winter—February. Note: it is safe to plant or do any of the tasks listed for regions cooler than yours.

USDA Zone 9-10: danger of frost continues:

- Plant out asparagus, artichoke, and horseradish roots.
- Cool-weather transplants can be set out into the garden: beets, broccoli, Brussels sprouts, cabbage, carrots, chard, collards, Italian sprouting broccoli, kale, kohlrabi, leaf lettuce, mustard, onion seedlings and sets, parsley, Irish potatoes, radishes, and turnips.
- Sow cool-season seed directly in the garden: Asian greens, beets, carrots, leaf lettuce, peas, and turnips. Protect seedlings with a row cover if weather is chilly.
- In warm, sandy soil, plant potatoes that have been pre-sprouted (chitted).
- Indoors keep tomato, pepper, and eggplant seedlings beneath bright lights.
- Indoors, sow seed of warm-weather crops: bush and pole beans, lima beans, cantaloupe, sweet corn, cucumbers, eggplants, peppers, pumpkin, squash, tomatoes, tomatillos, watermelons, and tender herbs such as dill, fennel, and basil. Most of these crops will require 7 to 8 weeks of growing before they will be large enough to transplant into the garden.
- Do not place any warm-season plants in the garden until the night temperatures stay warmer than 60°F—50°F if protected at night.
- Remove winter mulch from perennial vegetable beds—covering asparagus, horseradish, and rhubarb.
- In southern regions where all danger of frost has passed set out starts: tomatoes, eggplant, peppers, and tomatillos (be ready to protect these crops should the temperature drop).

USDA Zone 8: frost possible:

- Prepare planting beds with plenty of aged compost. Turn the soil to a depth of 8 to 12 inches adding aged compost or organic planting mix. This will ensure the soil is well drained.
- Where the ground can be worked, direct seed or plant asparagus and artichoke roots, beets, black-eyed peas, bok choy, broccoli, cabbage

plants, carrots, cauliflower plants, collards, endive, kale, kohlrabi, leek, lettuce, mustard greens, onion sets or plants, parsley, peas, Irish potatoes, radish, spinach, Swiss chard, and turnip.

- Check the average date of the last frost in your area before setting out transplants; protect them if the weather is unsettled.

- Start tomatoes and peppers indoors; place flats or pots beneath bright lights as soon as they sprout.

- As soon as weather turns mild, remove winter mulch from perennial vegetable beds—covering asparagus, horseradish, and rhubarb. If you see signs of green growth remove half of the mulch and a week later remove the rest.

USDA Zone 7: freezing temperatures likely:

- Start early tomatoes indoors under lights.

- Start from seed indoors by mid-month: artichoke, broccoli, Brussels sprouts, cabbage, cauliflower, celery, eggplant, peppers, fennel, kale, kohlrabi, leeks, lettuce, mint, onions, oregano, peppers, early potatoes, radishes, rhubarb, spinach, tomatoes, and turnips.

- Set seed potatoes in a warm place to encourage sprouting.

- Harden off cabbage family seedlings in a cold frame.

- Outdoors where the soil is workable, set out asparagus roots, beets, bok choy, broccoli, cabbage, cauliflower, collards, horseradish, lettuce, mustard greens, onion sets, parsley, peas, radishes, rhubarb, spinach, Swiss chard, and turnips. Plant early potatoes in trenches or hot bed.

- Use portable plastic hoop tunnels to protect crops if the weather is chilly—less than 50°F.

USDA Zones 3-6: snow and ice likely:

- Start indoors under lights: artichokes, broccoli, cabbage, cauliflower, celery, leeks, mint, onions, oregano, and thyme.

- Sow strawberries indoors.

- If winter is subsiding you may be able to start cool-weather crops in a cold frame: broccoli, cabbage, cauliflower, celeriac, celery, fennel, leeks, lettuce, onions, peas, early potatoes, radishes, rhubarb, shallots, spinach, turnips.

- Prepare planting beds as soon as the soil has dried; prepare beds for peas, potatoes, and other early crops.

LATE WINTER GARDEN TASKS

- Review garden notes from last season and update planting map.

- Create your new garden map and planting schedule.

- Plan crop rotations and successions for the upcoming season.

- Inventory old seeds and order new seeds for the coming year.

- Check viability of stored seeds.

- Clean and organize seed starting supplies; containers, soil mix, grow lights, heat mats.

- Check supplies of fertilizers and organic spray; replace any that are outdated.

- Purchase organic soil amendments.

- Get soil tested if not done last autumn.

- Check garden for overwintering insects and fungal diseases.

- Add aged compost, aged manure, leaf molds, and earthworm castings to planting beds if the weather permits.

- Renew mulch in areas where it is thinning.

- Ready cloches, plastic hoop tunnels, cold frames, and hoop houses.

- Keep an eye on the weather and forecasts; protect plants with row covers if temperatures drop below 28°F.

- Water plants well before freezing temperatures occur; make sure plants are mulched to protect them from cold.

- Ventilate the cold frame when daytime temperatures warm to 60°F or warmer.

- Organize, clean, and sharpen garden tools.

COOL-SEASON CROPS FOR PLANTING IN LATE WINTER

Cabbage. Cabbage is easy to grow and can be eaten raw or cooked. Cabbage also stores well either in the root cellar or in the form of sauerkraut. There are many cabbage varieties to choose from—green or red, smooth leaved or ruffled-leaved savoy, round-head, cone-shaped, and flattened-head. And consider days to maturity—early season, mid-season, and late season; late maturing cabbage (more than 90 days) is the best choice for storing in a root cellar for winter use; early- and mid-season varieties are usually planted in spring for fresh use midsummer and autumn. Here are a few varieties that are easy to grow:

- 'Dynamo': 70 days to maturity, early season, split resistant, grows well in all regions.
- 'Early Jersey Wakefield': 63 days to maturity, heirloom variety that resists splitting.
- 'January King': 160+ days to maturity, cold-hardy, great flavor, French heirloom.
- 'Savoy Express': 55 days to maturity; sweet-flavored, crinkle head.
- 'Ruby Perfection': 85 days to maturity, mid- to late-season, stores well.
- 'Super Red': 115 days to maturity, early season, split resistant, good flavor.

Broccoli, cauliflower, kohlrabi are good choice for planting in late winter or early spring for harvest before summer heat. There are 60-days-to-maturity-or-less varieties for each of these vegetables. All like to start and come to harvest in cool weather. Plant these in a cold frame or under a plastic hoop tunnel or start these crops indoors up to 10 weeks before the last frost then transplant them to the garden as early as 4 to 6 weeks before the last frost. Plant these cabbage-family crops in compost rich soil that is well-drained and workable—not too wet after winter rains or snow. Here are a few excellent growers for spring planting:

- **Broccoli:** 'Arcadia' (63 days); tolerates heat and cold; 'Packman' (55 days) deep green, tight florets.
- **Cauliflower:** 'Snow Crown' (58 days), tolerate heat and cold, smooth head; 'Amazing' (68 days) self-blanching standard.
- **Kohlrabi:** 'Early White Vienna' or 'Early Purple Vienna' (55 days) white fleshed; 'Kolibri' (45 days) reliable grower.

Planting leeks and a leek planting calendar. Sow leek seeds indoors 8 to 10 weeks before you want to set seedlings into the garden. Transplant leeks into the garden 3 to 4 weeks before the last frost in spring. Sow seeds in trays filled with seed starting mix. Set seed starting trays under fluorescent shop lights or in a sunny window. Keep the starting mix just moist; do not let it dry out. Seedlings 4 inches tall or taller are large enough for transplanting. The soft roots of leeks do not like compacted soil. Turn the soil at least 6 to 8 inches deep with a garden fork before setting out transplants. If the soil is heavy clay or filled with pebbles and stones, plant leeks in a raised bed. Set leek seedlings in a trench 4 to 6 inches deep and about 6 inches apart—closer if you plan to harvest them young. Trim off the top inch of leafy growth at transplanting time to encourage new growth. Backfill the trench as the plants grow tall keeping the developing base of the plant just covered. Pushing loose soil up around the base or putting a paper or plastic cylinder around the stem will keep stalks white and tender; this process is called blanching.

In mild winter regions, plant leeks in late autumn or winter.

In cool–but not cold–winter regions plant leeks in late summer and autumn for spring harvest. Plant them again in spring for autumn or winter harvest.

In cold winter regions transplant leeks into the garden three weeks before the last spring frost or later.

Leeks require 75 to 130 days from sowing to harvest depending upon the variety. Leeks can be harvested at just about any stage of growth though as a rule they will be most flavorful when young and

31

tender and about ½ inch round or later when the shanks have grown thick and round. Two outstanding varieties are 'King Richard' (75 days) and 'Lincoln' (70 days).

Planting horseradish. Set out horseradish crowns or root cuttings 4 to 6 weeks before the average last frost date. Set horseradish in rich well-drained soil in full sun. Prepare the soil to a depth of 10 to 12 inches and remove stones and lumps that might cause the roots to split. Add sand and compost to the planting bed to keep the soil loose. Horseradish prefers a soil pH of 5.5 to 6.8. Set crowns just at soil level. Place root cuttings in shallow trenches 3 to 4 inches deep and cover with 2 to 3 inches of soil. Slice root cuttings at a 30° angle or plant with the narrow end down. Space roots 24 to 36 inches apart. Horseradish planted in the garden should be contained with wooden, metal, or masonry borders set at least 24 inches deep around the bed. (Horseradish roots can spread through the garden rapidly if not contained.) Horseradish is a perennial and will require its own planting bed for up to ten years.

HARVEST BY ZONE:
Late Winter / February

Most crops coming to harvest in February were planted late last summer or autumn. They overwintered in the garden or were grown under cover.

- **USDA Zones 7-10:** arugula, Asian green, beets, broccoli, Brussels sprouts, cabbage, carrots, cauliflower, celery, chervil, chives, cilantro, collards, fennel , green onion, kale, leeks, lettuce, mâche, mustard, parsley, parsnips, peas, potatoes, radicchio, radishes, sorrel, spinach, strawberries, Swiss chard, thyme, turnips.

- **USDA Zones 4-6:** arugula, beets greens, broccoli, Brussels sprouts, cabbage, chicory, Chinese cabbage, carrots, chives, garlic, kale, leeks, mâche, parsnips, radicchio, spinach, Swiss chard, baby turnips.

- **Crops in storage:** beets, cabbage, carrots, celeriac, garlic, kohlrabi, onions, parsnips, potatoes, rutabaga, sweet potatoes, turnips, and winter squash. Inspect stored vegetables and fruits and discard any that show signs of decay.

March

Early Spring

Planting Indoors and Out

March brings the end of winter and the beginning of spring. Spring for the northern hemisphere will arrive on March 20, the vernal equinox. On this day, the sun rises directly in the east and sets directly in the west. There will be exactly 12 daylight hours from sunrise to sunset. In the northern hemisphere, every day hence will grow just a little bit longer until summer.

March is a month of transition in the vegetable garden. In the warmest regions–United States Department of Agriculture (USDA) Plant Hardiness Zones 10 and 9–spring has arrived and planting is underway or can begin during March. In USDA Zones 8 and 7, preparation for spring planting can begin in earnest this month, but sowing and transplanting out into the garden may be delayed by continuing cold weather. In USDA, Zones 6, 5, 4, and 3, winter weather and cold temperatures will likely keep you out of the garden this month. (To know which planting zone you live in see Appendix 3, pages 171-180, and find the town or city nearest you.)

PREPARING TO PLANT OUTDOORS

Planting outdoors when the soil is workable. Don't sow seed or plant outdoors in spring until the soil is workable. Here's the test for workable soil: squeeze a handful of soil in the palm of your hand; when you open your hand if the soil remains a cold, wet clump, it is not workable. You should wait a few weeks to test again. But if the soil in your fist crumbles when you open your hand, it is workable—it's safe to plant cool-season crops.

As soon as the soil is workable in spring, you can:

- **Direct sow:** collards, kale, lettuce, parsnip, peas, radish, rutabaga, spinach, turnips.
- **Transplant out:** broccoli, Brussels sprouts, cabbage, onion.

Planting by nature signals—phenology. Plant growth is determined in part by temperature and day length. When the temperature and day length are right for one plant it may be right for others. You can use perennial plants as natural indicators that conditions are right for planting vegetables. Natural indicators include leafing out, bud formation, and flower blooms of certain plants. One of the most widely used plant indicators is the lilac. When lilacs leaves swell just beyond the leaf bud scale, it's safe to plant cool-season plants such as peas, lettuce, and spinach. When lilacs are in full bloom—when nearly 100 percent of the plant's flower clusters are fully open—it's safe to plant tender, warm-weather crops such as corn, tomatoes and basil. Tracking the regular cycles of plants and animals is called phenology—which comes from a Greek word meaning "science of appearances." (Read more about lilacs and phenology on page 46 in April.)

Hedge your bets. Whenever you are unsure about the weather, sow or plant just a few short rows early. If the weather turns bad your loss will be small. Be prepared to re-sow if the weather does not cooperate and seeds don't sprout. Alternatively, start plants in the cold frame or under a plastic hoop tunnel and remove the protection when you know the weather and temperatures have settled.

PREPARING PLANTING BEDS

Preparing outdoor planting beds. Garden planting beds can be readied for seed sowing and planting when the soil is workable. Workable soil should be prepared to a depth of at least a foot.

- **Double-dig new planting beds:** Double-dig when preparing new beds. To double dig: remove the soil to a depth of a spade—about 12 inches, then loosen the soil beneath with a spading fork or dig the soil with the spade to a depth of a second 12 inches. Break up any large clumps and clods and remove all stones. Double-digging is a one-time sweat equity investment in your planting beds.

- **Renew existing planting beds:** Use a garden fork to loosen the soil in existing planting beds. (Avoid working in planting beds when they are wet.) Spread 2 to 4 inches of aged compost across the planting bed; or spread 1 inch of well-rotted manure and 1 or 2 inches of aged compost across the bed. Let wind and rain work the soil amendments into the bed for a few weeks or even month or two. Earthworms and soil microorganisms will break down the compost and manure renewing natural nutrients in the soil.

Protecting planting beds early in the season. If the weather has been wet or cold and it has been difficult to work in the garden, place clear plastic sheets over the planting beds for a week or more. This will allow the soil to warm and dry. You can also protect planting beds from early season wet and cold weather with a plastic tent or hoop tunnel.

Raised and mounded bed advantages. Raised beds (often bottom boxes) and mounded beds (mounded soil) offer some distinct advantages over growing vegetables at ground level. Here are the advantages of raised and mounded beds:

- Increase the depth of loose, crumbly topsoil; especially important for root crops.
- Stay 8 to 10 degrees warmer than the surrounding ground.
- Dry faster than ground beds; this is important if you live where it rains often.
- Well-drained; rain and irrigation does not puddle on the soil surface.
- Raises plant roots above clay or sandy soil.
- Well suited for wide row planting.
- Easy to plant, easy to tend, and easy to harvest; less stooping and bending.

- Soil is never compacted by the gardener stepping in to the bed.

How to make a raised bed. A raised bed is simply an open-bottomed box filled with soil, aged compost, and planting mix. You can make a raised bed by setting four 4x4 inch posts at each corner of the planting bed and then attaching 2x6 inch or 2x12 inch planks between each post. A raised bed can be square or rectangular. It can be any width or length you like, but you should be able to reach to the center of the bed without stepping in to it. The raised bed can be any height you like: 6 inches, 12 inches, or more. You can also make raised beds out of bricks, cement blocks, logs, or bales of hay.

How to make a mounded bed. A mounded bed is a raised bed without a frame. Mark where the mounded bed will stand by driving four stakes into the soil to mark the four corners of the bed. A bed 24 to 36 inches wide is about right. Turn the soil inside the designated bed to a depth of at least 8 inches. Next, go along the outside edges of the bed and shovel to the center of the bed loose soil from the ground on all sides. You can also add aged compost and commercial planting mix to the bed. Add as much soil as needed to form the height of the bed—6 inches to 8 inches or more. Use a rake to flatten the crown of the mound, creating a flat planting surface. A few days before planting sprinkle 10-10-10 organic fertilizer across the mounded bed and lightly turn it under with the rake to a few inches deep. You have created a mounded bed ready for planting seeds or transplants.

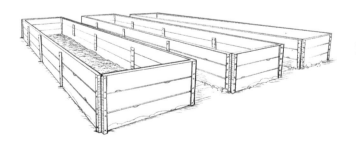 

Wooden raised beds and mounded soil planting beds allow the soil to warm sooner in spring for an early start to the growing season.

Below ground planting beds for hot regions. Just as an elevated raised or mounded bed can work to warm the soil early in spring; depressed, below ground planting beds can be used in very hot regions. Trench gardening was first practice by the Southwest desert native people. A trench can be used to capture rain water or to hold irrigation water. The temperature at the bottom of a trench is cooler than soil at ground level. A frame can be erected over a trench and can be draped with shade cloth to keep plants cooler. To grow in a trench, you will need to prepare the planting area just as you would a ground level planting bed. Turn and amend the soil with aged compost and organic matter to a depth of 12 to 24 inches before planting.

PLANTING ZONE-BY-ZONE: March / Early Spring

Beginning with the warmest regions first, here is a seed starting and planting guide for late-winter—March. It is safe to plant or do any of the tasks listed for regions cooler than yours.

USDA Zone 10: warm weather

- Transplant to the garden tomato, pepper, eggplant, and tomatillo seedlings.
- Direct seed warm-season crops: beans, corn, cucumbers, lettuce, melons, okra, pumpkin, summer spinach, squashes, sweet potatoes, and watermelon.

USDA Zone 9: frost possible:

- In frost-free regions, set out seedlings of cabbage, eggplant, melon, okra, pepper, pumpkin, squash, and tomato seedlings started indoors.
- Be prepared to protect crops from temperatures cooler than 60°F with cloches, row covers, or plastic hoop tunnels.
- Direct seed beets, beans, carrots, cauliflower, celery, collards, corn, cucumber, fava beans, French tarragon, garlic, kale, kohlrabi, leeks, lettuce, onions, oregano, parsley, parsnip, peas, potatoes, radishes, salsify, summer spinach, and thyme.

- Protect young plants from temperatures cooler than 60°F.
- Before transplanting out summer crops warm the soil with plastic sheeting, horticultural fleece, or cloches.
- If not started indoors already, start tomatoes, peppers, eggplant, and sweet potato slips.
- If potting up seedlings started indoors, move plants to next largest container.
- Chit (sprout) seed potatoes; allow cuts to heal for two weeks before planting.
- Plant potatoes, onion sets, and shallots when the soil temperature is 60°F.
- Thin seedlings.

USDA Zone 8: frost possible:

- When the soil is dry and workable, plant asparagus crowns, onion sets, and early potatoes. Prepare planting holes adding a layer of aged compost.
- Top-dress asparagus beds with aged compost and well-rotted manure.
- Sow in the garden beets, broad beans, carrots, cauliflower, kohlrabi, lettuce, green and spring onions, parsnips, peas, radishes, shallots, spinach, and turnips.
- Plant new strawberries; put cloches over strawberries if you want an early crop.
- Direct seed herbs: chervil, dill, fennel, parsley, pot marjoram, and sorrel. Lift and divide overgrown clumps of bergamot, chives, and fennel.
- Dig well-rotted manure into runner bean trenches.
- Indoors sow tomatoes, peppers, and eggplant; also start sweet potato slips.
- Adjust the height of seed-starting lights or turn seedlings in the windowsill daily; water and fertilize indoor seedlings.

USDA Zones 6 and 7: freezing temperatures likely early—frost likely late:

- Place cloches or plastic hoop tunnels in position to warm up the soil.

- Move broccoli, cabbage, and cauliflower seedlings to a cold frame to harden off.
- When the soil is workable sow outdoors beets, Brussels sprouts, carrots, dill, lettuce, parsley, parsnips, peas, onions, radishes, spinach, and Swiss chard; cover beds with horticultural fleece if hard frosts persist.
- Sow broad beans under cloches.
- Sow early peas in a sheltered spot; make a second sowing in two weeks.
- Plant early potatoes and onion and scallion sets. Sow onion and scallion seed.
- Plant asparagus, horseradish, and rhubarb.
- Work soil thoroughly for a fine seedbed.
- Sow indoors broccoli, Brussels sprouts, cabbage, cauliflower, celery, kale, kohlrabi, mint, okra, and Swiss chard.
- Start indoors or in hotbeds seed of tomatoes, peppers, eggplant, and basil.
- Begin sowing herbs indoors or in a warm cold frame or green house.

USDA Zone 5: freezing temperatures likely:

- Put seed potatoes in a warm, bright windowsill to encourage them to sprout
- Prepare cold frame and hot bed for sowing half hardy vegetables by forking over the soil, which should be light and loamy. Start tender seeds in the hotbed towards the end of the month. Be sure to open the frame and ventilate on warm days.
- At the end of the month, move broccoli, cabbage, and cauliflower transplants outdoors to a cold frame. Cover the frame with a blanket or tarp if a hard freeze threatens.
- Start tomato and pepper seeds indoors.
- Plant new asparagus and rhubarb beds when soil is workable; fertilize established ones with a blanket of compost.
- Plant potatoes.
- Mid-month start indoors seed of basil, bok choy, broccoli, Brussels sprouts, cabbage, cauliflower, celeriac, celery, eggplant, endive, fennel, kale, kohlrabi, lettuce, okra, peppers, Swiss chard, and tomatoes.

- If the weather is mild toward the end of the month, sow outdoors arugula, Asian greens, beets, carrots, cilantro, fava beans, lettuce, onion sets, parsnips, peas, radishes, salsify, spinach, and turnips. Be sure the location has good drainage.

USDA Zone 3 and 4: freezing temperatures continue:

- Seed sowing indoors gets under way this month. Sow mid-month or later artichokes, broccoli, Brussels sprouts, cabbage, cauliflower, celeriac, celery, kohlrabi, leeks, mint, onions, oregano, shallots, and thyme in pots or flats inside. Give seed 12 hours of sunlight. Transplant them to larger pots as soon as they become crowded or get their second pair of true leaves.
- Start cabbage, broccoli, Brussels sprouts, cauliflower, celery, leeks, onions, and parsley indoors beneath lights.
- Trim the tops of onion and leek seedlings to an inch or so high, to keep them stocky.
- Late in the month, start indoors seeds of tomatoes, peppers, eggplants, and okra; use individual peat pots.
- If the weather permits place plastic over planting beds to begin warming the soil.

INDOOR SEED STARTING

Pepper, eggplant, okra seed starting indoors. Time indoor seed starting of peppers, eggplant, and okra so that these crops are ready for transplanting into the garden after nighttime temperatures are 55°F or warmer—usually two or three weeks after the last frost in spring. Count backwards from the expected last frost eight to ten weeks; that's when you want to sow pepper, eggplant, and okra seed indoors.

Pepper, eggplant, okra varieties to grow. Here are some easy to grow varieties:

- **Sweet Peppers:** 'Ace' (50-70 days) large, bell pepper, grows in cool regions; 'Gypsy' (65 days) long, sweet, All American Selection; 'Sweet Banana' (70 days) eat grilled or raw; 'Sweet Chocolate' (70 days) purple-brown, very sweet.

- **Hot Peppers:** 'Anaheim' (80 days) mild hot pepper; 'Cayenne Long Slim' (75 days) very hot, bright red; 'Jalapeño (70 days) medium hot, matures bright red.

- **Eggplants:** 'Black Beauty' (74 days) heirloom standard, large, tender fruits; 'Rosa Bianca' (73 days) plump, round, mottled heirloom, excellent flavor.

- **Okra:** 'Burgundy' (55 days) tender, burgundy pods; 'Cajun Delight' (55 days) green pod, high yield, All American Selection.

OUTDOOR TASKS IN EARLY SPRING

Turn under cover crops. Cover crops planted last autumn should be turned under several weeks ahead of planting. Spade or till the cover crop so that the green side is down. Alfalfa, buckwheat, and annual ryegrass are cover crops that once turned under become green manure. Green manure is both a fertilizer and soil conditioner; the organic matter adds bulk to sandy soil and break-up clay soils. The roots of cover crop green manures reach deep into the soil and bring nutrients back up to the topsoil while holding moisture near the surface for the roots of new crops.

Remove winter mulches. Mulches spread across fallow planting beds in autumn to protect the soil from winter rains and erosion should be lifted in early spring. Mulches covering perennial vegetables such as asparagus, rhubarb, and strawberries should be pulled back as well. Removing winter mulches will expose planting beds to the sun; beds can begin to warm ahead of spring planting. Compost winter mulches or spread the mulch over wet or muddy pathways.

Row covers and floating row covers. Use row covers to protect seedlings and young plants in spring. Row covers are commonly made form spun bonded polyester or polypropylene fabric–often called horticultural cloth or fleece. Heavyweight covers are used to extend the growing season by keeping plants up to 10°F warmer during the day and 2° to 3°F warmer at night. Lightweight floating rows covers are used to shield plants from insects and diseases in spring and summer—and may provide one or two degrees of protection from cold. Row covers can be draped over hoops or frames set above rows of plants (to form protective hoop tunnels) or they can be laid loosely or floated over plants. (Early in the season leave enough fabric loose so that the cover can float up as plants grow.) Row covers can be anchored in place with garden staples, lengths of board, bricks, or soil. Row covers set over hoops can be replaced with plastic sheeting when temperatures dip below 40°F to create a plastic hoop tunnel; the temperature in a plastic hoop tunnel will be 10 degrees or more warmer than the outside air temperature.

Chicken wire to protect seedlings and young plants. Keep a roll of chicken wire and a roll of clear plastic sheeting handy to help protect young seedlings and plants from unexpected frost or cold temperatures. Use the chicken wire to fashion a frame over or around seedlings. Fold the wire in half to form a "tent" or cut a section of chicken wire to form a cylinder to place around plants. Next drape sections of clear plastic sheeting or row covers over or around the chicken wire to make a temporary greenhouse to protect plants.

Divide rhubarb. Rhubarb is propagated by dividing large root clumps. Dig up roots in autumn or early spring when they are dormant. Use a spade or knife to slice the root clump into pieces or use your hands to separate the twisted roots. Make sure each root piece has at least one bud and then replant. It's best to replant the divisions right away—but they can be stored in the refrigerator. Add aged compost to each new planting hole; place the root or crown 1 to 2 inches below the surface and be sure that buds are facing up. Mark the planting spot. Rhubarb roots commonly grow crowded and need dividing or thinning about every 5 years—usually when plant start sending up smaller, thinner leaf stalks

Planting horseradish. Horseradish is best planted in spring or autumn. Plant dormant root cutting or pieces; choose pieces that are straight with a crown of buds at the top. Horseradish prefers humus-rich, loose soil. Set pieces 12 to 18 inches deep. Horseradish is a rapid spreader. To keep roots from running through the garden just below the surface, set a bottomless container such as a plastic bucket or trash can in the soil 20 to 24 inches deep; plant roots inside the bottomless container which will act as a root barrier.

Planting onion sets. Onion sets are started onion bulbs. Plant onion sets (bulbs) in well-worked, soft soil. Add 10-10-10 organic fertilizer to the planting bed a week or so before planting onions set; rake the fertilizer under to a depth of 1 or 2 inches. Plant sets pointed side up; push them into the soil to the full depth of the set. The onion will develop roots from the bottom of the set and the onion bulb will grow up from the bottom of the set; at harvest time two-thirds of the developed bulb will be above the ground (the bulb does not grow down any further than the bottom of the planted set). Plant sets 3 to 4 inches apart, closer if you plan to thin the onions as scallions; the harvest thinning of scallions will aerate and loosen the soil which will help the remaining bulbs as they mature. Tamp down the soil above each set making sure the set makes good contact with the soil.

Onions from seed. Start onions from seed in flats in late winter or early spring. Onion starts can go in the garden in late spring. Once onion seedlings are about 5 to 6 inches tall use a scissors to trim the top; you can trim away a couple of inches. This will force bottom growth and the development of a strong root system. Onions started from seed in early spring will be mature in early autumn.

Onion guide. Here's a guide to onions you can grow from small to large in size:

- **Shallots:** small, mild and slightly nutty flavor.
- **Yellow onions:** medium-size, firm, best for storing.
- **White onions:** grow big and sweet when started early.
- **Red onions:** very large, tangy onions for hamburgers and sandwiches; Bermuda types.

Sprouting sweet potatoes for planting. Sweet potatoes require a long, frost-free growing season (120 days or more). To have sweet potatoes ready for the garden, start them indoors. Here's how: cut a sweet potato in half lengthwise and set the two cut sides down in few inches of potting soil in an aluminum baking tray; moisten the soil first. Place the sweet potato halves and tray in a clear plastic bag and tie the end shut. When leaves sprout in a few weeks, remove the tray from the plastic bag and place the new plants in a sunny window. Keep the soil just moist as the leaves continue to grow. In about 8 weeks, you will have sweet potato slips (young plants) ready for transplanting to the garden. Two varieties to grow are 'Beauregard' which is a large, meaty dark burgundy-purple root with smooth-texture and 'Vardaman' a large, deep orange tuber that is flavorful.

Asparagus upkeep. At the end of winter cut down the dry, brown stalks that were asparagus ferns last summer and autumn. Soon the asparagus crowns (roots) will send up new spears. You'll want the asparagus patch cleared before the new stalks begin to appear. With the stalks gone, remove weeds from the planting bed and rake up any litter. Next lightly sprinkle 10-10-10 organic fertilizer around the stubble of each plant; below the surface are the dormant crowns which will soon begin to grow.

Strawberries. As winter cold disappears, gradually remove mulch from established strawberry plants and cover them with a row cover to encourage early blooming. Remove or replace strawberry plants heaved by frost. You also can protect strawberry plants from frost and freezing weather with cloches.

Chitting potatoes. Chitting potatoes means to pre-sprout potatoes ahead of planting. Chit potatoes in a cool, frost-free, light place. Choose potatoes about the size of a hen's egg or cut a large potato in half. Make sure each "seed" potato or potato piece has one or more eyes. Place your "seed" potatoes in the hollows of an empty egg carton or a shallow box—eyes up. New sprouts will emerge from the eyes. These sprouted seed potatoes are ready for planting outdoors.

Growing potatoes in containers. Potatoes are easy to grow in large containers: bushel baskets, wooden or plastic barrels, plastic or metal trash cans, wire cages, and even heavy-duty plastic garbage bags.

A container for potato growing should be at least 2½ to 3 feet tall and 3 feet across with holes for drainage in the bottom and sides. A container 2 feet across can support four plants. Place a few inches of soil at the bottom of the container then lay seed potatoes on the soil and cover them with a few inches of soil or aged compost. Once the plant has begun to grow and reached about 6 inches tall, add soil, compost, or straw mulch to cover all but 3 inches of the plant—just a few leaves poking through the soil. Again, let the foliage grow another 6 inches and repeat. Continue this process until the container is filled. If you use heavy-duty garbage bag, simply roll the bag up until it is filled. When harvest time comes, turn the container on its side and let the potatoes spill out.

Potato varieties to grow. Plant potatoes in early to mid-spring in cool climates; plant in autumn in warm climates. Start with certified organic, disease-free seed potatoes. Here are a few varieties to grow:

- 'All Blue' (late season harvest): indigo skin with white flesh, flavorful.
- 'Gold Rush' (mid-season harvest): sweet-flavored baking potato.
- 'Kennebec' (late season harvest): smooth brown potato, crisp flesh, stores for months.
- 'Red Norland' (early season harvest): new potato favorite; bake, boil, roast; red skin, white flesh.
- 'Yukon Gold' (early to mid-season): very popular; small to medium size tuber; stores well.

Jerusalem artichoke tubers can be planted where the soil is workable. Grow Jerusalem artichokes in a dedicated bed at least 3 feet from other vegetables. These plants grow tall and can shade nearby crops and the tubers multiply so give them room.

Herbs. Sow cool-weather herbs in the garden as soon as the soil is workable. These include chervil, dill, fennel, parsley, pot marjoram, and sorrel. Perennial and biennial herbs can be lifted, divided, and replanted now. Look for any overgrown clumps of bergamot, chives, and fennel.

Cutworms and seedlings. Cutworms feed at night on seedlings and young plants, usually severing the stem at or just below the soil line causing the plant to fall over. Cutworms can completely consume seedlings. Cutworms attack most early-season vegetable and flower seedlings, shoots, and transplants. During the day, cutworms rest in the soil at the base of plants; they are usually found curled up into a C-shape. Cutworms are the larvae of several species of night-flying moths. The moths are brownish or gray with 1½-inch wingspans. The larvae are plump, gray or brown, hairless caterpillars often with shiny heads. Protect seedlings and transplants from damage by using cutworm collars. A collar can be made of cardboard, plastic cup, or a small tin can with both ends removed. Press the collar an inch into the soil, leaving an inch or two exposed. The collar will exclude cutworms from the plant stem. Cultivation can expose cutworms to cold and birds. A drench containing *Steinernema* parasitic nematodes can be poured into planting beds; the nematodes will attack cutworms.

MORE THINGS TO DO IN EARLY SPRING

- **Scatter wood ash** around the onion, carrot, and radish beds or seedlings to keep root maggots away.
- **Slugs and snails.** Before slugs, snails, and pill bugs invade your leafy greens, head them off with beer traps; they are attracted to yeast in beer and will drown in the trap.
- **Monitor soil moisture.** Keep the soil just moist; do not let it go dry. Water in dry regions regularly and deeply. Avoid wetting plant foliage. Protect recently planted vegetables and herbs from drying winds.
- **Weeds.** Keep the garden free of weeds.
- **Thinning.** Thin young seedlings. Keep in mind the size of plants at maturity. Thin so that the outer leaves of plants just touch or slightly overlap at maturity.
- **Pests and disease.** Check plants for signs of pests or disease every few days. Check leaf axils and the undersides of leaves for the signs of insect pests or their eggs.

- **Chives.** Divide chives by digging up plants and teasing apart roots. You can also use a hand fork to divide a clump of chives.
- **Tools.** Check and clean tools now; sharpen blades and make repairs.
- **Poles and trellises.** Get your wire and wooden trellises and planting poles in order or get new supplies for the coming season.

PLANTING A CONTAINER VEGETABLE GARDEN

Planting a container vegetable garden is not much different than planting your in-ground vegetable garden. The same seasonal requirements apply–plant cool-season crops in early spring or late summer; plant warm-season crops in spring and summer.

Because your container garden space is limited in size–including the depth of the soil for root growth–first, select a container that is big enough for the crop you want to grow, next choose crop varieties or cultivars that will grow well in containers. You will have success with vegetables that are described as "compact," "bush," or "dwarf."

The advantages to container gardening are many:
- All you need to start is a trowel, premixed soil, and container.
- Care is easy: container gardens rarely get weeds; diseased soil is easily tossed; water is almost always close by since most container gardens are on patios, porches, or balconies
- Containers are mobile: you can take advantage of sun and seasonal changes; plants are more easily sheltered from cold.
- Harvest is quick: place your containers near the kitchen.
- Almost every plant that grows in your in-ground garden will grow in your container garden provided the container is large enough.

Because container gardens offer so much freedom, add to the adventure by growing gourmet varieties that you do not commonly find at the farm market or produce store. For a list of vegetable varieties well suited for container growing see Appendix 5, pages 195-196.

How big does a container need to be to grow vegetables? Here are suggested container sizes for vegetables you might want to grow in containers (if you want to grow more than one plant in a container add three-quarters again the width to the container sizes listed here):

- Artichoke: 18″ wide × 24″ deep.
- Beans, Lima: 12″ wide × 8-10″ deep.
- Beans, Snap: 12″ wide × 12″ deep.
- Beets: 6″ wide × 6-12″ deep.
- Broccoli: 8-12″ wide × 20″ deep.
- Brussels sprouts: 12″ wide × 18-20″ deep.
- Cabbage: 8-12″ wide × 12″ deep.
- Carrots: 10″ wide × 10″ deep.
- Cauliflower: 8-10″ wide × 10″ deep.
- Chard: 12-18″ wide × 12″ deep.
- Chinese cabbage: 12″ wide × 12″ deep.
- Collards: 12″ wide × 12″ deep.
- Corn: 36″ wide × 18″ deep; 3 plants per container to insure pollination.
- Cress: 8″ wide × 6-8″ deep.
- Cucumber: 12″ wide × 16″ deep.
- Edible Flowers: 6″ wide × 8-10″ deep.
- Eggplant: 16″ wide × 18″ deep.
- Endive, Escarole: 8″ wide × 6-8″ deep.
- Garlic: 10-12″ wide and deep.
- Herbs: 6″ wide × 8-10″ deep.
- Horseradish: 5 gallons or larger.
- Kale: 8″ wide × 8″ deep.
- Kohlrabi: 12″ wide x 10″ deep.
- Leeks: 12″ wide x 10″ deep.
- Lettuce: 8″ wide × 6-8″ deep.
- Mustard: 12″ wide x 8-12″ deep.
- Onion: 12″ wide x 12″ deep.
- Parsley: 6″ wide × 8″ deep.
- Peas: 12″ deep × 12″ wide.
- Peppers: 16″ deep × 18″ deep.

- Potatoes: at least 20 gallons.
- Pumpkins: 24″ wide x 18″ deep.
- Radicchio: 8″ wide × 6-8″ deep.
- Radishes: 12″ wide x 12″ deep.
- Spinach: 12″ wide x 12″ deep.
- Squash, summer: 24″ wide x 18″ deep.
- Squash, winter: 24″ wide x 18″ deep.
- Strawberries: 12″ wide x 12″ deep.
- Sweet Potato: 20 gallons or larger.
- Tomatoes: 24″ wide x 24-36″ deep.
- Turnips: 10-12″ wide × 12″ deep.

PLANTING HERBS

Herbs are highly adaptable they will grow in the garden, on a balcony or patio, and even indoors. An herb garden can be very small or as large as space allows. Herbs for cooking are especially rewarding; they offer great fresh flavor at very little expense. In a small space you can grow "pot herbs" for bulk use in cooking pots, "salad herbs" for raw seasoning, and "sweet herbs" for flavorings. Here is a simple checklist to start an herb garden:

Sunny location. The ideal site for an herb garden is a sunny spot with protection from the prevailing breeze. Most aromatic herbs are Mediterranean in origin, so a site with 6 to 8 hours of sun is best.

Close to kitchen. A location close to the kitchen door will make it convenient for picking herbs just as they are needed. A quiet location will make your herb garden a peaceful spot to get away from a hectic day.

Well-drained, nutrient-rich soil. Herbs grow best in soil that is rich in organic matter and well drained. Puddles of water should not remain after a rain. Add compost and well-rotted manure to the planting bed; this will ensure the soil is rich in nutrients as well as loose and well-draining. Turn the soil to about 8 inches deep and remove all debris and stones. Use a potting soil for containers. If you are planting in ground that you suspect may not be nutrient rich,

add a granular 10-10-10 organic fertilizer across the bed.

Plan before you plant. Draw a sketch of your garden before you plant. Be sure your herbs are easily accessible from paths—never more than arm's length away. You can plant herbs in straight rows or whimsical curvilinear ribbons; you can plant herbs alongside colorful annual flowers or perennials in existing flower beds. And you plant herbs in pots and containers.

Perennial and annual herbs. Plant annual herbs such as basil and chives where they can be easily replaced each year. Plant perennial herbs such as rosemary and sage where they have room to grow for several years to come. One plant of each perennial or evergreen herb is enough for most family gardens.

Essential culinary herbs. Here are a few herbs that many cooks consider essential: Parsley and chives for flavorful garnishes, sweet marjoram for flavoring, basils for both sweet and spicy flavorings, tarragon for its delicate and distinctive flavor, Florence fennel for its sweet swollen stems, sages for their many flavorful uses, dill for flavoring, coriander for its seeds and leaves, and thymes for a variety of flavors.

Sow seed or set out transplants. Some herbs can be easily started from seed; others must be set out as seedlings. (Herb seedlings are often started by commercial growers who can propagate seed or cuttings under ideal growing conditions.) You can start your own seed in a small container filled with moist potting soil. If possible germinate herb seeds indoors under grow lights shining 12 hours a day. Keep the soil moist until the seeds germinate. When seedlings have formed their first true leaves and grown to 4 inches tall they can be transplanted into the garden or containers. Don't set young plants outdoors until two or three weeks after the last frost.

Transplanting. When transplanting herb seedlings into the garden dig a hole slightly larger than the transplant's root ball and make sure to set the plant even with the soil surface–not deeper. Fill and lightly tamp the soil, and water well. Be sure to protect young seedlings from direct sunlight and wind for the first week to 10 days.

Temperature outdoors. Herb seeds can be started in the garden, but it's important to wait until the soil and air temperatures average about 70°F. Nearly all herb seeds need warm temperatures to germinate and to grow from seedlings to maturity. If you are growing herbs where temperatures are chilly be sure to protect them under a cloche, plastic hoop tunnel, or cold frame.

HARVEST BY ZONE:
Early Spring / March

Most crops coming to harvest in March were planted late last summer or autumn or in a cold frame in late winter. They overwintered in the garden or in the cold frame.

- **USDA Zones 9-10:** arugula, Asian greens, asparagus, broccoli, Brussels sprouts, cabbage, carrots, cauliflower, celery, chives, cilantro, dill, fava beans, fennel, French tarragon, garlic, kale, leeks, lettuce, onions, oregano, parsnips, peas, potatoes, radicchio, strawberries, Swiss chard, thyme, turnips.

- **USDA Zones 7-8:** arugula, beets, broccoli, cauliflower, fennel, kale, lettuce, mâche, peas, Swiss chard.

- **USDA Zones 3-7:** asparagus, chives, green garlic, parsley, scallions. Grown under cover: baby turnips, beet greens, kale, radicchio, salad greens, spinach, Swiss chard.

April
Mid-Spring

Seed Sowing and Transplanting

Mid-spring is a time of transition in the vegetable garden. Weather extremes from snow flurries to hot weather can occur in the Northern Hemisphere. In cold-winter regions, spring weather may still be several weeks away. In warm-winter regions, the last frost has already passed and gardens are warming.

The timing of planting is important in the vegetable garden. Frost and cool weather can harm warm-weather crops sown or transplanted into the garden too soon. Some cool-weather crops can thrive where there is still the threat of frost, but in southern regions where the last frost is past warming temperatures may mean the end of seeding or transplanting of cool-weather crops and the start of the warm-weather vegetable planting season. Keep an eye on weather forecasts during this time of transition.

You can use the bloom time of shrubs and trees in your neighborhood to tell you when it's safe to plant vegetables in the garden. The flowering of trees, shrubs, and perennial plants is determined by day length and temperature—both soil and air temperature. The same is true for vegetables.

As mentioned in the last chapter, experienced gardeners often look to lilacs to tell them when it is safe to plant vegetables in the garden. Here is the lilac "planting calendar" for the vegetable garden:

Lilac begins to leaf out: direct sow seed of cool-weather vegetables such as peas, lettuce, and spinach; direct sow cold-tolerant herbs such as parsley and chervil.

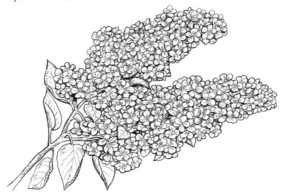

Blooming lilacs are one way nature signals the start of the vegetable planting season.

Lilac flower spike is in full bloom: direct sow seed of basil, corn, tomatoes, and warm-season crops.

Nature Cycles and Vegetable Garden Planting

Lilacs are not the only plants that offer signals. Once again phenology (as explained in the March chapter) is the study of the natural cycles of plants and animals. Vegetable gardeners can look to the leafing out and blooming of several different shrubs and trees to know when to sow vegetables in the garden. Here are shrub and tree bloom times that can be used to signal vegetable seed sowing times in your garden:

- **Green Bean:** direct sow when lilacs bloom.
- **Broad bean:** direct sow when flowering quince, saucer magnolia, grape hyacinth, and narcissus are in full bloom.
- **Beet:** direct sow when forsythia and dandelions begin to bloom.
- **Broccoli:** direct sow when flowering quince, saucer magnolia, grape hyacinth, and narcissus are in full bloom.
- **Brussels sprouts:** direct sow when forsythia and dandelions begin to bloom.
- **Carrot:** direct sow when forsythia and dandelions begin to bloom.
- **Cauliflower:** direct sow when flowering quince, saucer magnolia, grape hyacinth, and narcissus are in full bloom.
- **Celeriac:** direct sow when flowering quince, saucer magnolia, grape hyacinth, and narcissus are in full bloom.
- **Celery:** direct sow when flowering quince, saucer magnolia, grape hyacinth, and narcissus are in full bloom.
- **Chervil:** direct sow when forsythia and dandelions begin to bloom.
- **Corn:** direct sow when redbuds, flowering dogwoods, flowering crabapple are in bloom and lilacs are in full bloom.
- **Corn salad:** direct sow when flowering quince, saucer magnolia, grape hyacinth, and narcissus are in full bloom.
- **Cucumber:** direct sow when redbuds, flowering dogwoods, and flowering crabapple bloom and lilacs are in full bloom.

- **Endive and escarole:** direct sow when forsythia and dandelions begin to bloom.

- **Eggplant:** set out plants when peony, black locust, and goldenchains tree are in full bloom.

- **Florence fennel:** direct sow when flowering quince, saucer magnolia, grape hyacinth, and narcissus are in full bloom.

- **Kohlrabi:** direct sow when forsythia and dandelions begin to bloom.

- **Leek:** direct sow when forsythia and dandelions begin to bloom.

- **Lettuce:** direct sow when forsythia and dandelions begin to bloom.

- **Lima bean, bush:** direct sow when Chinese wisteria blooms.

- **Lima bean, pole:** set out plants when peony, black locust, and goldenchains tree are in full bloom.

- **Melon:** direct sow when redbuds, flowering dogwoods, flowering crabapple are in bloom and lilacs are in full bloom.

- **New Zealand spinach:** direct sow when Chinese wisteria blooms.

- **Okra:** set out plants when peony, black locust, and goldenchains tree are in full bloom.

- **Parsley:** direct sow when forsythia and dandelions begin to bloom.

- **Parsnip:** direct sow when forsythia and dandelions begin to bloom.

- **Pea:** direct sow when forsythia and dandelions begin to bloom.

- **Peppers:** set out plants when peony, black locust, and goldenchain trees are in full bloom.

- **Onion (sets, seed):** direct sow when forsythia and dandelions begin to bloom.

- **Potato:** plant when daffodils and dandelions begin to bloom.

- **Pumpkin:** direct sow when redbuds, flowering dogwoods, and flowering crabapples bloom and lilacs are in full bloom.

- **Radish:** direct sow when forsythia and dandelions begin to bloom.

- **Salsify:** direct sow when forsythia and dandelions begin to bloom.

- **Soybean:** direct sow when Chinese wisterias bloom.

- **Spinach:** direct sow when forsythia and dandelions begin to bloom.

- **Squash:** direct sow when redbuds, flowering dogwoods, and flowering crabapple bloom and lilacs are in full bloom.

- **Sweet potato:** set out plants when peony, black locust, and goldenchain trees are in full bloom.

- **Swiss chard:** direct sow when forsythia and dandelions begin to bloom.

- **Tomatillo:** set out plants when peony, black locust, and goldenchain trees are in full bloom.

- **Tomato:** set out plants when peony, black locust, and goldenchain trees are in full bloom.

- **Turnip:** direct sow when forsythia and dandelions begin to bloom.

- **Watermelon:** set out plants when peony, black locust, and goldenchain trees are in full bloom.

- **Zucchini:** direct sow when redbuds, flowering dogwoods, and flowering crabapple in bloom and lilacs are in full bloom.

Succession Plantings of Crops: Make succession plantings any time after the first planting dates but keep in mind the number of days for a crop to reach maturity. Also consider increasing or decreasing air temperature as the season progresses; i.e. cool-weather crops must come to harvest before the warm temperatures arrive in late spring or summer and warm-weather crops must mature before cool and chilly temperatures arrive in autumn.

PLANTING BEDS AND WIDE ROWS

Narrow planting beds. A vegetable garden planting bed should be easy to work. Consider a planting bed no wider than the reach of your arm from either side of the bed. If the depth of each planting bed is no more than the length of your reach, you will never have to step into the bed once it's established. This makes working your garden less messy and protects the soil, worms, and soil microorganisms from being disturbed or compacted. A garden bed you can work from the edge is called a narrow bed; it's not too wide. If the reach of your arm is 24 inches and you can work the planting bed from both sides, a narrow planting bed 48 inches across or less is right; if your reach is 18 inches, your planting bed should be 36 inches wide across or less. If you can work the planting bed from only one side, the narrow bed will be no wider than your reach across—18 inches or 24 inches. The length of a narrow bed should be no more than the distance you want to walk from one side to the other. When considering the length of a planting bed keep in mind that you may want to carry tools and a hose from one side to the other, so don't make the walk a chore.

You can reach to the center of a narrow bed without stepping into the growing soil. Wide rows are placed across the narrow bed.

Wide rows. Planting wide rows across a planting bed will allow you the optimal use of garden space. (A traditional single straight line row like you would see on a farm leaves unused space on either side of the row. Farmers use that space to run tractors through their fields. In a home garden that space and soil is wasted if not planted.) A wide row can span the width of a narrow bed. A wide row can grow one, two, three, four or more plants across. A wide row across a 36-inch wide bed is enough space to grow 6 leaf lettuce plants. The same row could grow 3 lettuce plants and 3 spinach plants or 1 pepper plant

and 6 radishes. A wide row can grow three times the number of plants as a single row.

Advantages of wide row planting:

- Grow two to three times more what you would grow in a conventional single row.
- Best use of garden space for growing; unused space between rows is eliminated.
- Close spaced plants in wide rows create their own living mulch; the soil is cooler in hot weather and soil moisture evaporation is reduced.
- Crops are easily harvested from the edge of the row; no stepping into planting beds.
- Different crops and varieties are easily interplanted; varieties with differing days to maturity can be harvested in succession or staggered.

Equidistant planting also called intensive planting. Equidistant planted vegetables produce the most food. To plant traditional rows you stake out rows with a taut string and space the seeds or seedlings at the distance recommended by seed packets or plant labels. Traditional row gardens leaves 6 to 12 inches or more between rows; that's unused soil. In equidistant or intensive planting, seeds and seedlings are set not in rows but at a distance that allows each plant to reach its mature size and just overlap with each of its neighboring plants. Plants are set equidistant in all directions—spacing is closer than straight row recommended distances found on seed packets. When intensively planted, seeds and seedlings are spaced to just overlap at maturity or to just touch at three-quarters maturity—every inch of growing ground becomes productive. Intensive planted crops are commonly grown in wide rows set in narrow beds. Less open space between growing plants means more production.

Planting on a triangular grid. Plants set equidistant from each other in wide rows form naturally staggered or offset rows; they form a triangular grid pattern when viewed from above. When grown equidistant from one another plants of equal size at maturity will appear to be set at the three points of an equilateral triangle. Equidistant planting in a triangular grid pattern provides the most efficient use of space allowing gardeners to grow the greatest number of plants in a given area (16 percent more plants than plants set on a square grid).

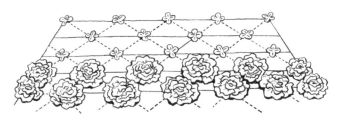

Planting on a triangular grid creates staggered rows and allows for equidistant planting; your garden will be more productive.

Equidistant plant spacing. There are several ways you can accomplish equidistant planting. First you must know the approximate size of each plant at maturity. Here are recommended distances between plants set equidistant in a wide row; these distances reflect the size of each plant at maturity:

- Beans: 4-6″
- Beets: 2-4″
- Cabbage: 15″
- Carrots: 2″
- Cauliflower: 15″
- Celery: 6-8″
- Chard: 8-12″
- Chinese cabbage: 12-18″
- Collards: 15-18″
- Endive: 6-12″
- English peas: 4-6″
- Garlic: 4-8″
- Kale: 12″
- Kohlrabi: 5-8″
- Leeks: 6″
- Lettuce: 6-9″
- Mustard: 4-6″
- Onions: 3-5″
- Parsley: 6-8″
- Parsnips: 3-4″
- Peppers: 24″
- Radishes: 2-4″
- Rutabagas: 6-8″
- Southern peas: 6″
- Spinach: 4-6″
- Tomatoes: 24-36″
- Turnips: 2-6″

For more on planting distances see Appendix 2, pages 166-167.

DIRECT SEEDING IN THE GARDEN

Direct seeding. Start sowing cool-season vegetable seeds in the garden without the protection of a plastic hoop tunnel as soon as the weather has moderated when day and night temperatures are 50°F or warmer. If you are in doubt, check the soil temperature with a soil thermometer to make sure the soil has warmed to greater than 41°F; few seeds will germinate if the soil

temperature is colder—warmer is better. Delay planting outdoors if the soil is too cold.

Direct sow hardy and half-hardy vegetables and herbs first: beets, broccoli, Brussels sprouts, cabbage, carrots, celery, chard, endive, parsnips, smooth coated peas (wrinkled pea seeds later), potatoes, salsify, spinach, and turnips. Sow early peas in a sheltered spot. Protect cabbage, lettuce and other vulnerable leafy vegetables with cloches, plastic hoop tunnels, or inverted flower pots if the nights are expected to get cold. Seeds of beets, carrots, and parsley should be soaked for two hours in warm water before planting. Plant potatoes as soon as the ground is workable. Cut the tubers into 3 or 4 pieces, each with several good "eyes", and set them in trenches, about 3 inches deep and 2 to 3 feet apart.

Broadcasting or scattering seed. Small seeds are commonly broadcast or scattered by hand across the planting bed. Scatter small seed evenly across the planting bed or in shallow seed rows or trenches. Cover the seeds by raking fine soil over them to the recommended depth—soil cover should be equal to about twice the depth of the seed diameter. Firm the seed in place with the palm of your hand or a flat board, or the back of a rake. Seeds must make close contact with the soil to germinate.

Sowing seed in dry soil. If you are starting seed in the garden during a dry spell, germination and growth will be speeded if you first sprinkle the bed or fill the trench or seed row with water. As soon as the water has seeped into the soil, you can sow your seed and cover them with loose dry soil then gently moisten the planting bed.

Temperature for warm-season crop seed sowing. When day time temperatures average 60° to 65°F or greater, warm-season crops can be sown directly in the garden or transplanted out. Warm-season crops include: beans, corn, cucumbers, eggplant, peppers, melons, squash, and tomatoes.

Direct seed sowing checklist for mid-spring:
- Sow cool-weather crops first. Cool-weather leaf and flower crops include: bok choy, broad beans, broccoli, Brussels sprouts, cabbage, cauliflower,

chard, kale, lettuce, peas, and spinach. Cool-season root crops include beets, carrots, kohlrabi, leeks, onion sets, parsnips, early potatoes, radishes, scallions, shallots, and turnips.

- Sow early peas (with unwrinkled skins) first in a sheltered spot. Add phosphorus and potassium to the soil for good pod yield.

- Protect cabbage, lettuce and other vulnerable seedlings with cloches, hot caps, plastic hoop tunnels, or inverted flower pots if the nights are expected to get cold.

- Choose a sheltered spot with moist soil, to make the first sowing of carrots. Seeds of beets, carrots, and parsley should be soaked for two hours in warm water before planting.

- Direct-seed onions and shallots as soon as the soil can be worked. Plant onions and shallots in a sunny spot in compost-rich, well-drained soil.

- Direct sow lettuce, endive, escarole, and spinach. Sow successive crops every 2 weeks into autumn. Plant heat-tolerant, slow-bolting loose-leaf cultivars such as 'Green Ice', 'Simpson Elite', and 'Red Oakleaf'; plant summer Batavia lettuce 'Deer Tongue' and Bibb lettuce 'Buttercrunch'. Other heat-resistant leafy crops are 'Coral' escarole, 'Tres Fine' curly endive, and 'Hector' spinach.

- Make successive sowing at 10 to 14 day intervals of beets, carrots, lettuce, turnips, runner beans, green beans, endive, radishes, and kohlrabi.

- Direct sow radishes throughout the season; begin now. Sow new crops every 2 to 3 weeks. Keep the soil evenly moist for best yield. White daikon cultivars should be planted in late spring or summer, not spring; daikons bolt in cool weather.

- Plant 1-year-old asparagus roots (called crowns) in early to mid-spring. Dig new planting beds 18 to 24 inches deep adding aged compost and well-rotted manure. Dedicated asparagus beds will produce fresh asparagus spears for 20 years. Soil pH should be 6.5 to 7.5; asparagus does not like acid soil. Plant at least 25 roots. First harvest of a few spears will come one year after planting; three years after planting harvest will begin in earnest. When purchasing asparagus crowns, choose male plants—not female. Female asparagus plants produce more spears, but the spears are smaller than spears produced by male plants; that's because female plants must use energy to also produce berries or seed.

- When day time temperatures average 65°F or greater, warm-weather crops can be sown or transplanted out. Warm-weather crops include: basil, beans, corn, cucumbers, eggplant, peppers, melons, okra, squash, and tomatoes.

TRANSPLANTING SEEDLINGS INTO THE GARDEN

Transplanting vegetables: Crops started indoors are ready for transplanting out in the garden when they are about 4 inches tall or slightly taller. When it's time to transplant seedlings make sure the soil in the garden has been prepared in advance. Dig planting holes, properly spaced, before you begin transplanting. Set plants in the ground no deeper than they were in the container; this will help prevent stem rot which sometimes comes with banking soil too high around plant stems. If the weather is not right for transplanting, it is best to pot up young seedlings into the next largest container to avoid roots becoming cramped. Timing is everything when it comes to transplanting; the outdoor soil and air temperatures must be right and the weather should be settled.

Transplanting tips:

- Transplant seedlings when they are young and stocky; avoid setting out plants that have become leggy and spindly. Younger plants transplant better than older plants.

- Harden off seedlings started indoors before transplanting out to the garden.

- Water plants the day before transplanting.

- Transplant out seedlings on a day that is overcast rather than bright and sunny. Shade transplants set out on sunny days.

- Measure and mark the spots and dig holes for transplants ahead of setting out. Make sure the

Support the stem of the seedling as you ease it out of its pot; set it in a hole half again as big as the root ball and gently firm in the soil.

plants are properly spaced—consider the size and spread of each plant at maturity.

- Moisten the planting hole before setting out transplants; moisten the seedlings root ball as well.

- Set out only young, healthy plants. Toss old and weak plants into the compost pile.

- Firm the soil in around transplants so that roots make good contact with the soil in the new planting bed.

- Water in plants thoroughly after transplanting. Water young plants regularly and deeply. Keep the soil just moist—not wet. Avoid wetting plant foliage when you water; this will help keep diseases out of the garden.

- If you have any doubt about whether it is safe to set transplants into the garden then transition the seedlings by placing a plastic hoop tunnel, cloche, or hot cap over the plants for several days to a week or more.

- Protect recently planted vegetables and herbs from drying winds.

- Feed seedlings with manure or compost tea after planting. Soak compost or well-rotted manure in water. You can use the resulting "tea" as a liquid fertilizer.

Selecting plants at a nursery:

The alternative to starting seed indoors or in the garden is to plant plants started by a grower. You can purchase grower-started seedlings at a garden center or nursery. Seedlings for transplanting into the garden are commonly started weeks in advance. Starting your own seed is the least expensive method of growing vegetables, but sometimes buying seedlings from a grower is the best course especially if you are tight on space and time. Here's what to look for if you decide to buy seedlings from a garden center or grower:

- Choose seedlings that are dark green and have stocky, straight stems.

- Choose plants that are vigorous and healthy looking.

- Choose compact plants with leaves spaced close together on the stems.

- Choose plant with healthy new growth at the top.

- Avoid plants that are top heavy.

- Avoid seedlings with yellowish or purplish leaves.

- Avoid plants that are stretched, leggy, or limp.

- Avoid plants that have damaged leaves or stems.

- Avoid plants with leaves that are soft or mushy or plants with brown, dry leaves of leaf edges.

- Avoid plants that look wilted or stressed.

PLANTING ZONE-BY-ZONE: April / Mid-Spring

Beginning with the warmest regions first, here is a seed starting and planting guide for early spring— April. It is safe to plant or do any of the tasks listed for regions cooler than yours.

USDA Zone 10: warming conditions

- Direct-sow or plant out tender warm-season vegetables and herbs.
- Plant sweet potatoes and okra now.
- Feed seedlings with liquid fertilizer after planting.
- Thin seedlings of earlier plantings.
- Remove bolted cabbage family crops and leafy greens from the garden and compost them.
- Plant cilantro, lemongrass, and oregano after parsley, coriander, and dill go to seed.

USDA Zones 7-9: frost possible

- Direct-sow or plant out successions of cool-weather vegetables and herbs where temperatures will remain moderate, 75°F or less; sow cabbage, carrots, cauliflower, celery, endive, kohlrabi, lettuce, radishes and turnips.
- If the weather is mild and you do not expect frost, set out warm-season seedlings such as bush and pole beans, cucumbers, eggplant, sweet corn, melons, peppers, tomatoes, and squashes. Don't rush planting of summer crops until you are sure the last frost is past.
- Plant out bay, hyssop, lavender, mint, rosemary, rue, and sage. Make further sowings of dill, fennel, parsley, and pot marjoram. Layer creeping stems of thyme to root new plants. Sow basil indoors.
- Plant early potatoes.
- Start sweet potato slips to transplant out next month.
- Thin seedlings of earlier plantings.
- Stop picking asparagus spears so that the plants do not exhaust themselves. Plant asparagus crowns.
- Continue to plant onion sets in the north.
- Feed seedlings with liquid fertilizer after planting.
- Water garden if weather is dry. Weed as needed.
- Plant new strawberries. Put cloches over strawberries if you want an early corp.
- Remove rhubarb flowers as soon as they appear; this allows the plant to continue strong growth.

USDA Zones 3-6: danger of frost and freeze

- Prepare the soil for early planting. Spread aged compost and manure, and fertilizers across planting beds.
- Place cloches and black plastic sheeting across planting beds to warm the soil. Use horticultural fleece or floating row covers to protect early crops.
- Start sowing vegetables without protection if you live where the weather is mild; check the seed packets to make sure they are suitable for early sowing.
- Where the weather remains chilly, sow early crops in cold frames, plastic hoop tunnels, or beneath cloches. You can also protect seedlings from chilly nights or frost with hot caps, inverted flower pots, cardboard boxes, or newspaper tents.
- Direct-sow or plant out cold-tolerant vegetables and herbs. Sow fava beans, beets, Brussels sprouts, carrots, cauliflower, endive, lettuce, onion sets, parsnips, early peas, potatoes, radishes, scallions, shallots, spinach, Swiss chard, and turnips.
- Soak beet, carrot, and parsley seed for 2 hours in warm water then drain and wash thoroughly in cool water before sowing. Mix beet, carrot, and parsley seed with dry sand to facilitate sowing.
- Harden off cabbage, broccoli, cauliflower , celery, and kohlrabi seedlings for a week before setting them out in the garden under cloches
- When the weather permits, set out new asparagus, rhubarb, and strawberry plants under cloches.
- Sow tomato, pepper, eggplant, cucumber, and melon seed in hotbeds or indoors if you haven't done so already. Apply a fungicide if damping off has been a problem in the past.
- Chit (sprout) 'seed' potatoes (small tubers) of early varieties. Plant potatoes as soon as the ground is workable. Cut the tubers into 3 or 4 pieces each with several good eyes, and set them in trenches about 3 inches deep and 3 feet apart. Soil should be well dug and fertilized, but not limed.

- Make a second sowing of early peas two weeks after the first sowing. Make successive sowing of cool-season crops every 10 to 14 days—beets, carrots, onions, spinach, Swiss chard, and turnips.

- Where the weather is mild, set out transplants of beans, cucumber, corn, eggplant, melon, parsley, pepper, squash, and tomato. Don't set out warm-season crops too soon particularly if late spring cold spells are common in your region.

MID-SPRING GARDEN TASKS

Early crops. As soon as the soil is workable plant garlic, kale, leaf lettuces, onion sets and seeds, radishes, spinach. These crops can be planted in blocks. Choose the planting bed that gets the most sun where the soil has dried out from winter.

Seed starting in a plastic hoop tunnel. Hardy, cool-season vegetables can be started in a plastic hoop tunnel or portable cold frame. Amend the planting bed with aged compost, turn it, and rake it even and fine. You can use this covered bed to start seedlings that will later be transplanted to other parts of the garden. Cabbage family crops—cabbage, broccoli, Brussels sprouts, cauliflower, collards, and kale—can be started under a plastic hoop tunnel. Plants started in a plastic hoop tunnel will transplant easily; they are already acclimatized to outdoor temperatures and soil. (Warning: plastic hoop tunnels and cold frames can heat up on clear warm days; be sure to open the hoop tunnel or frame midday on warm days.)

Broadcast sowing early crops. Beets, carrots, chard, lettuce, onions, peas, spinach, and turnips can be planted outdoors as soon as the soil is workable. Plant these crops in wide beds. Broadcast or sprinkle the seed across the planting bed; a 16 to 24-inch wide block or band will be right for these crops. Don't worry if broadcast seed seems to be a little heavy seeded; more seed is better than less—you can thin later. Press seed firmly into the soil with a flat board or the back of your hand; seed must make good contact with the soil. Sprinkle a quarter inch or more soil over the top of the seeds. Lightly water the seedbed after sowing. When seedlings come up you can thin the block by pulling a steel rake across the block uprooting some of the seedlings leaving rows of others in place.

Radish markers. Radishes sprout faster than any other vegetable. If you want to mark a row or block of just sowed seed, sprinkle radish seed at the end of the row or along the edges of the block. If you intermix radish seeds in rows or blocks with other seeds, the radishes will be harvested before other crops freeing up space and leaving the soil aerated for the longer to harvest crop. A good combination is radishes interplanted with carrots; when the radishes are lifted the carrot roots can expand into the loosened soil just vacated by the radish roots.

Radishes to grow include:

- 'Cherry Belle' (22 days to harvest): classic, red, round, mildly pungent.

- 'Easter Egg' (28 days to harvest): multi-colored roots—white, purple, red, pink, lavender skinned.

- 'French Breakfast' (20 days to harvest): long, cylindrical, red with white tip.

- 'White Icicle' (30 days to harvest): pure white, 4 to 6 inches long, good summer grower.

Soil test and liming. If your pH soil test shows the soil is acidic—below 6.5 for most vegetables—add lime to the soil. Ground limestone is slow to break down, so the true effect of liming will not come for a few months. Where the soil is naturally acidic, liming may be required every 4 to 5 years. You can lime planting beds in the spring or autumn. Lime does not hinder or interfere with seed germination.

Earthworms. Earthworms benefit the soil and plants in three important ways: (1) they burrow through the soil and dirt clods increasing soil aeration which benefits plant roots; (2) they break down organic matter—eating leaves, grass clipping, and soft vegetation remains; (3) their excrement—called "castings"—is rich in nutrients plants need. Earthworms rise or descend into the soil with the surface temperature; they thrive where the soil temperature is between 55° and 75°F. Stepping into planting beds and working the soil can send earthworms deeper, but when the soil goes undisturbed they will return to soil rich in organic material that is in the temperature range they prefer.

Planting garlic. You can plant cloves from garlic heads purchased at a grocery store or farm market as long as they have not been treated to prevent sprouting. Garlic requires a long season for optimal yield; garlic's long season of growth must include 6 or more weeks of chilly weather for optimal bulb or head production. Spring planted garlic (set out 6 weeks before the last frost) will reach maturity in about 100 days, but bulbs will not be as large as autumn planted garlic. To plant garlic: separate the cloves in a garlic set or head. Plant each clove broad side or root side down every 3 to 4 inches. A 12-inch by 36-inch wide row should be enough for a plentiful harvest. The largest cloves will produce the largest garlic.

Garlic types and varieties to plant: There are three botanical groups of garlic:

- Softneck garlic: The necks of this garlic type are soft and pliable at maturity. Softneck is the strongest-flavored garlic. It is less winter hardy than hardneck garlic but stores better. 'Silverneck' is a soft-neck suited to cool climates. 'Red Torch' is a softneck suited for warm climates.

- Hardneck, also called Rocambole, and Spanish garlic: This garlic has a stiff central stem or neck which curls at the top forming a 360° coil. It has a mild flavor. Hardneck garlic takes nine months to reach harvest. 'German Porcelain' is a hardneck type. 'Killarney Red' is hardneck garlic.

- Elephant garlic: Elephant garlic is not true garlic; it is a type of leek. This plant gets its name from its size; it has large fist-size bulbs weighing up to ½ pound or more. Elephant garlic has a mild flavor.

Milk jug cloches. Cut the bottoms off plastic gallon-size milk jugs to use them as cloches to protect tender warm-season seeds and seedlings. Place the jug over young tomatoes, peppers, eggplants, and melons; mound some soil up around the bottom of the jug to insure it stays warm inside. Leaving the jug cap off during the day will insure ventilation and keep the temperature inside from getting too warm.

A simple cloche: remove the bottom and top of a plastic milk jug and set it around the young plant to protect it from early season chill.

Screwing the cap on at night will protect seedlings from a heavy frost.

Cloches and hot caps are small glass, plastic, or paper covers placed over plants or seeds to protect them from cold or bad weather. Cloches and hot caps are commonly used at the beginning or end of the growing season when there are big swings in the daytime and nighttime temperature. These protective devices can add 3 to 4 weeks to the growing season. The temperature inside a cloche or hot cap will be 2 to 5 degrees warmer than the outside temperature; that is enough to protect a plant from an early or late frost. Cloches and hot caps can also protect fragile plants from wind and heavy rains. Cloches and hot caps can be simply made from materials you find around the house—plastic jugs or plastic sheeting is most common. Commercial cloches are made of glass or heavy translucent plastic including hard plastics such as Plexiglas and fiberglass and soft plastics such as polyethylene and Mylar. Use heavy plastic for long life; use soft plastic when you plan to move the cover often. A word of warning: cloches and hot caps—especially those made of plastic and glass—heat up quickly on warm, sunny days. The temperature under a cover can quickly grow too hot for plants. Don't leave cloches in place over plants on sunny or mild days.

Potting-up tomatoes. Potting up means transplanting a plant from a smaller container to a larger container. Tomatoes started indoors are commonly potted up as they wait for the outdoor temperatures to warm in spring. To pot-up a tomato, pinch off all but the very top branches; you are going to bury all but the top branches in the new pot (be sure to select a pot deep enough). Place an inch or two of potting soil in the bottom of the new pot and set the root ball on the soil—make sure the potting soil and the root ball are just moist. Now, fill in potting soil around the stem up to just below the top leaves of the plant. New roots will grow along the length of the stem where you pinched off the branches. This will give the tomato a strong root system. Always pot-up tomatoes that are spindly or leggy.

Potting-up peppers, eggplants and others. Any crop started indoors can be potted-up as it waits to go into the garden. Potting-up insures that young plants to not become root bound and that they have plenty of shoulder room—that they do not grow crowded in flats or small containers. Vegetables commonly started indoors and potted up are peppers, eggplant, tomatoes, celery, melons, and squashes. When tomatoes are potted up their lowest branches are nipped off and the stem is buried up to just below the top two or three branches or sets of leaves; don't do this with other crops. Set peppers, eggplants, celery, melons, and squashes in the new pot slightly higher in the soil than they sat in the previous pot—then fill in soil around the root ball.

Planting peas. Plant peas in a block that is easy to work from the edges, a 3 × 3 foot or 4 × 4 foot block is about right. Sprinkle the seeds across the planting bed or sow them at 1 to 3 inch intervals then rake soil over the top of the seed to a depth of about 1 inch. Before sowing, toss the seed in a bag of inoculant—inoculant is a bacterial powder that helps peas and beans fix nitrogen in their roots. (Bacteria called Rhizobia works with nodules on the roots of peas and beans to chemically convert—"fix"—nitrogen from the air to make it available for the plant.) Peas planted close together will support one another and do not need a trellis or stakes. Close planting also keeps the soil cool and weed-free. Peas are self-fertilizing.

Peas: types and varieties. Peas can be classified as indeterminate (climbing) or determinate (bush or dwarf). The taller the plant grows, the larger the yield. Tall types require a fairly long, cool spring and often do not mature until summer. Tall peas should be grown on poles, fences, or trellises. Some peas are for shelling, some have edible pods, and others can be shelled or eaten pod and all. Shelling peas can be used fresh or dried and used in soups. Edible pod peas are called snow or sugar peas. Peas that are shelled and eaten fresh are called green peas, garden peas, or English peas. There are many varieties of bush and pole peas; here are some to try:

- **Garden peas:** 'Knight' and 'Dakota' are harvested early; 'Lincoln' is a sweet heirloom; 'Green Arrow' is a flavorful climber; 'Tall Telephone' is a sweet climber; 'Alaska' is a short-season variety; 'Little Marvel' and 'Wando' are small bush varieties.
- **Snow peas:** 'Oregon Giant' is large podded; 'Mammoth Melting Sugar' is long podded.
- **Sugar peas:** 'Super Sugar Snap' is a sweet climber; 'Sugar Snap' is a pole pea; 'Sugar Ann' is a bush pea.

Planting potatoes. Here's how to plant potatoes step-by-step:

- Create a furrow or dig individual holes 4 to 5 inches deep. New potatoes form above the seed potato so you want at least 4 to 5 inches above the seed potato for new potato growth. Set holes for each seed potato at least a foot or two apart; if planting in rows set rows 3 feet part.
- Set small seed potatoes in the bottom of the furrow or hole. Large seed potatoes should be cut into quarters or pieces with two or three "eyes" per piece. Sprinkle sulfur on the cuts of pieces (you can get sulfur at a drug store); sulfur keeps the cut pieces from rotting. Also let the cut pieces sit a day or two so that the cut can toughen or "heal".
- Sprinkle bone meal at the bottom of the furrow or hole (or superphosphate 0-20-0); bone meal is rich in phosphorus which is important for root growth. Cover the bone meal or fertilizer with a few inches of soil so the seed potato does not sit directly on the phosphorus.
- Set the seed potato cut side down so that the eyes or sprouted buds are facing skyward—the direction they will grow.

- Cover the seed potato with 4 to 5 inches of loose soil and firm the soil in the back of your hand or the back of a hoe.

- As soon as the first leaves sprout, begin "hilling" the new growth. Hilling means drawing soil up to nearly cover the leaves. Hilling adds additional soil above the seed potato for the formation of new potatoes.

Planting squashes, melons, and cucumbers on mounds. Vining crops can be planted on mounds. (Create mounds as soon as the soil is workable but wait until two or three weeks after the last frost to sow seed.) Use your steel rake to mound up soil from the surrounding ground. A mound 6 inches high and 36 inches across is good. Mounds warm quickly in spring and stay warm through the growing season; this is important for vining crops. (You can also plant squashes, melons, and cucumbers on mounds.) Space mounds at least 3 feet apart or more. Scoop out a 10-inch diameter hollow or bowl in the center of the mound. Sow 3 or 4 seeds or set 2 or 3 plants in the hollow and backfill. Sprinkle a few radishes into the hollow as well; quick germinating radishes will attract leaf eaters that might otherwise bother young vining crops. Cover the seed with an inch or two of soil. Place a hot cap or small plastic dome or hoop tunnel over the planted seeds until the seeds germinate. Continue to protect young seedlings from cool temperatures until 3 weeks after the last spring frost.

MORE MID-SPRING TIPS

- **Pests.** Watch for pests. Look out for aphids on broad beans and root flies on cabbages, carrots, and onions. Pinch out the tips on broad beans to encourage good pod set and to deter attack from aphids. Place beer traps at the base of leafy greens to kill slugs, snails, and pill bugs. Place cardboard collars around seedlings to exclude cutworms.

- **Diseases.** Good plant care is the best defense against disease. Do not work around wet plants. Plant diseases are easily spread on tools and clothing when a gardener moves around plants with wet foliage. Keep the garden free of all plant debris; fallen leaves and dead plants can harbor diseases.

- **Watering.** Water regularly and deeply. Water in newly transplanted crops and then shade them from the sun and wind until they are established. Avoid wetting plant foliage. Protect recently planted vegetables and herbs from drying winds.

- **Weeds.** Cultivate between plants and rows. Get rid of small weeds as soon as they appear.

- **Thinning.** Thin out overcrowded seedlings. Remove overcrowded seedlings by cutting the weaker seedlings off at the soil level with a scissors; this will ensure the roots of remaining plants are not disturbed or uprooted.

- **Feed seedlings** with compost tea or dilute fish emulsion after planting. Soak compost in water. You can use the resulting "tea" as a liquid fertilizer.

- **Support young plants.** Sticks or netting can support growing peas. Corn can support itself if planted in several short rows in a rectangle or block; block planting will also aid pollination.

- **Frost protection.** Cover seedlings and warm-weather crops with horticultural fleece if night frost is forecast.

- **Succession planting.** To get the most out of your vegetable garden, successive plantings of crops are a way to extend the season. Plant leafy greens and root crops as early as possible and then plant successions of these crops every week to 10 days. Quick-maturing crops are best for successive planting: lettuce, radishes, spinach, chard, peas, beets, and carrots in cool weather, and later in warm weather string beans and sweet corn.

- **Asparagus.** In the northern regions, the first asparagus are starting to appear; cut the stems when they are 4-6 inches high. Where the harvest has already been underway for 3 to 4 weeks, stop cutting spears before plants begin to exhaust themselves. Prepare asparagus beds and plant asparagus crowns for next year.

- **Rhubarb.** Remove rhubarb flowers as soon as they appear before they rob the plant of food and energy.

- **Potato** plants should be earthed up as they grow. Mound soil up around the plant leaving just the top few leaves exposed.

- **Celery** should be fed about 3 weeks after plants are set out; use compost tea of dilute fish emulsion. Keep celery moist by regular irrigations. Black heart celery disease is caused by alternate drying and wetting of soil.

- **Compost pile.** Turn the compost pile when it thaws. Begin a new compost pile during the spring if you don't already have one. Add dry leaves, grass, and non-fatty kitchen scraps to the pile.

DROUGHT-TOLERANT VEGETABLES FOR DRY SUMMER REGIONS

If you live where water is scarce or where summers are long and dry, choose vegetables that do not demand a lot of water. Below is a list of drought tolerant vegetables that are very good performers. One note, even plants that do not require a lot of water still require some water. Once these plants are well established—meaning their roots have begun to grow deep, they will get by with slow, deep watering once every 7 to 10 days. Here are vegetable varieties for dry summer regions:

- Amaranth: green leaves used as vegetables; use thinnings raw in salad, steam like spinach.
- Moth bean: nutty flavor, popular in India.
- Garbanzo bean, also called chickpea: bean for making humus and use in salads.
- Tepary bean: grows in desert and near desert conditions, a common bean.
- Black-eyed pea, also called cowpeas: use bean to make vegetable soup.
- Yard-long asparagus bean: long, thin, crunchy pod often used in Chinese cooking.
- Snap beans and pole beans: require a short growing season and can draw on residual soil water.
- Swiss chard
- Black Aztec corn: use black kernels for roasting.

- Eggplant
- Mustard greens: tangy, spicy salad green.
- Purslane: use as a salad green.
- Okra
- New Zealand spinach: a warm weather spinach use just as cool-weather spinach.
- 'Pearson' tomato: old fashion flavor, used often for canning.
- 'Early Girl' tomato: medium size, tasty.
- 'Super Roma' tomato, 'Golden Nugget' tomato.
- 'Sugar Baby' watermelon: sweet tasting ice box watermelon.

Planting vegetables in dry regions. Set plants at least 1½ times or greater the spacing distance recommended on seed packets. When fewer plants are in the garden there will be more water to go around. For example, tomatoes that might normally be planted on 4 foot centers should be planted on 5 or 6 foot centers. (It is important to note that seeds must germinate under normal conditions; that is they must receive moisture to begin life and grow. Give seeds and seedlings all the water they need until they are established.)

HARVEST BY ZONE: Mid-Spring / April

Crops listed here were planted last autumn or winter or in early spring:

- **USDA Zones 9-10:** amaranth, artichokes, arugula, Asian greens, asparagus, basil, beans, beets, broccoli, cabbage, carrots, cauliflower, celery, chives, cilantro, collards, dill, fava beans, fennel, French tarragon, garlic, kale, kohlrabi, leeks, lettuce, mustard, onions, oregano, peas, potatoes, radicchio, rhubarb, spinach, strawberries, Swiss chard, thyme, turnips.

- **USDA Zones: 7-8:** arugula, Asian greens, asparagus, beets, chervil, chives, fennel, green onions, kale, lettuce, parsley, peas, rhubarb, radishes, and spinach.

- **USDA Zones 5-6:** arugula, beets, carrots, kohlrabi, lettuce, parsley, radishes, spinach.

- **USDA Zones 3-6:** arugula, carrots, chives, lettuce, parsley, parsnips, radishes, spinach.

ORGANIC FERTILIZERS AND SOIL AMENDMENTS

Organic fertilizers come from natural sources–plants, animals, and rocks. Organic fertilizers are the most natural way to feed plants. Add organic fertilizers to planting beds several weeks in advance of planting. Earthworms and soil microbes break organic fertilizers into small nutrient particles that plants can use. A relatively safe organic fertilizer is 5-10-10 which has a lower percentage of nitrogen than phosphorus and potassium. High nitrogen fertilizers can burn plant roots if over-applied. Cow, chicken, and rabbit manure can be used as fertilizer—they are higher in nitrogen than phosphorus and potassium. If you apply manure to planting beds, be sure it has aged by at least a couple of months and is free of weed seed.

Synthetic fertilizers are chemical based—commonly made from petroleum products. Synthetic fertilizers are fast-acting (unlike organic fertilizers). They can be added shortly before or after planting. Synthetic fertilizers can easily burn plant roots if over applied. Follow carefully label instructions.

Soil amendments are used to condition or improve soil texture—that is to make the soil lighter by breaking up clay soil or heavier by adding organic bulk to sandy soil. Most, but not all, soil amendments add some nutrients to the soil. Compost and leaves are common organic soil amendments.

Organic fertilizers and soil amendments. Here are a few common organic fertilizers and soil amendments:

- **Bat guano**: Bat guano (feces) is harvested from caves and powdered. Adds nitrogen and phosphorus; stimulates soil microbes; average NPK: 10-3-1.
- **Bone meal**: Steam processed bone, a slaughterhouse by product. Adds phosphorus; average NPK 1-11-0.
- **Colloidal rock phosphate**: By-product of mining rock phosphate. Adds phosphorus; average NPK 0-2-0.
- **Compost**: Decayed plant and organic materials. Adds organic matter and nutrients to soil; average NPK 4-4-4. Compost includes grass clippings and leaves from deciduous trees.

- **Cow manure**: Cow and steer manure. Adds nitrogen and organic matter and some other nutrients to the soil (about 17 percent organic matter); average NPK: 0.6-0.2-0.5.
- **Fish Emulsion**: Liquid fertilizer processed from fish waste. Nitrogen rich and adds micro nutrients to soil; average NPK: 5-2-2.
- **Kelp meal**: Dried, ground seaweed, an ocean product, also called seaweed meal. Adds potassium and also calcium, sodium, sulfur, and organic matter; average NPK: 1.0-0.5-2.5; contains a broad array of vitamins, minerals, and soil-conditioning elements.
- **Limestone, dolomitic**: A lime that contains about half calcium carbonate and half magnesium carbonate. Soil balancer, calcium (25 percent), magnesium (8 percent). Lime raises calcium level in soil and will slowly raise the soil pH at the same time. It also adds calcium and magnesium to the soil. Perform a soil test before adding lime to the soil.
- **Poultry manure**: Droppings from chickens, turkeys, and other domesticated birds. Adds nitrogen and lesser amounts of phosphorus and potassium and organic matter; average NPK: 1.1-0.8-0.5. Compost poultry manure before adding it to the soil; fresh manure is high in nitrogen and can "burn" plants.
- **Rock phosphate**: Finely ground skeletal remains of prehistoric animals add phosphorus; average NPK: 0-3-0.
- **Worm castings**: Manure of earthworms. A source of organic matter and small amounts of many nutrients; average NPK: 0.5-0.5-0.3.

PEST CONTROL EARLY IN THE SEASON

Spring brings the start of the insect pest season. Insects are ectothermic which means their body temperature is regulated by sunlight and the outside temperature; they are "cold-blooded" so their body temperature depends on the external environment. When the weather warms in spring, insects emerge from winter dormancy and begin to feed and reproduce. The life cycle of insects closely parallel the life cycle of most plants. Just as plants begin to grow with the upturn of temperature in spring, so, too, are insects looking for food which plants can provide in whole or in part. Pest insect control begins in spring and continues until temperatures turn cold again.

Here are few tips to control insect pests:

- Healthy plants are most resistant to insect pest attack; start plants in rich potting mix and transplant them to planting beds rich in aged compost; keep the soil just moist as plants grow.
- Plant insect-resistant varieties; check plant labels and catalog descriptions. Choose healthy starts at the garden center; avoid plants with leggy stems or yellowish leaves.
- Check plants regularly for pest insects and diseases. Many insects lay eggs on the undersides of leaves.
- Hand-pick and destroy pest insects and their eggs; early morning is a good time to spot insects feeding.
- Keep the garden free of weeds; weeds host and feed many pest insects.
- Plant in wide rows and blocks; healthy plants growing close together fend off insect invasions.
- Early crops are less plagued by insects; they are planted and grow before the start of life for many warm-season insects. Midsummer vegetables commonly have the most pest problems.
- Remove damaged leaves or plants weakened by pests; dispose of insect-infested plant material in the trash, not the compost pile.
- At the end of the season remove all plant debris and residue from the garden; insects often overwinter in plant debris. Turn the soil and leave it exposed to freezing weather; this will kill insect pest eggs and larvae in the soil.

PESTS TO WATCH FOR

Aphids attack just about all vegetables. Aphids suck the juices from leaves leaving them curled, deformed, and yellow. As they move from plant to plant, aphids can also spread diseases. Aphids are very small, pear-shaped insects. There are many kinds of aphids so they can be just about any color; often they are lime green. They feed on the most tender parts of a plant—young growth, buds, stems, and the undersides of leaves. Aphids are easily knocked off of plants with a strong blast of water. Beneficial insects such as lady bugs and lacewings eat aphids. A reflective mulch of aluminum foil placed underneath plants will confuse aphids and they will fly away.

Flea beetles. Flea beetles emerge in spring. They attack basil, beans, beets, broccoli, Brussels sprouts, cabbage, cauliflower, chard, Chinese cabbage, collards, corn, eggplants, kohlrabi, muskmelons, peppers, potatoes, radishes, rutabagas, spinach, tomatoes, turnips, watermelons, and other vegetables. The flea beetle is a shiny black insect 1/10 of an inch long. Adults and larvae chew many, many tiny holes in leaves and transmit viral and bacterial diseases including early blight to potatoes and bacterial wilt to corn. The larvae feed on roots of plants. Control flea beetles by dusting plants with diatomaceous earth, pyrethrum, or rotenone for serious infestations. Apply spinosad or *Beauveria bassiana* to kill beetles. Juvenile nematodes will destroy flea beetle larvae.

Leafminers attack beets and spinach. Leafminer maggots feed between the upper and lower surfaces of leaves creating tunnels or mines that appear irregular and white or brown on the surface. Spinach and beet leafminers are most active in spring when they attack young beets and spinach. By midsummer, a second species, the vegetable leafminer attacks tomatoes and other crops. Adult leafminers are black bristled gray or black flies usually with yellow stripes about 1/10-inch long. Larvae leafminers are stubby, green translucent maggots about 1/8- inch long. Leafminer flies emerge from the soil in spring to lay eggs on the undersides of leaves or directly inside leaf tissue. The eggs are white, cylindrical and appear in clusters. The tiny maggots emerge and feed their way through the middle of leaves for one to three weeks. When maggots finish feeding they emerge from the leaves and drop to the soil to pupate for two to four weeks. There are several generations of leafminers from spring to late summer. Row covers can be put over target crops to exclude leafminer flies. Spraying the undersides of leaves with horticultural oil will suffocate eggs.

May

Late Spring

Starting Warm-Season Crops in the Garden

May is the month when the vegetable garden begins to look more and more like the summer garden. By mid-month most warm-season crops can be sown or transplanted out in the garden without worry. But if you live in a short growing season region keep crop protecting devices – plastic hoop tunnels and row covers—at the ready. By the end of May, tender crops can go into the garden almost everywhere without worry. Whether set in the garden early or late, crops started indoors should be hardened off before they are transplanted into the garden this month.

Hardening off. Hardening off is a term gardeners use to mean acclimatizing indoor started plants to outdoor conditions. Tender (cold sensitive) crops started indoors are hardened off by being set outdoors for an hour or two and then an hour or two more over several days. This process of gradual exposure to outdoor temperatures can be carried out over two or three weeks, so that plants acclimatize to the outdoors gradually. Set young seedlings started indoors outside on a porch or patio for a few hours each day. Young plants started under a plastic hoop tunnel or cold frame can be hardened off by lifting the cover for a few hours each day. Increase exposure to outdoor temperatures and sunlight each day until plants are exposed to outdoor temperatures and sunlight all day. At the end of the hardening off process, plants can be exposed to nighttime temperatures without protection as long as temperatures do not dip below 50°F.

During May you can:
- Sow seed of tender vegetables directly in the garden as soon as the last frost is past.
- Set out tender vegetables started indoors once the last frost is past—earlier if protected.
- Sow or set out tender herbs after the last frost.
- Continue succession sowings of cool-season vegetables where summers do not get hot.

LATE SPRING PLANTING AND PREPARATION

Turn the soil before planting. Just before sowing seed or setting out transplants turn the soil or lightly cultivate planting beds one more time. Germinating seed and transplants will root quickly in loose, well-aerated soil. Lightly moisten the soil the day before planting.

Use a dibble or trowel to create the planting hole for each seedling.

Transplanting seedlings. When setting seedlings in the garden, do this:
- Dig a hole one and a half times the depth and width of the plant root ball.
- Put a handful of aged compost or a teaspoon of 5-10-10 organic fertilizer in the bottom of the hole; lightly cover fertilizer with soil before setting the transplant in the hole.
- Place the root ball in the hole and fill in soil and firm the soil around the roots to make good contact.
- As you fill in the soil, create a small basin around the transplant to hold water.
- Let water seep into the soil, then add some more.
- Keep the soil around new transplants moist for at least three or four days.
- If snails, slugs, earwigs, or cutworms are a problem in your garden, set a cardboard or newspaper collar in place around each seedling; sink the collar (a ring around the stem) one or two inches into the soil with another two inches exposed surrounding the seedling; the paper collar will disintegrate in a month or so.

Thinning young seedlings. Seed that is broadcast (sprinkled) across wide planting beds can be thinned once seedlings are about a half inch to one inch high.

Draw a steel rake across the bed uprooting seedling with the tines creating rows about 1 to 3 inches apart. This is an easy way to thin carrots, beets, lettuce, and other greens.

Staggered planting across a wide row. To plant the greatest number of plants across a wide row, stagger the plants in a 3-2-3 formation or a 2-1-2 formation depending on the size of the plant at maturity and the size of the planting bed. Very large growing plant such as vining tomatoes can be planted in a single stagger or zig-zag 1-1-1-1.

Early-season plant care tips:

- Water often early in the season when roots are shallow; soil moisture evaporation can leave the soil dry; dry soil can interrupt plant growth.

- Cultivate to about ½ inch deep; this is just to break the soil crust and allow rain and irrigation to soak down to roots. Light cultivation will also uproot weeds without harming vegetable roots. Keep in mind plant roots extend out as far as the plant's outermost leaves.

- Mulch around plants after the soil has warmed—usually three or more weeks after the last frost in spring. In warm-winter regions where the soil does not freeze during winter, mulch as soon as plants are set out.

Watering early in the season. Watering new sowings and transplants is very important. Slow or interrupted growth because the soil goes dry can be disastrous for transplanted seedlings and crops grown from seed. Normal growth depends upon an even supply of water. Check the garden daily to make sure the soil stays evenly moist. Put your finger in the soil, if it comes away just moist, soil moisture is good. If your finger comes away from the soil dry, water immediately.

Weeding in early season. Hand pull weeds or use a hoe or weeder to uproot weeds as they appear. Do this often so that weeds do not set down deep roots. If you use a hoe, cultivate about ½ inch below the surface; let the hoe glide across the planting bed just disturbing the soil surface and lifting new weed seedlings. Onions, shallots, leeks, and garlic have shallow root systems so be very careful around these crops that you don't get too close to plants and their shallow roots.

Weeds compete with vegetables and herbs for water and nutrients so knock down the competition.

Asparagus planting tips. Plant 25 to 30 asparagus crowns for a family of four. Two-year-old crowns will have more roots than one-year-old crowns and will come to harvest sooner. Plant crowns in a trench 12 inches deep. At the bottom of the trench sprinkle plenty of aged compost then form mounds 6 inches high spaced 2 feet apart. Plant crowns 2 to 4 inches deep; alternate the depth one plant to the next by a couple of inches (this will extend your harvest later—spears from the shallow crowns will appear first). Crowns should be at least 2 inches deep so that planting beds can be cultivated in spring without disturbing the roots. Spread crown roots over the mound evenly in all directions. Fill in the trench with soil and be sure to mark each row. Do not harvest asparagus the season you plant crowns or the following season; allow roots to store energy. The second season after planting harvest only spears the thickness of your little finger or larger. Keep in mind, asparagus is a long-lived perennial vegetable; it can be in the garden for 20 years or more so plant asparagus in a dedicated bed. Varieties that resist rust and fusarium disease are 'Jersey Giant', 'Jersey Knight', and 'Jersey Prince.'

Preparing for beans. Where the soil is workable, you can prepare a planting bed for bush, pole, and runner beans. Dig a trench 18 inches wide and about 12 inches deep. Loosen the soil with a garden fork and add a 3 to 4 inch layer of aged manure or compost to the bottom of the trench. You also can add hoof and horn fertilizer or blood meal. Then fill the trench with 3 to 4 inches of soil and a second layer of compost and then the remaining soil. Mark the trench with stakes or garden flags. The site is now ready for sowing beans late next spring. When you order or purchase beans for next season get both bush and pole beans; bush beans come to harvest over a 2 to 3 week period; pole beans have a long harvest time of several weeks if picked regularly. Here are several varieties to try:

- **Bush beans:** 'Black Valentine', 'Bush Blue Lake', 'Provider', 'Royal Burgundy', 'Top Crop'.
- **Pole beans:** 'Blue Lake', 'Fortex', 'Kentucky Wonder'.

- **Filet bean:** 'Romano', 'Pension', 'Roma II'.
- **Shell beans:** 'Flagrano', 'Taylor Dwarf', 'Tongue of Fire', 'Kentucky Wonder'.
- **Dry beans:** 'Jacob's Cattle', 'Midnight Black Turtle', 'Vermont Cranberry'.
- **Runner beans:** 'Hestia', 'Painted Lady', 'Prizewinner', 'Scarlet Runner'.
- **Soybeans:** 'Chiba Green', 'Midori Giant'.
- **Lima beans:** 'Fordhook 242'.

See bean varieties to grow on pages 186 and 195.

Prepare to plant eggplant, melons, squash, and zucchini. Early in May prepare the planting spots for tender eggplant, squashes, melons, and zucchini. Dig holes 12 inches square, 12 inches deep, and 3 feet apart. Add a forkful of well-rotted compost or manure to the bottom of the hole and then refill the hole. Draw soil from the surrounding area to form a mound over each hole. At the end of the month, sow three seeds on each mound. When the seedlings come up, clip away the two weakest and leave the strongest seedling to grow on. If you are planting starts, set one on each mound in early June.

Lettuce and salad crops. Make further sowings of salad crops–lettuces and spinach–to maintain a continuous cut-and-come-again harvest. Continue to sow lettuce and spinach ever two weeks until about six weeks before maximum daytime temperatures are expected to average about 80°F. Where summer temperatures do not average 80°, continue successive sowings until about six weeks before the first frost is expected. Sow heat-tolerant New Zealand spinach where summers are hot. This crop is a summer substitute for spinach in warm-summer regions. New Zealand spinach is tolerant of sandy, salty soil. It loves sun and doesn't like shade. Mature plants spread 1 to 2 feet.

Onions—block planting. Broadcast onions seed across a wide row. When seedlings are 1 inch tall, thin the block by drawing a metal rake across the wide row; this will uproot some seedlings and create rows of seedlings to grow on. When plants are 6 inches tall and pencil-thin you can begin to harvest green onions as you need them for salads and seasoning; thin between plants as you harvest giving the remaining plants room for bulb growth; as the season progresses harvest small-bulb scallions as you need them again leaving room for bulb development of the remaining plants. By the end of the season the leaves will be 12 to 18 inches tall and you will have hamburger-sized onions for slicing and storing. (The taller the green tops, the bigger the bulb.)

Potato planting tips: Avoid planting potatoes where potatoes or tomatoes grew last year; potatoes and tomatoes come from the same plant family and so are susceptible to the same soil borne diseases. Check the soil pH; potatoes prefer acid soil and a pH of about 5.0 (most vegetables prefer a pH of 6.5); a low pH protects potatoes from "scab" which is a potato blight that causes skins to become rough and discolored. Potatoes planted in trenches and well-covered with soil grow larger than potatoes grown under mulch near the surface. New potatoes form above seed potatoes; keep this in mind when you plant seed potatoes—allow room for the new potatoes to grow above the seed potato. Once young potato plants are established and growing you can hill up soil covering all but a few leaves. Hilling up allows potato plants to sprout and grow new tubers protected by warming spring soil. Potatoes should be protected from late frosts. Set floating row covers of spun poly over potato plants when night temperatures are predicted to dip. (More about planting potatoes in containers in March.)

Strawberry planting. Grow strawberry plants from seed, runners, or crown; crowns are divisions of existing plants that have roots.

- Sow seed indoors 8 weeks before setting out new plants in early spring. Sow seed ¼ inches deep in lightly moistened seed starting mix. Seed will germinate in 7 to 14 days at 65-75°F. Transplant seedlings to the garden when plants are 6 to 8 weeks old the soil temperature is at least 60°F and all danger of frost is past.
- Runners are sections of stem that include at least one node. Runners will root at nodes along a stem. Runners are easily harvested from mother plants; simply find a node that has rooted and cut the stem or runner away from the mother plant. Plant new runners in spring about 2 weeks after the last frost.

- Set out root divisions or "crowns" also in early spring about 2 weeks after the last frost. Plant each crown so that the topmost roots are ¼ inch below the surface and leaves are set just above the soil level. A buried crown will rot.

If possible, plant strawberries on hills or raised mounds so that runners run away from the crown of the plant down the hill. Space plants 12 inches apart in every direction. Plant strawberries in a dedicated bed; plants will live about 2 to 3 years or so, but established plants are always sending out runners to establish new plants.

Strawberry types. There are three basic types of strawberry plants—June bearing, everbearing and cultivated wild strawberries. For a full season of fruit you may want to plant more than one type (there are several named varieties among each type).

- **June-bearing** types produce on crop each year in late spring or early summer. Varieties include 'Allstart', 'Chandler', 'Earliglow', 'Jewel', 'Sequoia' and 'Surecrop'.
- **Everbearing or day neutral** types flower and set fruit over a long season with harvest peaking in early summer and continuing into autumn. Varieties include 'Fort Laramie', 'Ogalla', 'Ozark Beauty', and 'Quinault'.
- **Cultivated alpine and wild strawberries** varieties include 'Baron Solemacher', and 'Yellow Alpine'.

Pest control. Pests become active in late spring. Begin scouting the garden every day or two for pests and take appropriate action. Knock aphids off plants with a stream of water. Protect tender shoots from cutworms with paper collars around newly set seedlings. Control slugs and snails by placing sandpaper collars around seedlings. Place loosely rolled wet newspaper "traps" around the garden to collect snails, slugs, and earwigs; these pests seek a cool, moist place to hide during the day.

Growing veggies in containers. Many varieties of vegetables and almost all herbs can be grown in containers. If you have limited or no yard space or if the soil where you live is difficult, container gardening is a very good alternative. Grow vegetables and herbs in containers on the patio, deck, or porch. Choose a container large enough for the vegetable or herb you want to grow. Choose miniature, dwarf, or compact vegetable varieties; you will find these in most seed catalogs. (See more on pages 195-196.) Salad greens and most herbs are well suited for container growing. Choose a container that has ample space for the plant at maturity and is deep enough for root growth. If you know the height of a vegetable or herb at maturity a container half again as deep will be right for root growth.

Herbs planting. Set herb transplants into the garden after the last frost. Herbs started indoors for transplanting to the garden include: bay, cilantro, dill, garlic chives, hyssop, lavender, sweet marjoram, mint, Greek oregano, rosemary, rue, sage, summer and winter savory, and thyme. Basil and lemon grass are also started indoors and transplanted to the garden but it is best hold off transplanting these very tender herbs until nights are at least 60°F. Plant herbs in full sun in compost-rich, well-drained soil.

- **Basil seedlings** can be set out late this month when the danger of frost has passed. Set seedlings about 15 inches apart and water well in the early stages until the plants are established. Sow basil seed 1 inch deep in garden beds that have warmed.
- **Cuttings.** Take cuttings 3 to 4 inches long of pot marjoram, rosemary, sage, and thyme from last year's growth. Strip the lower leaves from the cutting, and with a sharp knife cut straight across the stem below a joint. Dip the cut end of the stem in rooting hormone and set cuttings into sand-filled flats or into open, sandy soil to root. If the weather is cold or windy, give cloche protection.
- **Division.** Mint and thyme which has overgrown pots or have become straggly in the garden can be divided or rooted now. The tiny roots at each joint on the runners will grow new roots if buried in fine soil.

TOMATO PLANTING TIME

Prepare to plant tomatoes. Early in the month, prepare planting spots for tomatoes. Dig holes 12 inches square, 12 inches deep, and 2 to 3 feet apart. (Space holes 2 feet apart for determinate bush tomatoes; 3 feet or more apart for indeterminate vining tomatoes.) Add a forkful of well-rotted compost or manure to the bottom of the hole and then refill the hole. Draw soil from the surrounding area to form a mound over each hole. Tomatoes starts can be safely set in the garden when nighttime temperatures average 55°F, toward the end of this month or early in June. Tomatoes planted earlier should be protected from cold nights.

Tomato transplanting. Dig a hole as deep as the tomato is tall in its container. Sprinkle 5-10-10 organic fertilizer in the bottom of the hole and lightly cover with soil. Strip off all but the very topmost leaves of the tomato seedling. Bury the entire stem except for the topmost leaves. Firm in the soil and create a small basin to hold irrigation water around each seedling. The buried stem will generate new roots and the plant will put its energy into new root and thicker stem growth.

Two ways to plant a tomato: upright or horizontally in a shallow trench. New roots will grow from the buried stem. Trench planting exposes the roots to greater solar warmth and spurs quick growth.

Trench planting tomatoes. If you live in a cool or slow to warm spring region, consider trench (horizontally) planting tomatoes. A tomato planted horizontally in shallow trench will root, blossom, and fruit faster than a tomato planted vertically in a hole. The roots of a trench-planted tomato will absorb more solar heat than a hole-planted tomato; the roots of a trench-planted tomato are exposed to more soil moisture since they are growing horizontal to the surface. Here's step-by-step how to trench-plant a tomato:

- Dig a shallow trench about 2 inches deep and about 12 inches long. Sprinkle 1 inch of aged compost or a tablespoon of 5-10-10 organic fertilizer along the bottom of the trench. Cover the fertilizer lightly with soil so that the plant does not make direct contact with the fertilizer.
- Remove all the leaves from the stem of the tomato seedling except for the very top ones.
- Remove the seedlings from its container cupping the root ball in one hand; support the stem between two fingers.
- Set the bare stem on its side along the length of the trench at least 2 inches below the surface; new roots will grow along the length of the stem. Because the stem is just below the soil surface, the warm soil will encourage new root growth in less than 10 days.
- Wrap a torn section of newspaper around the stem near the leaves forming a collar or barrier to keep cutworm from chewing on the stem. (The collar will be half buried, half-exposed.) Place a small mound of soil under the leaf cluster and bend the stem gently upward.
- Fill in the trench along the length of the stem and firm in the soil. Where the stem turns upward and vertical make sure the paper collar is exposed.
- Moisten the soil thoroughly along the length of the buried stem.
- Set a stake or cage in place soon after planting so that you avoid severing the newly buried stem.
- Within a day or two of sun exposure, the stem will straighten and grow vertically up toward the sun.

Tomato planting strategy for a long harvest. To stretch your tomato harvest, plant tomatoes with differing days to maturity at the same time: early-season tomatoes will be ready for picking in 55 to 65 days from transplanting; mid-season varieties will be ready in 70 to 85 days after transplanting, late season varieties will be ready 90 to 120 days after transplanting. Grow a couple of each. Grow marble-sized cherry tomatoes for salads and snacking; grow plum-shaped tomatoes for canning and sauce; grow medium-sized and beefsteak varieties for slicing.

Tomatoes and red plastic mulch. Red plastic mulch reflects the far-red spectrum of light. Far-red light triggers a natural growth regulator in tomato plants. The growth regulator triggers increased shoot and root growth; fruit yield will be increased by 12 to 24 percent according to USDA and university research. Red plastic mulch, like black plastic mulch, also will warm roots, decrease the loss of soil moisture, prevent soil and water splash which can cause disease, and keep down weeds.

Plant supports. Tomatoes, cucumbers, beans, melons, and squashes will take a lot of space in the garden if you let them run. Vertical supports—vertical gardening—will get these crops off the ground allowing for a cleaner harvest and increased yield. Here are a few ways to train crops up:

- **Stake:** wood or metal stakes 6 to 8 feet long are a good choice for training up tomatoes and beans. Drive the stake 18 inches or more into the ground if possible; this will keep the stake from tipping late in the season. Prune plants to the stoutest one or two stems and tie them loosely to the pole with elastic garden tape, strips of cloth, or soft garden twine. Beans can be trained up tripod stakes tied at the top.

- **Cage:** Choose a cage at least 18 to 24 inches across and 5 to 6 feet in height for vining tomatoes or cucumbers. Shorter cages can protect peppers and eggplants. Use construction mesh with holes large enough for your hand to reach through and harvest fruit or buy pre-made galvanized metal cages.

- **Trellis:** Wooden or metal trellises 5 feet tall can support beans, peas, cucumbers, and tomatoes. Be sure to attach support each trellis with stakes well anchored in the ground. Choose a trellis with cross pieces wide enough for your hand to fit through to reach fruit on the opposite side.

PLANTING ZONE-BY-ZONE: Late Spring / May

Beginning with the warmest regions first, here is a seed starting and planting guide for late-spring—May. It is safe to plant or do any of the tasks listed for regions cooler than yours.

USDA Zone 10: warming conditions

- Set out plants of tomatoes, peppers, and eggplants if not already done; plant deep, water well and shade for 3 days

- Succession plant warm-season crops such as beans, squash, and zucchini where heads of cabbage, lettuce, mustard and other cool-weather crops have been harvested.

- Protect developing tomatoes and peppers from sunscald by setting up shade cloth frame.

- Side-dress corn, cucumbers, beans, tomatoes, peppers, and eggplant with organic fertilizer as fruit begins to form.

- Plant okra in wide rows with stalks every 2 or 3 feet. Cut pods before they mature, so the plants will continue to bear all season.

- Keep soil in planting beds evenly moist.

USDA Zone 9: warming weather

- Sow or transplant out warm-season crops: bush and pole beans, lima beans, beets, cabbage, cantaloupes, casaba, cauliflower, celery, sweet corn, cucumbers, eggplants, leaf lettuce (in shade), New Zealand spinach, okra, peanuts, black-eye peas, crowder peas, peppers, pumpkins, radish, salsify, edible soybeans, squash, sunflowers, sweet potato slips, Swiss chard, tomatoes, and watermelon.

- Plant heat-loving vegetables in deeply composted holes.

- Stake or cage tomatoes, eggplants, peppers, and pole beans when plants are about one foot high. Train cucumbers on trellises.

- Prune tomatoes already in the garden. Prune early tomatoes to 2 stems and stake with 5 foot stakes. Pinch out suckers that develop between the main stalk and the branches while they are small.

- Mulch long-season crops such as tomatoes with 4 inches of aged compost or clean hay.

- Be on the lookout for potato bugs, cabbage worms, tomato fruit worm and vegetable weevils. Check the underside of leaves for Mexican bean beetle, bean leaf beetle, spot and striped cucumber beetle, pickle worms on cucumbers and cantaloupe. Also look for blister beetles, squash lice, and young harlequin bugs. These pests can be destroyed by hand or by spraying with natural insecticides such as neem oil, pyrethrum, rotenone, or Bt (*Bacillus thuringensis*).

- Spray tomatoes with Bordeaux mixture if fungal leaf spot appears. Here's the recipe for Bordeaux anti-fungal mixture: mix 1 gallon of water, 3⅓ tablespoons of copper sulfate and 10 tablespoons of hydrated lime. Mix thoroughly before you spray. Make successive plantings of vegetables every 10 days.
- Mulch heavily with compost to help retain soil moisture and improve soil tilth.
- Irrigate thoroughly once a week. Gently dig around roots to see if plants have sufficient moisture. Water at the base of plants.
- Don't work with plants when they are wet. Fungal diseases are easily spread in drops of water.

USDA Zone 8: gradual warming, frost still possible

- Prepare outdoor site for cucumbers, eggplant, peppers, squashes, tomatoes, and zucchini. Prepare squash and cucumber mounds with plenty of well-rotted manure and compost.
- If the weather is warm, direct-sow French and runner beans, long-rooted beets, squash, pumpkins, cucumbers, cauliflowers, sweet corn, peas, endive, green beans, leaf lettuce, Chinese cabbage, and chicory. If the weather is chilly, sow these indoors for planting out next month.
- Be prepared to protect seedlings under a plastic hoop tunnel or row cover.
- Plant potatoes. Mound soil around young shoots to protect them from frost.
- Make furthers sowings of lettuces and summer spinach.
- Transplant out Brussels sprouts and leeks for autumn harvest.
- Sow indoors tender warm-weather herbs such as basil
- Take cuttings of pot marjoram, rosemary, sage, and thyme.
- Divide any straggly mint and thyme plants.

USDA Zone 7: frost likely

- Sow indoors broccoli, leeks, kohlrabi, and cauliflower for planting out in early summer.
- Sow cabbage outdoors in fertile soil.
- Plant onion sets, potatoes, and asparagus crowns.
- Harden off young plants from early spring sowings of cauliflower, leeks, onions, lettuce, peas, and broad beans before planting out.
- After mid-month sow indoors or under a plastic hoop tunnel seeds of beans, corn, cucumber, melons, okra, squash, and zucchini.
- Set out plants of tomato, eggplant, pepper, and sweet potato slips under a plastic hoop tunnel; these crops must be protected from temperatures less than 60°F.
- Thin beets, carrots, lettuce, radishes, spinach.

USDA Zones 2-6: frost likely, freezing possible

- When sowing or planting outdoors, bear in mind that the soil temperature as well as air temperature is important. Few seeds will germinate if the soil temperature is below 45°F, so use a soil thermometer to check before you sow.
- As soon as the soil can be worked, add soil amendments: aged compost, aged manure, planting mix, humus, organic fertilizer; turn the soil and prepare for planting and sowing.
- Continue to sow in cold frames, plastic hoop tunnels, or beneath cloches early crops: lettuce, beets, and carrots.
- If the weather is mild, sow hardy and half-hardy vegetables outdoors; sow broad beans, cauliflower, Brussels sprouts, onions, peas, radishes, spinach, and parsnips.
- Set out starts of cabbage, broccoli, and cauliflower plants for late-season harvest.
- Sow indoors broccoli, leeks, kohlrabi, and cauliflower for planting out in early summer.
- Plant onion sets and asparagus crowns.
- Chit 'seed' potatoes. Plant potatoes when frost danger has passed.
- Use horticultural fleece or cloches to protect seedlings.

- Remove runners from strawberries. Plant new strawberries. Put cloches over strawberries if you want an early corp.
- Side dressings of complete fertilizer or aged compost will help along young plants.
- Cultivate after watering. Shallow cultivation to keep the vegetable garden soil from caking.
- Remove perennial weeds root and all from the garden; a portion of root left behind can regenerate the weed.
- Protect younger plants from cutworms by placing a collar around each stem; cover young plants with hot caps at night.
- Dig aged compost and well-rotted manure into trenches for planting celery and runner beans.
- Sow perennial and biennial herb seeds outdoors.

Intercropping: Short broad leaf lettuce interplanted with tall vertical growing onions. The lettuce will be harvested before large onion bulbs mature.

INTERCROPPING AND SUCCESSIONS

Intercropping and succession planting explained. Intercropping and succession planting are two ways to get more production out of your garden. Here's what these terms mean:

- **Intercropping (also called interplanting)** is placing a quick-maturing crop in the spaces between slower-maturing crops.
- **Succession planting** is sowing or planting a new crop in the same spot where a precious crop was growing and was just harvested.

Intercropping—also called interplanting—allows for two crops to grow simultaneously in the same bed. The two crops are commonly planted at the same time but one—commonly a smaller growing plant at maturity—comes to harvest well before the other larger plant. The larger plant is often called the "main crop" because it's larger and it's time in the garden is longer. For example a bush tomato plant will fill a space 24 inches in diameter in 60 to 80 days, but for 5 to 7 weeks that the tomato is in the ground it may only need 8 to 15 inches diameter space—the same for a neighboring tomato. That means for 4 to 6 weeks there are 10 to 15 inches or more of unused space in the planting bed between the two tomatoes. In that time, a smaller fast growing plant such as radishes, lettuce, or spinach can be intercropped and grow from seed to harvest in the shadow of the tomato. In fact, two or three lettuce plants can grow to maturity in that space.

Small crops to intercrop under larger crops. A main crop plant does not need its mature footprint of space in the garden for its entire life—only for the final weeks as it reaches maturity. That means space around the plant is vacant for many weeks before the plant matures and comes to harvest. Quick-maturing small crops to plant around and under larger crops include leaf lettuce, radishes, green bunching onions, beets, turnips, spinach, and mustard greens. Slow maturing large crops include tomatoes, corn, squash, melons, eggplant, peppers, and cabbage.

How to intercrop. First determine which crop is the slower maturing, larger crop—that becomes your main crop. Use the breadth of the main crop at maturity to lay out your planting bed or blocks in the planting bed—remember you will set each main crop plant equidistant from its neighboring main crop plants using equilateral triangle templates (Read more on equidistant planting in April). With siting of the main crop in place, you can then plan and plant the secondary intercrop—again plant the secondary crop plants equidistant from one another and the main crops plants using equilateral triangle templates. Looking from above the plant centers will be set on equilateral triangular grids.

How to plan succession crops. To plan a succession of crops use the number of days each crop takes to grow from seed to harvest or from setting out transplants to harvest and the number of days each crop remains in the garden at harvest stage. For example, leaf lettuce can grow to maturity in 40 days and be harvested on the 40th day—thus needing 40 days in the garden; a vining tomato may require 80 days from transplanting to reach its harvest time, then fruits will continue to mature on the plant for another 25 days; that tomato plant will need 105 days in the garden. Using the above example, if your growing season is 250 days long, you can plant leaf lettuce on the day of the last frost and harvest the lettuce in 40 days; you can then set out a tomato seedling in the same spot and grow it on to harvest in 80 days; the tomato fruits will continue to mature over another 25 days until no more fruits are ripening; then you can remove the tomato plant from the garden and sow cabbage seed for harvest in about 100 days just before the first frost in autumn. Now add up the days each crop required in the garden: 40 + 80 + 25 + 100 = 245 days. There are 5 days to spare in the 250-day growing season.

Use the Planting and Harvest Planning Chart on pages 166-167 to determine how much time each crop will require in the garden—that is the number of days to harvest and the number of days or weeks a harvest lasts from one sowing.

Planning seasonal successions. To perfect succession planning and planting you need to know the average number of days in the growing season, the average date of the last frost in spring, the average date of the first frost in autumn (see Appendix 2), the number of days to harvest for each crop, and the

number of days of harvest for each crop. You also must know when during the season each vegetable prefers to grow—in cool weather or warm weather. As well, it's important to know which crops can't tolerate frost and freezing temperatures and which crops can't tolerate warm temperatures. Cool-season crops must mature before the weather warms; many warm-weather crops can't tolerate a chill let alone a frost. For a simple succession of three crops, you would be advised to: (1) plant a cool-season crop in early spring that takes less than 50 days to mature; (2) follow with a warm-season crop—knowing the number of days to harvest from planting and the number of days in the harvest period; (3) end the season with a second cool-weather crop—usually quick maturing varieties so that they come to harvest before the first freeze.

Season successions. Here are a few examples of seasonal successions:

- Replace radishes with New Zealand spinach or leaf lettuce or endive.
- Replace early lettuce with carrots or beets.
- Replace early peas with beans.
- Replace spring lettuce with okra or tomatoes.
- Replace spring peas with pole beans, cucumbers, or asparagus beans.

Succession of varieties. Another method of succession cropping is to plant different varieties of the same crop, some maturing early, some maturing mid-season, and some maturing on the same day. For example plant an early-maturing bush tomato, a mid-season maturing vine tomato variety, and a late-maturing heirloom variety. This type of succession planting requires setting each variety in a different block in the planting bed—although for small crops you could mix the varieties together.

Staggered succession block and row planting is planting the same variety several days or weeks apart; for example plant radishes in a wide row or block today then plant a second row or block in two weeks and a third row or block two weeks after that. When the first block is harvested, replant it with radishes again. Then go on to harvest the second block and the third block in order and in turn come back to the replanted first block. Staggered succession planting of the same variety requires replenishing soil nutrients—-as simple as adding aged compost to the planting bed—before planting again.

Cool-Season Crop Successions:

Here are a few tips for crops that can be planted again in late spring:

- **Beets.** Sow seeds of long-rooted beets–'Cylindra' and 'Rodina' are two–once the weather has warmed. Sow seeds 1 inch apart and cover with ¼ inch of compost. Later, thin plants to 3 inches apart. Keep soil evenly moist to produce tender roots.

- **Brussels sprouts.** In cool-summer northern regions, set out Brussels sprouts starts in late spring for summer-to-autumn harvest. In warm-winter regions, wait to plant Brussels sprouts in late summer and autumn. Set plants 1½ to 2 feet apart. Keep plants growing vigorously by keeping the soil evenly moist.

- **Carrots.** Sow main crop carrots after the last frost. Carrots grow best in light, sandy, stone-free soil. The varieties 'Imperator' or 'Gold Pak'–which grow roots to 9 inches long–are good choices in light soil. In shallow, rocky, or clay soil, plant the varieties 'Chantenay' or 'Nantes' with roots that grow 6 or 7 inches long. Sow successive crops at three-week intervals.

- **Cauliflower.** Cauliflower grows best in cool summer regions where temperatures don't get warmer than 75°F. Growing temperatures in the mid-60s°F are optimal. Set out cauliflower starts when both the soil and air temperature is at least 50°F. Plant cauliflower starts 24 inches apart in rows 24 inches apart. Place a bottomless paper cup around each stem to protect the plants from cutworms.

COMPANION PLANTING

Companion planting means growing certain plants together with the hope and intent that one will benefit another or that both will benefit each other.

Companion planting is a bit of art and science; not all of the claims for companion planting have been scientifically proven, but anecdotal evidence and collected garden wisdom seem to support keeping some plants close and others at arm's length. One of the most helpful influences one plant may have for another is the ability to repel pests and or attract beneficial insects. Other plants–mostly legumes–aid other plants by helping to enrich the soil. If you decide to give companion planting a try, keep in mind that companion plants do not need to be bosom buddies. Vegetable garden companions will still have a positive impact even if they are many feet away or several planting beds apart. Here are several vegetables and their companions:

- **Asparagus:** tomatoes repel asparagus beetles; nasturtiums, parsley, and basil enhance growth.

- **Beans:** potatoes repel Mexican bean beetles; rosemary repels insects, catnip repels flea beetles. Beets, carrots, peas, cauliflower, cabbage enhance the growth of bush beans; eggplants, cucumbers, radishes enhance the growth of pole beans.

- **Cabbage** (and cabbage family crops—broccoli, Brussels sprouts, cauliflower, collards, kale): Celery repels cabbage worms, onions deter maggots; rosemary, sage, thyme repel most insects. To enhance growth plant beets, carrots, bush beans, lettuce, spinach, cucumbers, kale, potatoes, aromatic herbs, dill, sage, mint, chamomile, and nasturtiums.

- **Carrots:** beans and peas add nutrients to the soil; onion, leeks, chives repel carrot flies; rosemary and sage repel most insects. Tomatoes, peppers, leaf lettuce, and red radishes enhance growth.

- **Cucumbers:** beans and peas add nutrients to the soil; radishes repel cucumber beetles. Corn, tomatoes, cabbage, lettuce, sunflowers, dill, and nasturtiums enhance growth.

- **Lettuce:** beets, carrots, radishes enhance leaf lettuce growth.

- **Melons:** corn enhances growth; nasturtiums and radishes repel cucumber beetles.

- **Onion** (and onion family crops—bulb onions, garlic, leeks, scallions, shallots): growth enhancers include beets, tomatoes, broccoli, peppers, kohlrabi, lettuce, cabbage, leeks, summer savory, carrots, strawberries, chamomile, parsnips, and turnips.

- **Peppers:** tomatoes, eggplant, onions, carrots, parsnips enhance growth.
- **Potatoes:** beans and corn repel most insects; to enhance growth plant: cabbage, peas, marigolds, horseradish at corners, parsnips.
- **Squash:** corn and nasturtiums enhance growth.
- **Strawberries:** lettuce, spinach, beans, onions, and borage enhance growth.
- **Tomatoes:** asparagus and basil repel insects; peppers, celery, onions, carrots, cucumbers, parsley, mint, chives, marigolds, and nasturtiums enhance growth.

FERTILIZERS

Fertilizers contain the minerals that nourish plants. Nitrogen, phosphorus, and potassium are the three "major" plant nutrients. Nitrogen (N) promotes photosynthesis and green leafy growth—important for lettuce and leafy crops. Phosphorus (P) promotes flowering, fruit ripening, and root growth—important for fruiting crops such as tomatoes and peppers. Potassium (K) aids plant vigor, fruit formation, and tuber and root growth. The minor plant nutrients are: calcium, iron, boron, and magnesium; all of these are important for good plant growth. Fertilizers can be divided into two major types: organic and inorganic fertilizers.

- **Organic fertilizers** contain nutrients in a natural form. Organic fertilizers include fish emulsion, seaweed solutions, compost tea, and manure tea. Organic fertilizers decompose and release nutrients slowly.
- **Inorganic or synthetic fertilizers** are man-made chemicals commonly synthesized from petroleum derivatives. Inorganic fertilizers are usually more concentrated and faster acting then organics.

Reading a fertilizer label. The label on a fertilizers package will tell you the percentage of nitrogen, phosphorus, and potassium in the package—in that order—commonly labeled NPK (the chemical element symbols for each, N=nitrogen, P=phosphorus, K=potassium). A 10-10-10 fertilizer contains 10 percent nitrogen, 10 percent phosphorus, and 10 percent potassium equaling 30 percent of the package's total contents; the other 70 percent of the package's content may include minor nutrients but mostly it is made up of an inert substance to carry or help spread the nutrients.

Best fertilizers for vegetables.

- **Leaf and root crops:** The best fertilizer for leafy crops will be a fertilizer with a high percentage of nitrogen; nitrogen aids green growth; a 5-5-5 or 10-10-10 fertilizer would be ideal for leafy crops; (these are also balanced fertilizers because the percentage of each major nutrients is equal.) Nitrogen-rich organic fertilizers include animal manures, cottonseed meal, fish emulsion, and blood meal.
- **Fruiting crops:** The best fertilizer for tomatoes, peppers, cucumbers, beans, peas, and fruiting crops will be a fertilizer low in nitrogen, higher in phosphorus (for fruit and roots growth) and potassium, such as 5-10-10. Organic fertilizers high in phosphorus are bone meal, colloidal phosphate, phosphate rock; organic fertilizers high in potassium are wood ashes, greensand, and granite dust.

Compost is not a fertilizer per se; it is a soil amendment; however, compost contains nearly all major and minor plant nutrients. When you amend the soil with aged compost you are also feeding the soil.

HARVEST BY ZONE:
Late Spring / May

Late winter and early spring planted crops can be harvested as soon as they are big enough to eat— baby carrots, loose leaf lettuce, arugula, endive, and spinach leaves. Spring onions can be harvested as soon as the bulbs begin to swell. Harvest leafy crops cut-and-come-again, that is cut the outer, largest leaves now and allow the center smaller leaves to grow on for harvest later. Pick early peas as soon as the pods start to swell; pick them regularly for a longer harvest.

- **USDA Zone 10:** amaranth, artichokes, arugula, Asian greens, asparagus, basil, beans, carrots, chard, chives, cilantro, corn, cucumbers, eggplant, fava beans, French tarragon, garlic, kale, lettuce, okra, onions, oregano, peas, potatoes, rhubarb, strawberries, summer squash, thyme, tomatillos, tomatoes, watermelon, zucchini.

- **USDA Zone 7-9:** arugula, artichokes, Asian greens, asparagus, beans, beets, broccoli, cabbage, carrots, cauliflower, collards, garlic scapes, fava beans, kale, kohlrabi, lettuce, mizuna, peas, potatoes, radishes, rhubarb, rutabagas, scallions, spinach, strawberries, Swiss chard, turnips.

- **USDA Zones 5-7:** arugula, Asian greens, asparagus, beets, Brussels sprouts, cabbage, chives, fava beans, fiddleheads, garlic scapes, green onions, kale, kohlrabi, lettuce, parsley, radishes, rhubarb, scallions, spinach, Swiss chard, turnips.

- **USDA Zones 4-6:** arugula, asparagus, greens, garlic, green onions, kohlrabi, lettuce, peas, radishes, spinach.

June
Early Summer

Summer Begins

June is the month to set out heat loving crops–zucchini, summer squashes, cucumbers, melons, and tomatoes. Plant these crops on slight hills where the soil stays warmest. Work a spade-full of compost or well-rotted manure into each hill or planting hole before planting. Also, plant this month at least a week or two after the last frost heat-loving peppers, eggplants, and okra.

Keep summer vegetables evenly moist. Water transplants every day until they are well rooted. Don't let tomatoes, peppers, eggplants, melons, zucchini, squashes, or cucumbers go dry–this will impede quick and even growth which is essential for tender and sweet tasting fruits at harvest.

PLANTING SUMMER CROPS

Bean planting. Green snap beans and beans for drying can be sown or transplanted into the garden as soon as the soil reaches 60°F. Cold soil will slow down bean growth so don't plant too early. For optimal growth, the soil should be moist but not wet–too little or too much water can leave beans susceptible to diseases and pests. Avoid overhead watering. Feed beans every two weeks for the first six weeks with compost tea. (Make compost tea by soaking a small bag or sock full of aged compost in a bucket of water until the water turns the color of tea). Pole snap beans to grow include 'Blue Lake' (60 days), 'Kentucky Wonder', and 'Scarlet Runner'. Bush snap beans to grow include 'Bountiful' (55 days), 'Contender' (49 days), and 'Tenderette' (58 days). Good bean varieties for drying include 'Yellow Eye' (90 days), 'Soldier' (85 days), and 'Navy' (100 days). (For more suggested varieties of all crops, see Appendix 5, pages 186-197.)

Lima beans. Lima beans thrive in warm dry weather. Plant lima beans at least two weeks after the last frost in spring. In cool-summer regions try 'Jackson Wonder' (66 days) and 'Eastland Baby' (70 days); in warm-summer regions plant 'Dixie Butterpea' (75 days), 'Fordhook 242' (75 days), and 'Burpee's Improved Bush Lima' (75 days). For a long harvest and the best yield, pick lima beans regularly. Butter beans are a type of lima bean. (As mentioned in Chapter 1—January, specific vegetable varieties recommended in this book are tried-and-true standards that you can find for sale at a nearby garden center or online.)

Sweet corn planting. Sow sweet corn when all danger of frost is past. Sow seeds any time average temperatures are expected to stay within a range of 45°F at night to a high of 85°F during the day. Prepare the planting area in advance by working in an inch of well-rotted manure and aged compost. Sow seed 1½ inches deep in groups of three, at intervals of 18 inches apart. Sprinkle 10-10-10 organic fertilizer at the bottom of each planting hole or furrow and lightly cover with soil before sowing the seed. Thin to the strongest plant a couple of weeks after the seedlings emerge. Sow corn in a number of short rows arranged in a rectangular block. Block sowing will facilitate pollination; corn is pollinated by wind-borne pollen, which cannot travel far. To keep birds from stealing just planted seed and to protect young seedlings, roll a 2-foot wide length of chicken wire along each row and then bend it to create an upside down V or tent which you can place over the length of the row. Keep this wire protection in place until plants are established—about 6 inches tall. Feed corn with a side-dressing of compost tea or organic fertilizer when plants are 6 inches tall and a second time when plants set tassels. Favorite sweet corn varieties include 'Country Gentleman' (90 days), 'Peaches & Cream' (70 days), and 'Krispy King' (78 days).

Cucumber planting. Cucumbers thrive in warm weather. Sow cucumber seeds or set out seedlings started indoors after night temperatures average 55°F and all danger of frost is past. Prepare the growing site in advance: dig holes 12 inches square, 12 inches deep, and 3 to 4 feet apart for trailing plants, 12 inches apart to grow plants on stakes or a trellis. Add 3 to 4 inches of well-rotted compost or manure to the bottom of the hole and then refill the hole. Draw soil from the surrounding area to form a mound about 4 inches high if you plan to let the cucumbers trail. To train cucumbers up, set out stakes or a trellis at planting time. Pinch out the growing tips of cucumber plant when seven leaves have formed. This will keep the plant at a manageable size. Once flowers appear, water cucumbers regularly; avoid washing soil away from the roots. Feed cucumbers every two weeks with compost tea or liquid manure once the first fruits have started to grow. See page 188 for a list of slicing, pickling, and other cucumbers to plant in your garden.

Pre-sprout cucumber and melon seeds. Cucumber and melon seeds are slow to germinate; they have very hard seed coats. Pre-sprouting cucumber and melon seeds can speed germination. Here's how:

- Moisten a paper towel and sprinkle seed on top of it.
- Roll the paper towel and then roll it again inside a damp terry-cloth hand towel.
- Place the towel inside a plastic bag and seal the bag.
- Set the bag in spot where the temperature is evenly warm all day—the top of the refrigerator is a good place.
- Check the seeds every day for germination. Plant sprouted seeds into small containers to grow on.

Melon and squash planting. Melon and squash seedlings can be transplanted into the garden 2 to 3 weeks or more after the last frost in spring when the soil temperature is at least 60°F. They can go into the garden earlier if protected by a plastic hoop tunnel or cloche. To avoid transplant shock, seedlings should be about 4 weeks old at the time of transplanting. Dig holes 12 inches square, 12 inches deep, and 3 feet apart. Add a forkful of well-rotted compost or manure to the bottom of the hole and then refill the hole. Over each hole draw up soil from the surrounding area to form a mound. Sow three seeds on each mound. When the seedlings come up, clip away the two weakest and leave the strongest seedling to grow on. The roots will grow down into the compost-rich soil below. If squash bugs or cucumber beetles are a problem in your garden, you can place a wooden frame three feet square and one-foot high over each mound and cover it with cheesecloth or light spun-poly row cover to exclude the insects.

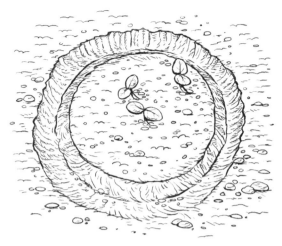

Plant melons and squash on elevated mounds. Grow three plants on each mound training the vines to grow in different directions.

Training melons. Melon plants should be limited to four side shoots each. Pinch away any additional shoots. Make sure the shoots you choose are growing out in opposite directions. When each side shoot has produced five leaves, pinch out the growing tip for that shoot. Soon you will have sub-laterals and flowers. To make sure your melon harvest is full later this summer: look for the flowers with a tiny bulge on the stalk right behind the petals–these are the female flowers. On a sunny day, take male flowers, remove their petals and brush them against the knob-like stigmas of the female flowers. When the fruits begin to swell, choose one fruit for each of the four side shoots–that is four melons per plant, and remove the others. For a list of melons and varieties to grow see page 189.

Pepper, eggplant, and okra planting: Be patient with peppers, eggplants, and okra. These crops require a soil temperature of 70°F, daytime air temperature above 70°F, and night air temperature above 60°F. Sun and heat are essential for these plants to reach flowering and fruiting. Set peppers, eggplants, and okra in the garden 2 to 3 weeks after the last frost in spring. These crops demand warm weather. They are slow, steady growers; even a chilly night can stall their growth. Here are tips for planting peppers, eggplants, and okra:

- Set plants in a staggered double row about 18 to 24 inches apart in all directions; at maturity the leaves of neighboring plants should just touch.

- Dig a hole for each root ball; the hole should be twice as deep and wide as the root ball.
- Place a handful of aged compost or a teaspoonful of 5-10-10 organic fertilizer at the bottom of the hole and lightly cover the fertilizer with soil. (You can also add a pinch of Epsom salt to stimulate root growth.) Tender roots should not come in contact with fertilizer.
- Cup the root of the young seedling with your hand as you slide it out of its container.
- Set the young plant into the ground just slightly deeper than it grew in the container; this will insure the roots are thoroughly covered.
- Place a paper or cardboard cutworm collar around the stem of each plant; the collar will be half-buried and half-exposed.
- Backfill the soil around the root ball and firm it in. Create a small basin of soil around the base of the stem.
- Water around each transplant thoroughly right after planting.

Zucchini and winter squash planting. Plant summer squash, zucchini, and winter squash when the days are warm and long. Soil temperatures greater than 70°F are optimal for direct seeding and growing summer and winter squashes. Retain as much of the soil ball as possible when transplanting squash and water in immediately. Squash are heavy feeders: choose an organic fertilizer high in nitrogen and moderate in phosphorus and potassium. Seaweed or fish emulsion is a good choice. Winter squashes share the same growing requirements as summer squash but need an additional three months of frost-free growing time. Use row covers to protect squash from chilly temperatures. 'Blue Hubbard' and 'Butternut' are favorite winter squashes (both take 110 days to harvest).

Sweet potato planting. Sweet potatoes grow best in warm, loose soil. Plant sweet potatoes in raised or mounded beds where the soil will warm quickly and stay warm through the season. Sprinkle 5-10-10 organic fertilizer over the planting bed or put a teaspoon in each planting hole. Use a dibble or the handle of a trowel to create a planting hole about 5 to 6 inches deep. Set the sweet potato slip (a slip is a sprouted sweet potato) into the hole and re-fill

the soil up to the top leaf cluster Firm in the soil and thoroughly water each slip. You can also snap off shoots and place them in water for several days until they form roots. Then plant the rooted starts.

FEEDING VEGETABLES

Sprinkling fertilizer along a row of plants or around each plant is called side dressing.

When to feed vegetables. A side-dressing of 5-10-10 organic fertilizer or a handful of aged compost will give vegetables a boost once they are established and ready to set blossoms. Make a furrow by drawing a circle 1 inch deep with your finger around the dripline of each plant (the dripline is the imaginary line from the outermost leaves down to the soil). Sprinkle fertilizer or aged compost into the furrow and cover. Here's when to side-dress vegetables:

- **Broccoli, cabbage, cauliflower:** when they start to form heads.
- **Eggplant, peppers, tomatoes, okra, zucchini:** when blossoms appear.
- **Brussels sprouts:** when sprouts are marble size.
- **Cucumbers, melons, winter squash:** when vines start to spread and run.
- **Summer squash, zucchini:** when blossoms appear.
- **Leaf lettuce, spinach, chard:** after the second crew-cutting of leaves to boost growth for a third cutting.
- **Corn, onions:** when plants are 4 to 8 inches tall and when tassels form on ears.

- **Potatoes, sweet potatoes:** before second hilling; cover fertilizer when you hill.
- **Leeks:** when plants are 12 inches tall.
- **Beans, peas** usually don't need a side-dressing of fertilizer.
- **Root crops** will benefit from the addition of phosphorus-rich bone meal spread across the planting bed before seed sowing.

CULTIVATION AND WEEDING

Cultivation benefits. Use a hoe (try a wing hoe or a warren hoe), rake, garden fork, or weeder to cultivate around young vegetables. Cultivation breaks up the soil crust which can get thick as the summer sun begins to beat on planting beds. Cultivation allows rain or irrigation water to seep into the soil; a hard soil crust causes water to run off. Aim to break up the soil to about ½ inch deep with whatever tool you use to cultivate. Regular light cultivation will also keep weeds from getting a foot hold in the garden.

Uncovering weed seeds. Hard-shelled weed seeds can sit below the soil surface for years. When they work their way close enough to the soil surface and get a bit of sunlight they germinate and grow. Regular shallow cultivation will bring dormant weed seeds to the surface where they can sprout then you can knock them off before they put down deep roots. Here are a few ways to keep weeds at bay in the garden:

- Turn the soil three or four times before planting in spring. This will bring weed seeds close to the surface where they will be exposed to early spring cold and die.
- Hand dig out the deep roots of perennial weed. Eliminate perennial weeds growing at the edge of the garden as well.
- Grow a cover crop of annual rye grass or buckwheat when you are not growing vegetables. These thick cover crops will suffocate weeds.
- Regular cultivation every 4 or 5 days during the growing season will uproot weeds before they get too big.

- Never allow weeds to flower; eventually the weed seed reserve in the soil will be exhausted.
- Make sure mulches used in the garden are weed seed free.
- Block plant or intensively plant the garden; close growing vegetables will shade out weeds.

Warm-weather cover crops. Sow warm-season cover crops in planting beds or parts of the garden where you are not growing vegetables during the summer. Cover crops will smother weeds, slow soil moisture evaporation, improve soil tilth, and add nutrients to the soil if they are members of the bean family. Bush beans are a good warm-weather cover crop so is buckwheat, soybeans, and Sudan grass.

Rake thinning. You can thin broadcast seed—carrots, beets, lettuce, radishes—by drawing a metal rake across your wide beds. Rake thinning will eliminate very young vegetable seedlings in the path of each rake tine. Run the rake about ¼ inches deep. Thinning will allow the seedlings that remain to grow on uncrowded. Rake thinning also eliminates weed seedlings and breaks the soil crust allowing oxygen to reach seedling roots.

TOMATO GROWING TIPS

Vine and bush tomatoes. Indeterminate vining tomatoes will out produce determinate bush tomatoes. Indeterminate tomatoes produce fruit continuously until the first frost in autumn; determinate tomatoes ripen fruit over a three to four week period and then stop. Time the planting of bush tomatoes for early summer and autumn harvests. Plant vining tomatoes for a long mid-summer to late autumn harvest.

Tomato planting. Set tomato seedlings into the garden in all locations this month. Set tomato transplants so that root balls are at least 1 inch below the soil surface. Firm in plants and leave a slight depression around each plant to water in thoroughly. In dry regions, make sure tomato roots stay moist by inserting a 4-inch pot in the ground next to each plant with the top even with soil level. Fill the pots with water regularly. You won't need to water the surrounding soil. Set a tomato cage around each indeterminate or vining plant or place a 4-foot stake alongside each plant tying the stems loosely to provide support. Determinate bush varieties do not require support. Pinch or cut away new lateral leaf branches (called suckers) that form in the V between the central main stem and leaf branches. Tomatoes sucker–or produce new branch growth–most of the season. Some new branches are necessary to shade fruit forming below from sunscald, but most will steal energy away from the plant and so need to be controlled. Indeterminate vining tomatoes will out produce determinate bush tomatoes.

Tomato plant ties. Use elastic garden tape, fabric roping, or strips of old cloth to tie tomato plants to their supports, Make sure the ties are secure to the support but loose around the stem of the plant; this will allow the plant to move during wind or rain. Use more than one tie if the main stem is long. If the plant has multiple main stems, tie in each one. Check back regularly to adjust ties or add new ones.

Tomato fruit set. Tomatoes are self-fertile; pollen falls from the male anthers within a flower to the female stigma. If the weather is very dry, the pollen may not stick on the stigma. If the weather is very wet, the anthers may not release pollen. The optimal temperature for tomato pollination is between 65° and 80°F. If the weather is cold fruit will not set. If the weather is hot, the pollen will die. You can assist tomato pollination: when plants are blooming and the temperature is optimal gently shake the flower clusters; this will encourage the release of pollen.

Tomato blossom-end rot. Blossom-end rot (dark, squishy rot and discoloration of the bottom of the fruit) is caused by inadequate soil moisture. When the soil goes dry, calcium which is needed for strong plant cell growth is not drawn up into the fruit with soil moisture. As a result, the cells in tomato fruits become weak, collapse, and rot. Keep the soil evenly moist throughout the growing season. (Blossom-end rot often occurs early in the season while the soil is still chilly and moisture is slow to be taken up by plants.) About two weeks after the last spring frost, add thick mulch around tomatoes to conserve soil moisture; use dry grass clippings or straw.

Pruning tomato suckers. A tomato sucker is new growth that forms in the V between the original trunk or main stem and a lateral branch. Left to grow on, a sucker will grow blossoms and fruit—almost like becoming a new plant of its own. Suckers left unpruned will result in top heavy plants that will topple or break when loaded with fruits. If you allow tomato plants to sprawl across the ground, pruning suckers is not necessary, but if you stake, cage, or trellis a tomato plant, pruning suckers will keep the

Pruning tomato suckers: pinch out new growth in the V between established stems. This will control leafy growth and allow for the development of larger fruits.

plant upright. Young suckers can be pinched away; older suckers are best removed with a sharp knife to insure a clean cut. Suckers can be rooted in potting soil to grow new plants. In addition to removing suckers, also remove any new shoots that form at the base of the plant once two or three main stems are established.

Plant supports. If you didn't set plant supports in place when you planted, do so before crops get too big. Here are the most common supports:

- **Cages:** use pre-made galvanized metal cages. Be sure to select a cage tall enough for the plant you are supporting. Indeterminate tomatoes will need a cage 4 or 5 feet tall or taller. You also can make a cage using plant stakes and galvanized construction mesh. Be sure the mesh is wide enough for you to reach your hand through at harvest time.

- **Stakes:** Set stakes at least 12 inches deep, deeper if you are supporting tall growing indeterminate tomatoes. You may need more than one stake per plant. Set stakes opposite the prevailing wind so that the stem can rest against the support when necessary. Staked plants usually require some training; that is training the main stem to the stake for extra support.

- **Trellis:** A wire or wooden trellis is a good choice for training up vines such as beans, peas, and cucumbers. Make sure the trellis is supported by a sturdy frame or stakes so that the weight of the vine and crop do not topple the trellis near harvest time. Make sure the spacing between supports is wide enough for your hand to reach through at harvest time.

Tomato sprawl. The alternative to training tomatoes to stakes or cages is to let them run free and sprawl across the garden. Sprawling tomatoes do not require training or pruning. At harvest time you will have more fruit than if you had pruned; because there are more unpruned fruits on each plant, the fruits will generally be smaller—but the yield will be greater. To protect sprawling tomatoes from wet soil and rot, set down weed block before you plant then cut an X in the weed block wherever you want to plant.

MORE EARLY SUMMER TIPS

Tender crop successions. Plan succession crops of tender warm-weather crops by looking ahead to the average first frost date in autumn. Count back the number of days to maturity for each crop that you want to grow. Depending on the number of days left in your growing season, you may be able to plant one or more crop successions beginning this month. Make sure there is room in the garden for the crops that you want to grow. If unexpected cool weather happens, you can expect crops will take a week or two longer to reach maturity than planned.

Crops for block planting. Blocks or a series of short rows can be planted across wide beds. Corn is best block planted; this allows for easy pollination. Winter squash is a good choice for block planting; vines can sprawl among one another; mature vines will shade out weeds. Parsnips can be block planted. (Parsnips will not be ready for harvest until next winter.) Bush beans and dry beans can be block planted for easy harvest later. Lima beans are slow growing, so plant them in a dedicated block. Greens like lettuce and spinach are good choices for block planting; block planted greens are easily harvested cut-and-come-again.

Salad crops. Salad greens–lettuce, mesclun, and spinach–do best in cool weather. In cool-summer regions, you can direct sow lettuce right through the summer. In mild or warm-summer regions, choose heat-resistant varieties. (See a list of heat-resistant salad crops on page 50.) Rapid growth is the key to tender and tasty lettuce and salad greens. To encourage fast growth, give leaf crops soil rich in well-aged compost and side-dress plants with compost tea every two weeks until harvest.

Crew-cut lettuce and greens. An alternative to cut-and-come-again harvesting lettuce and other greens is the crew-cut method. Cut-and-come-again harvest takes the larger outside leaves allowing the inner leaves to grow on to size. The crew-cut harvest method cuts all leaves straight across at the same time leaving an inch or two of crown or base; from that base, new leaves will grow for another crew-cut harvest. Crew-cut greens when they are 4 to 6 inches tall. Loose-leaf lettuce, spinach, and chard can all be crew-cut harvested. One loose-leaf lettuce plant can be crew-cut harvested as many as six times in one season.

Block plant peas in hot summer regions. Peas are a cool-season crop. If you want to try to grow peas in summer, sow seed close across a wide row block. The plants will grow together shading the soil and conserving cooling soil moisture. Closely planted peas will both cool the soil and cool themselves. The tangle of vines also will block weeds.

Feed and mulch the asparagus patch. After asparagus plants have been harvested, it's important to side-dress the patch, preparing plants for next year. Asparagus is a heavy feeder; the soil must be renewed. Sprinkle organic 10-10-10 fertilizer across the planting bed. Next cover the patch with 2-inch-thick mulch of aged compost. The compost and nitrogen-rich 10-10-10 fertilizer will help spur the growth of leafy ferns which manufacture food stored in asparagus roots for spear growth early next spring.

Strawberries: protection and propagation. Cover ripening strawberries with netting to protect them from birds. Place a mulch of straw beneath ripening berries so that they do not touch moist soil; this will limit fruit rot. (You can also grow strawberries in beds covered with weed block which will limit berry contact with soil.) To propagate new plants, remove runners from young strawberry plants near rooted nods or peg down strawberry runners growing from established plants and cover a portion of the runner with soil to induce rooting which will create a new plant. Keep strawberry beds just moist; do not overwater plants. Allow the soil surface to just dry between watering.

Strawberry harvest. Strawberries come to harvest between late spring and early autumn depending upon variety. Fruit is ready for harvest 4 to 6 weeks after blossoming—so mark your calendar. Harvest only fully red, ripe berries but pick them before they get soft; pick every other day—they ripen quickly. The harvest from one plant will last up to 3 weeks. Pick berries in the morning when they are plump from the evening dew before the sun begins to dry them. Cut each berry from the stem; do not pull the berry you may pull away a productive runner. Unwashed berries will keep in the refrigerator for 3 to 5 days; freeze whole strawberries for up to 2 months.

Herb harvest and maintenance. Most herbs planted in spring will be ready for picking in early summer: mint, sage, and thyme can be used fresh, also chives, fennel, parsley and sorrel. To freeze herbs for later use as flavoring: cut small sprigs from plants, wash, and blanch for one minute in rapidly boiling water. These can be placed in plastic bags and frozen for later use. Maintain herbs through the summer by regularly trimming plants even if you are not using the trimmings in the kitchen. Regular light pruning will keep herbs bushy and prevent spindly growth. Regular pruning and pinching of new growth will also keep herbs from flowering; leaves from herbs that flower will not be as flavorful. Once an annual herb such as basil, oregano, or tarragon flowers and sets seed, it will begin a slow decline toward the end of life.

White radishes cultivate the soil. 'White Icicle' radishes grow as long as 6 inches. They are mild flavored and grow to maturity in less than 30 days. Plant white icicles radishes in beds where the soil has been tough to cultivate (the radishes will do the job for you) or plant them between or beside other root crops. The radishes will come to harvest ahead of other roots and leave the soil loose and well aerated.

Container crops. Water vegetables and herbs growing in containers daily during hot, dry weather. Set supports for melons and tomatoes in containers. Feed plants in containers regularly, unless slow-release fertilizer granules were added to the soil before planting. Use a liquid fertilizer such as compost tea or fish emulsion. Turn hanging baskets regularly so that the plants develop evenly on all sides of the basket. Watch for pests and signs of disease.

Pansy and viola flowers are edible so are calendulas. Use these brightly colored flowers in salads and garnishes for their mellow flavor and candied scent; winter and spring blooming in mild-winter regions, spring through summer in colder regions.

Many herbs have edible flowers than can be used as a colorful garnish for salads and for both sweet and savory dishes. Herbs with edible flowers include basil, borage, chives, lavender, mind, rosemary, sage, and thyme.

PLANTING ZONE-BY-ZONE:
Early Summer / June

Beginning with the warmest regions first, here is a seed starting and planting guide for early summer—June. It is safe to plant or do any of the tasks listed for regions cooler than yours.

USDA Zone 10—warm to hot weather

- Plant succession crops of beans, beets, carrots, cauliflower, celery, corn, cucumber, melons, peppers, squash, tomato. These will continue to produce until November.
- Always turn and rake the soil between plantings. Add aged compost in space left vacant by harvested crops. Side-dress around growing crops with aged compost.
- Check stakes and supports for tall and climbing plants.
- Have shade cloth ready to protect crops when weather turns hot.
- Weed, water, and fertilize as needed.
- Watch for pests and signs of disease.
- If weeds or nematodes are a problem, cultivate the soil, add organic matter, wet the bed down, and cover with clear plastic for at least a month. Solar heat will collect beneath the plastic and kill weeds and pests.

USDA Zone 9—warm weather:

- When peas, mustard, spinach, carrots and other early crops are harvested, replant immediately with sweet corn, crowder peas, collards, beans, okra, tomato, eggplant, pepper, and sweet potato plants.
- Plant out vegetable seedlings sweet corn, eggplants, peppers, melons, squash, tomatoes, and zucchini.

- Sow seeds of autumn-harvest crops such as cabbages, Chinese cabbages, and cauliflowers in a nursery bed where they can be grown for later transplanting.
- Sow French beans, plant runner and pole beans outdoors.
- Replace peas with beans; substitute Swiss chard for spinach.
- Lift early potatoes. Plant potatoes.
- Cage tomatoes or tie them gently, but firmly, to stakes.
- Eggplants are easier to handle when tied to a stake.
- Pinch back new growth of tomatoes.
- Pinch out the tips on broad beans to encourage good pod set and to deter attack from aphids.
- Pick the first peppers young; later fruits will be larger and more numerous as a result.
- Mulch when plants are several inches high. A 4-inch summer mulch of clean straw or dry lawn clippings will save hours of weeding and watering.
- Transplanted plants need thorough watering and shading for the first few days in the garden.
- Check stakes and supports for tall and climbing plants.
- Water plants in the morning so they don't become susceptible to fungus and insect infestation.
- Watch for pest insects and signs of disease; watch for aphids on broad beans and root flies on cabbages, carrots and onions. Prevention is better than cure.
- Remove diseased plants as soon as disease appears; discard diseased plants in the trash.
- Order seeds for the autumn garden now; sow in mid-summer.

USDA Zone 5-8—warm weather; night chill possible:

- Harvest spring planted vegetables.
- Direct sow green beans, runner beans, pole beans, beets, carrots, sweet corn, cucumbers, lettuce, peas, pumpkins, rutabagas, spinach,

squash, and turnips. Where summers are cool, grow warm-season vegetables under plastic hoop tunnel to increase yield.

- Plant out vegetable seedlings such as cabbages, cauliflowers, celery, sweet corn, cucumbers, melons, squashes, tomatoes, and zucchini.

- Plant for succession; make successive sowing of runner beans, green beans, beets, carrots, endive, kohlrabi, lettuce, radishes, and turnips.

- Plant potatoes and earth up a mound of soil over young potato shoots to protect them from frost.

- Transplant out seedlings of Brussels sprouts, Chinese cabbage, and winter cabbages for autumn harvest.

- Plant out leeks and self-blanching celery starts.

- Hill up soil around stalks of corn before summer wind or rain storms.

- Place shade cloth over lettuce and other leafy crops to keep them from going to seed as the days lengthen.

- Stake tomatoes and poles beans soon after planting to avoid injuring their roots.

- Thin beets and carrots while they are small to prevent overcrowding and poor yield.

- Keep tomato, peppers, and melons growing steadily by keeping the soil just moist?

- Sow chervil and dill.

- Finish cutting asparagus by the middle of the month so that the plants do not exhaust themselves.

- Replace spring peas, lettuce, and potatoes with field peas, lima beans, or a summer cover crop of soybeans.

- Pinch out the tips on broad beans to encourage good pod set and to deter attack from aphids.

- Begin tying to supports and continue pinching out new growth of tomatoes.

- Side-dress half-grown plants like cabbage, broccoli.

- Cut and dry or freeze bunches of thyme, oregano, and mint.

- Take cuttings from rosemary and sage if not done last month.

- Water the herb garden freely during dry weather, although most herbs can survive droughts.

- Thin seedlings sown earlier.

- Thin plantings of corn and beans.

- Weed, water, and fertilize as needed.

- Mulch when plants are several inches high.

- Check stakes and supports for tall and climbing plants.

- Watch for pests and signs of disease. Handpick Colorado potato beetles and other pests. Look for squash bugs on the vine crops.

- Put straw down around strawberries to protect fruit.

- Cultivate lightly after rain or watering to keep crust from forming on soil.

USDA Zones 3-4—cool weather gives way to warming weather

- Set out tender summer vegetable starts, after hardening off and all danger of frost is past.

- Set out peppers and eggplant somewhat later when soil warms up.

- Direct sow runner beans, summer squash, pumpkins, cucumbers, sweet corn, peas, endive, green beans, leaf lettuce, Chinese cabbage, and winter squash.

- At end of month sow cabbage family in cold frame for autumn crop. Start seeds of cauliflower, broccoli, and Brussels sprouts for the autumn garden.

- Plant onion sets.

- Plant asparagus crowns.

HARVEST BY ZONE:
Early Summer / June

Crops coming to harvest now were planted in spring.

- **USDA Zone 10:** amaranth, artichokes, arugula, Asian greens, asparagus, basil, beans, chard, chives, corn, cucumbers, edamame, eggplant, fava beans, French tarragon, garlic, kale, melons, okra, onions, oregano, peas, peppers, rhubarb, southern peas, strawberries, summer squash, thyme, tomatillos, tomatoes, watermelon, zucchini.

- **USDA Zone 7-9:** arugula, artichokes, Asian greens, asparagus, beans, beets, broccoli, cabbage, carrots, cauliflower, celery, collards, garlic scapes, fava beans, kale, kohlrabi, lettuce, mizuna, peas, potatoes, radishes, rhubarb, rutabagas, scallions, spinach, strawberries, Swiss chard, turnips.

- **USDA Zones 5-7:** arugula, Asian greens, asparagus, beets, book choy, broccoli, cabbage, carrots, chives, cilantro, fava beans, green onions, kale, kohlrabi, lettuce, parsley, radishes, rhubarb, scallions, spinach, strawberries (June bearing), Swiss chard.

- **USDA Zones 4-6:** arugula, Asian greens, asparagus, beets, cabbage, carrots, garlic, green onions, kale, kohlrabi, lettuce, parsley, peas, radishes, rhubarb, spinach.

INSECT PEST AND DISEASE CONTROL

10 ways to naturally control pests and diseases:

1. Choose the best site and soil for the plants you are growing. This will reduce plant stress and susceptibility to disease and pests. Too much or too little sun, water, shade, and fertilizer can stress plants. Use aged compost to deliver all essential plant nutrients naturally. Compost-rich soil is well draining while holding soil moisture. Apply a 2-inch layer of aged compost to your garden twice a year.

2. Choose pest and disease resistant plant species or varieties. Check seed packets and plant labels for pest and disease resistance. Seed grower catalogs and websites will also list pest and disease resistance. In the garden mix plant families together to create diversity. This will help avoid the rapid spread of pests or diseases that attack specific plant groups. Keep a garden notebook; note problems and successes for future reference.

3. Prune or pinch to remove damaged and diseased leaves and branches. Pruning will also increase light and air circulation in the garden. Remove dead and diseased plants from the garden immediately.

4. Trap insects with lures—both visual and olfactory. For example, sticky traps that are yellow will attract cucumber beetles, whiteflies, cabbageworms, and thrips; the yeast in shallow pans filled with beer will attract snails and slugs. Rolled, damp newspaper will attract earwigs.

5. Keep the garden clean of plant debris. Pest insects often hide or shelter in dropped or dead leaves. Turn the soil between plantings to expose pests to the elements.

6. Handpick insect pests off plants. Handpick slugs, snails, caterpillars; drop these pests into soapy water. Shake very small insects such as flea beetles from plant leaves onto a piece of paper and dispose of them.

7. Use pest barriers such as floating row covers or sticky bands or copper strips to exclude pests from plants and planting beds. A "collar" or ring of tar paper or cardboard pushed into the soil around a plant will deter cutworms and slugs. Copper strips will deter snails and slugs.

8. Encourage beneficial insects to take up residence in the garden. Release lady beetles, lacewings, spined soldier beetles, praying mantis, or trichogramma wasps to help control pest insects. Grow plants that will provide nectar and pollen for beneficial insects; many beneficial insects are attracted to the herbs dill, caraway, fennel, spearmint, and lemon balm.

9. Some bacteria, fungi, or viruses—infectious microorganisms—can be used to injure or kill some garden insect pests. The most commonly used microbial insecticide is *Bacillus thuringiensis* (Bt) a species of bacteria that produces a toxin poisonous to many common insect pests. Check with a local nursery or garden center for microbial insecticides.

10. Most insect pests can be controlled with relatively nontoxic sprays. A forceful spray of water from the garden hose is one of the easiest ways

to dislodge pests. Insecticidal soaps, horticultural oils, and insecticides made from plant extracts such as neem, pyrethrum, or sabadilla are natural alternatives to synthetic pesticides.

Insect pest controls—no chemicals involved. Use the least toxic pest controls first. Here are a few:

- **Wood ashes:** spread around cabbage-family crops to discourage cabbage worms and slugs.
- **Cutworm collars:** set paper collars an inch into the soil around tomato, cabbage and other seedlings to exclude cutworms.
- **Soapy water:** to kill and control aphids.
- **Garlic or hot peppers solutions:** blend garlic or hot pepper with water to discourage flea beetles.
- **Ladybugs and trichogramma wasps:** these beneficial insects eat pest insects.
- **Cheesecloth or row covers:** fine netting will keep moths from laying eggs.
- **Beer traps:** the yeast in a small tin of beer set at ground level will attract and drown slugs.
- **Rolled wet newspaper:** set in the garden will attract earwigs and slugs during the day; fold and toss the trap in the trash.

Pesticides—non-toxic to toxic. Here are pesticides and their uses from least to most toxic.

- *Rotenone or pyrethrum*: controls bugs and beetles including potato beetles which chew cabbage family crops and salad greens and also tomatoes, cucumbers, and vining crops.
- *Dipel* spray or dust: controls cabbage worms, tomato hornworms, and corn earworms.
- *Sevin* spray or dust: controls chewing bugs and beetles including potato beetles which chew cabbage family crops, beans, greens, tomatoes, cucumbers, and vining crops.
- *Malathion* spray or dust: controls chewing bugs and beetles including potato beetles which chew cabbage family crops, beans, greens, tomatoes, cucumbers, and vining crops.
- *Diazanon* spray or granular: controls aphids, borers, leaf miners, sucking insects, and root maggots that attack eggplant, peppers, tomatoes,

cabbage family crops, and root crops including radishes, carrots, beets, turnips, and onions.

Slugs and snails eat seedlings and leave large ragged hole in the leaves of older plants. Slugs and snails belong to the mollusk family. They feed at night and leave shiny trails on foliage and soil. Nearly all vegetable seedlings are at risk as are leafy greens, beans, tomato fruits, and strawberry fruits. Handpicking by flashlight at night is one way to control slugs and snails. Set out a board propped up on small stones and moisten the soil underneath; slugs and snails will shelter under the board during the day; you can lift the board and destroy them. Keep the garden clean of debris under which slugs and snails can hide. The yeast in beer will attract slugs and snails; place beer in a shallow can at soil level; the pests will fall in and drown.

Colorado potato beetles chew leaves and strip foliage from plants. Adult potato beetles are about the size of your small fingernail; they have dome-shaped shells with black and yellow stripes. The larvae (which do as much damage as the adults) are dull reddish-orange and humped with black legs and heads. Potato beetles feed on potatoes, tomatoes, peppers, and eggplants. They usually appear in late spring and feed all summer and into early autumn. Handpicking is the most effective control of potato beetles; drop the pest in a bucket of soapy water.

Cabbage worms. The imported cabbage worm butterfly is a day-flying white butterfly that flits around the garden. The butterfly lays small oblong yellow eggs on the undersides of broccoli, cauliflower, Brussels sprouts and other cabbage family crop leaves. Cabbage worms are the larvae of the cabbage worm butterfly. A cabbage worm is a small, thin, velvety-green caterpillar that hatches from one of those eggs. Cabbage worms, also called imported cabbage worms, eat large holes in leaves and can quickly decimate an entire cabbage head. There are two generations of cabbage worms each year, the first in early summer and the second in mid- to late summer. Early planting of cabbage-family crops is one way to avoid cabbage worms. Other controls are handpicking, garlic or hot pepper spray, and the application of spinosad or *Bacillus thuringiensis* var. *kurstaki*, a biological insecticide (sold under the brand names Dipel and Thuricide)

ANIMAL PEST CONTROLS

Animal pests	Target plants	Damage	Control
Birds	Seeds, seedlings, fruit	Eat seeds, uproot seedlings, damage fruits	Bird netting to cover seedbeds and crops; shiny items such as aluminum pie pans, strips of aluminum foil.
Deer	Vegetables, flowers, tree bark	Eat crops and ornamental plants	Vertical fence of wire or plastic mesh 8-feet high; electric fence; repellents that include blood meal.
Gophers	Carrots and root crops, seeds, bulbs, entire plants	Create tunnels and mounds throughout the garden; eat crops	Trench to 18 inches deep around garden and install a barrier of ½-inch wire mesh 18-24 inches deep or build raised beds and line bottom of beds with mesh; lethal traps can be used.
Ground Squirrels	Leafy crops, seeds	Burrows around garden; squirrels can climb over barriers eat crops	Fence of wire mesh with exterior electrified wire or 4-foot-high mesh fence with 2-foot-wide skirt of smooth sheet metal; underground skirt will exclude burrowing squirrels; also sprung and humane traps.
Mice	Vegetables, flowers, roots	Feed on crops leave excrement behind	Keep garden free of grassy areas, hay, leaf mulches in which they hide; surround garden with woven fence ¼-inch mesh at least 12 inches high; traps (sprung and humane); poisoned bait along runways.
Moles	Grubs and insects	Raised tunnels; moles do not feed on plants they feed on grubs and insects (including pest insects) and earthworms	Trench around garden and install a barrier of ½-inch wire mesh or build raised beds and line bottom of beds with mesh; traps; repellents; poison bait in tunnels.
Pets: dogs and cats		Digging in the garden	Fence around garden; row covers or screen cages to protect seedlings and plants; lay chicken wire around or over freshly worked soil; repellents such as blood meal or cayenne pepper.
Rabbits	Vegetables, flowers, roots	Eat crops	Fence 3-feet high of 3-inch wire mesh; bury mesh 12 inches below ground to discourage burrowing; repellents; humane traps.
Raccoons	Vegetables, corn, melons, insects, fruit, nuts	Eat crops	Fence of chicken wire 4-feet-high with top extending 18 inches above fence post; unattached portion will keep raccoons from getting over; low-voltage electric fence; humane traps; repellents.
Rats	Vegetables, flowers, roots	Feed on crops; contaminate the garden with droppings, hair, parasites, disease	Traps (sprung and humane); cereal bait (safer than anticoagulant baits).
Skunks	Corn, insects and grubs found in garden	Vegetables, corn, fruits, berries, small rodents	Fence of 3-inch wire mesh—bend the bottom 12 inches of mesh under in a trench to discourage digging; humane traps; repellents.

Animal pests	Target plants	Damage	Control
Snakes	Snakes eat rodents and insect pests; only about 1% of garden snakes are poisonous		Discourage snakes by clearing away brush, wood piles, and rock piles near the garden; humane traps.
Voles	Most vegetables and their roots	Feed on vegetables, bulbs, tubers, gnaw tree bark; travel above ground creating paths; live in shallow burrows beneath plants	Same as raccoons (see above) and also poison bait
Woodchucks (gophers)	Tender vegetables, flowers	Feed above ground but will burrow under fences	Same as raccoons; also bury wire mesh below fence line to prevent burrowing; humane traps.

July

Mid-Summer

Summer Growing

Mid-summer is a busy time in the vegetable garden. Spring planted warm-season crops will begin coming to harvest this month. Look back at your spring planting records–when you planted each crop and the days to maturity for each variety. Schedule your harvest accordingly; cool or rainy weather during the growing time can set the harvest back by a week or two, but generally plan to get each crop out of the garden on the day it is scheduled to reach maturity.

Both in warm- to hot-summer regions and in mild-winter regions, there is plenty of growing season left to continue planting warm-season crops. Succession plantings of cucumbers, peppers, and tomatoes can go into the garden this month where the weather stays warm into early autumn.

In cool- to just warm-summer regions, mid-summer is the time to begin sowing and planting cool-season crops for autumn and winter harvest. If there is not time to get a second or third warm-season crop to harvest before the autumn cool down, turn now to planting cool-weather crops.

Look ahead to the first average frost date to decide which variety of each crop still has sufficient frost-free days to reach harvest. For example, bush tomatoes that require just 50 to 60 days to reach harvest after transplanting can still come to harvest without a problem if the first frost comes in October, but newly planted vining tomatoes that require 80 or more days to reach harvest may not have enough time to ripen before the first frost.

GROWING VEGETABLES IN HOT WEATHER

Most vegetables are sensitive to hot temperatures–just as they are sensitive to cold temperatures. Each vegetable crop grows best in its own range of temperatures. The optimal temperature range for self-pollinating peppers and eggplants, for example, is 70° to 85°F; pollen will not drop from the male to the female part of the flower and pollination will not when night temperature fall below 55°F. Conversely,

blossoms often drop due to heat stress when the temperature rises above 86°F. Bean blossoms may drop off if temperatures remain warmer than 86°F for more than a day or two. Tomato flowers may drop if the temperature rises above 90°F during the day or 75°F at night.

When temperatures rise above a plant's temperature range the plant will go dormant–that is quit growing (the same is true when temperatures fall below the range). If temperatures go too high, plants can suffer sunburn and sunscald and plant cells can experience chemical alterations, membrane damage, dehydration, and death. Most plant cells are killed at temperatures from 122°F to 140°F.

In hot summer regions shade cloth stretched over newly planted tomatoes protects the seedlings from scorching afternoon sun and helps conserve soil moisture.

Adequate water and shade can help reduce blossom drop and cell damage when temperatures are very warm or hot. Feeding and fertilizing should be decreased or stopped during very warm and hot weather.

Expect loss of blossoms or crops when temperatures deviate from a crop's temperature range.

Optimal growing temperatures—high end of range given first:

- 95°F to 65°F (optimal 85°F to 70°F): eggplant, hot peppers, okra, sweet potato, watermelon.

- 95°F to 50°F (optimal 75°F to 60°F): corn, cowpea, New Zealand spinach.

- 90°F to 60°F (optimal 75°F to 65°F): cucumber, muskmelon.

- 90°F to 50°F (optimal 75°F to 65°F): chayote, pumpkin, squash.
  - 85°F to 65°F (optimal 75°F to 70°F): sweet pepper, tomato.
  - 85°F to 45°F (optimal 75°F to 55°F): chicory, chives, garlic, leek, onion, salsify, shallot.
  - 80°F to 50°F (optimal 70°F to 60°F): bean, lima bean.
  - 75°F to 45°F (optimal 65°F to 60°F): artichoke, carrot, cauliflower, celeriac, celery, Chinese cabbage, endive, Florence fennel, lettuce, mustard, parsley, pea, potato.
  - 75°F to 40°F (optimal 65°F to 60°F): beet, broad bean, broccoli, Brussels sprouts, cabbage, chard, collard, horseradish, kale, kohlrabi, parsnip, radish, rutabaga, sorrel, spinach, turnip.

WATERING VEGETABLES

Summer watering . Water young vegetables every day until they are well established. Pay close attention to tomatoes, peppers, eggplants, melons, zucchini, cucumbers, and squashes; they need regular water when flowering and as their fruits fill out. Keep beans and peas just moist until they have flowered then water a bit more often. Lettuce, spinach, Brussels sprouts, cabbages, broccoli, and cauliflower do best when watered regularly. Water plants in the morning so they don't become susceptible to fungus and insect infestation. When the weather is dry, water summer crops so that moisture reaches deep to the roots. Long, slow watering is best. (Water long and slow by allowing water to gently soak into the soil at the base of each plant over 30 minutes or more using a hose or drip irrigation.) The best times to water are in the morning or evening when evaporation is low.

One inch of water. Garden guides often recommend giving vegetables 1-inch of water every week. How much is one inch of water? One inch of rainfall or irrigation will soak the soil to a depth of 4 to 5 inches. Burrow your fingers into the soil to check soil moisture. In hot weather you may need to water more often, in cool weather less. Soil moisture evaporation is most pronounced near the soil surface; if the soil is moist 4 inches down, vegetable roots should

have sufficient moisture for steady growth. Watering to 5 inches deep will insure deep root growth.

Critical watering times

- **Tomatoes, cucumbers, squash:** water during flowering and fruit development.
- **Peppers, eggplant:** water regularly throughout season.
- **Beans, peas:** water when plants bloom; water when pods start to develop and continue to harvest.
- **Corn:** water when tasseling and as cobs develop.
- **Lettuce, chard, spinach, and leafy greens:** regular water through growing season.
- **Cabbage, cauliflower, broccoli, kale, Brussels sprouts:** water when heads are developing.
- **Root crops—beets, carrots, radishes, parsnips, turnips:** water just when soil starts to dry out.
- **Onions, garlic, shallots:** regular water when bulbs are enlarging; stop water when leafy tops fall and brown.
- **Asparagus:** following harvest keep fernlike foliage well-watered.
- **Leeks:** regular water through growing season.

Watering tips:

- Water in late afternoon when plants wilt; plants wilted in the morning, need water right away.
- Avoid watering midday when evaporation is greatest.
- Lightly cultivate the soil in advance of watering; break the soil crust to allow water to seep deep, not run off.
- Check soil moisture by burrowing your hand 4 to 5 inches into the soil; if it's not moist at that depth, water—roots are not getting the moisture they need.
- Mulch around plants to slow soil moisture evaporation; use dry grass clipping or straw; mulch after you water thoroughly.

SUMMER MULCHING

Protect plants from hot weather by applying mulch during the summer. Apply three to four inches of compost, dry grass clippings, or straw around plants. Mulch will reduce soil temperature by 10°F or more. Soil temperatures of greater than 85°F can slow plant growth. Mulch also protects soil from being compacted over time by the drying of soil particles and the beating of rain or irrigation. A thin layer of mulch will protect soil microorganisms and other beneficial soil borne organisms from cooking in the summer heat. Almost all plants benefit from the protection of mulch. Vegetables that most benefit from summer mulching are eggplants, tomatoes, cauliflower, celery, and potatoes. These crops especially appreciate cool, loose, well-drained soil.

Applying mulch. Two cubic feet of compost mulch can cover an area of 8 square feet to 3 inches deep; one cubic yard of compost mulch covers an area of 108 square feet to 3 inches deep.

Mulch should be applied loosely and not compacted. Mulch should be kept back a few inches from the stems or crowns of plants and trunks of trees. If placed too closely, mulch can retain moisture and cause plant stems and trunks to rot.

Mulch benefits. Mulch can control insects and diseases. Straw mulch can reduce the number of adult cucumber beetles laying eggs at the base of plants. Mulch reduces or eliminated the spread of fungal spores often spread by the splashing of irrigation water or rain.

Straw mulch, shredded leaves, dry grass clippings, or aged compost tucked around plants will protect roots and save soil moisture in hot weather.

Types of mulch for hot weather vegetable gardens:

- **Aged compost.** Loose, aged compost applied as a 2- or 3-inch sheet across the soil will slow soil moisture evaporation and keep roots cool in hot weather. Aged compost adds a wide-range of nutrients to the soil and improves soil structure and the retention of soil moisture.

- **Shredded or chopped leaves.** A 4-inch layer of dried leaves can cool the soil by as much as 18 degrees. Raked dried leaves can be shredded by the passing of a lawn mower set at 3-inches high.

- **Grass clippings.** Dried and aged grass clippings free of seed or weeds will protect the soil and add nitrogen to the soil as it decomposes. Avoid fresh grass clippings more than ½ inches thick; fresh, moist clipping can mat and decay from the center causing a sour smell and too much heat. Lawn clippings used as mulch should be herbicide- and pesticide-free.

- **Straw.** Set loosely around plants to 4 inches thick, straw will protect the soil from summer heat while allowing water to easily reach planting beds. Straw set under strawberries or summer fruiting vegetables will protect crops from insects, soil splashing, and rots.

- **Pine needles.** Pine needles are effective in keeping rain or irrigation from washing away furrows and raised beds and lightly applied will protect newly seeded rows. Pines needles break down slowly.

- **Newspaper.** Four to six sheets of damp black and white newsprint paper will protect the soil and suppress weeds. Newspaper should be applied loosely. Paper is best topped with grass clippings or straw to keep it from drying out. Check to make sure the paper does not absorb irrigation or rain water.

- **Living mulch.** Vegetable crops closely spaced can form a leafy canopy that acts as living mulch protecting the soil from the heat of the sun and slowing the evaporation of soil moisture. Crops should be planted so that their leaves just touch or slightly overlap at maturity. Intensively planted crops require fewer square feet. Moisture transpiring from leaves is trapped as humidity below the leafy canopy.

Other mulches. Plastic mulches and plastic sheeting or films are not good choices for mulch in hot summer regions. They are likely to make the soil too warm. Black plastic absorbs solar radiation and radiates heat to the soil. Clear plastic transmits sunlight directly into the soil and holds the heat there. Plastic mulches are best used to help warm cold soil in early spring.

Aluminum foil or white plastic film can be used as mulch when the summer is not too hot. Light-colored mulch seems to blind aphids and keep them from landing on plants. Aluminum foil also will deter potato aphids, bean beetles, and squash borers.

WEED CONTROL

Weeds in the garden. A weed is any plant that grows in the garden that you do not want. Weeds steal water and nutrients from vegetable crops reducing yield. Weeds compete with vegetables for sun and provide a refuge for pests and diseases. The best strategy for weed control is to prevent weeds from germinating and eradicate those that do.

Easy organic weed control:

- Remove weeds and their roots as soon as they appear. Don't let them grow.
- Never let weeds flower.
- Smother weeds with 4 to 6 inches of mulch; use straw, dry grass clippings or a couple of layers of newspaper or cardboard.
- Spray weeds with vinegar.
- Scald weeds with boiling water.
- Plant vegetables intensively.

MID-SUMMER PLANTING FOR AUTUMN HARVEST

Plant in mid- to late-summer for autumn harvest. Plant cool-season crops for autumn (and winter) harvest. Cool-season crops get a quick start from seed or seedling in warm summer soil and come to maturity in the cool autumn days. For autumn harvest, choose crop varieties with shorter days to

harvest so they will be ready before the first freeze. Here is a list of autumn harvest vegetables:

- Arugula
- Asian greens
- Beets
- Broccoli
- Brussels sprouts
- Cabbage
- Carrots
- Cauliflower
- Celery
- Chinese cabbage
- Collards
- Corn salad (mâche)
- Endive
- Escarole
- Florence fennel
- Kale
- Leeks
- Lettuce
- Mustard
- Parsnips
- Peas
- Radicchio
- Radishes
- Rutabagas
- Spinach
- Turnips

Planting times for autumn harvest. As a general guideline here is a seed starting calendar for autumn crops by planting zone:

- USDA zone 5 and colder: sow seed from early to mid-June; transplant in early July.
- USDA zone 6: sow seed in mid-June or early July; transplant in late July.
- USDA zone 7: sow seed from mid to late June; transplant in early August.
- USDA zone 8: sow seed from early to mid-July; transplant mid-August.
- USDA zone 9 and 10: sow seed from mid-July to early August; transplant after mid-August.

Plan to transplant out into the garden seedlings that are 4 to 6 weeks old. To calculate the seed sowing date of autumn and winter harvested crops, add a week or two to the number of days to maturity of the variety you are growing.

When to Plant Your Autumn and Winter Garden

The chart on the next page will help you determine when to plant each crop directly in the garden for autumn and winter harvest. It uses the middle of each month as a marker. If the date of your average first frost varies by a week or two in either direction then simply adjust the planting dates by a week or two. To learn more about the average last and first frost dates where you live see Appendix 3: Frost Dates and Growing Season pages 169-180.

PLANTING DATES FOR AUTUMN AND WINTER HARVEST

Vegetables	If First Frost in Autumn Sept. 15	If First Frost in Autumn Oct. 15	If First Frost in Autumn Nov.15	If First Frost in Autumn Dec. 15
Arugula	July 5—Aug. 5	Aug. 5—Sept. 5	Sept. 5—Oct. 5	Oct. 5—Nov. 5
Asian greens	July 5—Aug. 5	Aug. 5—Sept. 5	Sept. 5—Oct. 5	Oct. 5—Nov. 5
Beans – Snap	June 10—30	July 15—Aug. 5	Aug. 5—Sept. 5	Sept. 1—Sept. 25
Beet	June 25—Jul. 15	July 25—Aug. 15	Aug. 25—Sept. 15	Sept. 25—Oct. 15
Broccoli	May 25—Jun. 30	July 1—Aug. 5	July 20—Aug. 25	Aug. 25—Sept. 20
Brussels sprouts	June 10—30	July 15—Aug. 5	Aug. 5—Sept. 5	Sept. 1—25
Cabbage	June 10—30	July 15—Aug. 5	Aug. 5—Sept. 5	Sept. 1—25
Carrot	June 25—July 15	July 30—Aug. 10	Aug. 20—Sept. 10	Sept. 15—Oct. 5
Cauliflower	June 10—30	July 15—Aug. 5	Aug. 5—Sept. 5	Sept. 1—25
Celery	June 10—30	July 15—Aug. 5	Aug. 5—Sept. 5	Sept. 1—25
Chinese cabbage	July 5—Aug. 5	Aug. 5—Sept. 5	Sept. 5—Oct. 5	Oct. 5—Nov. 5
Claytonia	July 20—Aug. 10	Aug. 20—Sept. 10	Sept. 20—Oct. 10	Oct. 20—Nov. 10
Collards	June 25—July 15	July 30—Aug. 10	Aug. 20—Sept. 10	Sept. 15—Oct. 5
Cucumber	June 10—30	July 15—Aug. 5	Aug. 5—Sept. 5	Sept. 1—25
Endive/Escarole	July 5—Aug. 5	Aug. 5—Sept. 5	Sept. 5—Oct. 5	Oct. 5—Nov. 5
Florence fennel	June 10—30	July 15—Aug. 5	Aug. 5—Sept. 5	Sept. 1—25
Garlic	July 20—Aug. 10	Aug. 20—Sept. 10	Sept. 20—Oct. 10	Oct. 20—Nov. 10
Kale	June 10—30	July 15—Aug. 5	Aug. 5—Sept. 5	Sept. 1—25
Kohlrabi	June 10—30	July 15—Aug. 5	Aug. 5—Sept. 5	Sept. 1—25
Leek	June 25—July 15	July 30—Aug. 10	Aug. 20—Sept. 10	Sept. 15—Oct. 5
Lettuce	June 10—30	July 15—Aug. 5	Aug. 5—Sept. 5	Sept. 1—25
Mâche	July 20—Aug. 10	Aug. 20—Sept. 10	Sept. 20—Oct. 10	Oct. 20—Nov. 10
Mibuna	July 25—Aug. 10	Aug. 25—Sept. 10	Sept. 25—Oct. 10	Oct. 25—Nov. 10
Mizuna	July 5—Aug. 5	Aug. 5—Sept. 5	Sept. 5—Oct. 5	Oct. 5—Nov. 5
Mustard	July 5—Aug. 5	Aug. 5—Sept. 5	Sept. 5—Oct. 5	Oct. 5—Nov. 5
Onion plants	July 5—Aug. 5	Aug. 5—Sept. 5	Sept. 5—Oct. 5	Oct. 5—Nov. 5
Onion seeds	July 5—Aug. 5	Aug. 5—Sept. 5	Sept. 5—Oct. 5	Oct. 5—Nov. 5
Onion sets	July 5—Aug. 5	Aug. 5—Sept. 5	Sept. 5—Oct. 5	Oct. 5—Nov. 5
Pak Choi	July 5—Aug. 5	Aug. 5—Sept. 5	Sept. 5—Oct. 5	Oct. 5—Nov. 5
Parsley	June 10—30	July 15—Aug. 5	Aug. 5—Sept. 5	Sept. 1—25
Parsnip	June 10—30	July 15—Aug. 5	Aug. 5—Sept. 5	Sept. 1—25
Peas	June 25—July 15	July 30—Aug. 10	Aug. 20—Sept. 10	Sept. 15—Oct. 5
Radish	June 10—30	July 15—Aug. 5	Aug. 5—Sept. 5	Sept. 1—25

Vegetables	If First Frost in Autumn Sept. 15	If First Frost in Autumn Oct. 15	If First Frost in Autumn Nov.15	If First Frost in Autumn Dec. 15
Rutabaga	June 10—30	July 15—Aug. 5	Aug. 5—Sept. 5	Sept. 1—25
Salsify	June 10—30	July 15—Aug. 5	Aug. 5—Sept. 5	Sept. 1—25
Scallions	July 5—Aug. 5	Aug. 5—Sept. 5	Sept. 5—Oct. 5	Oct. 5—Nov. 5
Shallots	July 5—Aug. 5	Aug. 5—Sept. 5	Sept. 5—Oct. 5	Oct. 5—Nov. 5
Sorrel	July 5—Aug. 5	Aug. 5—Sept. 5	Sept. 5—Oct. 5	Oct. 5—Nov. 5
Spinach	July 5—Aug. 5	Aug. 5—Sept. 5	Sept. 5—Oct. 5	Oct. 5—Nov. 5
Squash, summer	June 10—30	July 15—Aug. 5	Aug. 5—Sept. 5	Sept. 1—25
Swiss chard	June 25—July 15	July 30—Aug. 10	Aug. 20—Sept. 10	Sept. 15—Oct. 5
Tatsoi	July 25—Aug. 10	Aug. 25—Sept. 10	Sept. 25—Oct. 10	Oct. 25—Nov. 10
Turnips	July 5—Aug. 5	Aug. 5—Sept. 5	Sept. 5—Oct. 5	Oct. 5—Nov. 5

MID-SUMMER THINGS TO DO

Succession planting. Warm-weather vegetables can still be sown directly in the garden in most regions. Continue to direct-sow bush beans, French beans, pole beans, lima beans, beets, spring cabbage (in cooler regions), winter cabbage, cantaloupes, carrots, late cauliflower, collards, sweet corn, cucumbers, leeks, lettuces, okra, southern peas, rutabagas, spinach, summer squash, watermelon, and turnips. Plant pumpkins and winter squash in a shady spot, but where the vines will run into the sunlight. Set out more sweet potato slips. In regions where the weather remains warm well into autumn, you can sow eggplants, peppers, and tomatoes now.

Spring lettuce succession planting. Once the spring lettuce harvest has run its course you can turn the plants under by about 12 inches—the depth of a shovel blade. The greens will decompose quickly. Rake the planting bed smooth and sow seed for autumn harvest greens or roots. Successions for planting now include onion sets, for scallions, lettuces, and broccoli.

Summer planted herbs. Direct sow warm-season herbs including basil, dill, cilantro, sweet marjoram, summer savory, and parsley. Cut back bushy herbs and take cuttings of perennial herbs to start new plants.

Tie in tomatoes, feed, and mulch. Make sure staked tomatoes are tied into their stake before they grow too large and heavy. Use elastic plant tape or strips of cloth. The tie should be tight around the stake and a loose loop around the stem. Give each plant a side-dressing of 2 tablespoons of complete organic fertilizer such as 5-10-10 after the plants have set blossoms. Add mulch around the base of tomatoes to preserve soil moisture which is essential for steady fruit development.

Tomato pruning. Pinch outside shoots which grow from the axils of vining or indeterminate tomato plants. "Pinching" refers to removing the growing tips–usually about a half inch of growth. Pinch regularly through the growing season. Do not pinch out the side shoots on bush varieties. For bush tomatoes or tomatoes growing without cages place straw or peat on the ground beneath the plant to keep the fruits off the soil. Feed tomatoes regularly. Use shade cloth or an old sheet to protect tomatoes and peppers from sunburn.

Early blight and tomatoes. Early blight is a fungal disease that attacks tomatoes. An early symptom of early blight infection is the appearance of brown concentric-ringed spots on the lower leaves of the tomato plant. In hot, humid weather, early blight can spread rapidly. Control early blight by applying a fungicide every 7 to 10 days throughout the growing season. Use a copper- or sulfur-based fungicide that contains the bacterium *Bacillus subtilis*.

Training pole and runner beans. Train pole and runner beans up for an easy harvest. Here are two methods: (1) make a tepee of four 6 to 7 foot poles; drive poles at least 6 inches into the soil, setting each pole 4 feet apart; bind the poles at the top with garden twine. Plant a half dozen seeds at the base of each pole; later thin to the strongest 3 or 4; (2) set tall stakes in the ground at 3-foot intervals; tie string horizontally from one pole to the next at the top and the bottom; next, attach additional string vertically every 6 inches; sow 4 or 5 bean seeds below each vertical string; thin to the strongest 3 plants; train the vines up the strings.

Training cucumbers. To keep cucumbers from taking over the garden, train them up a trellis or cover a frame with chicken wire and set it at 45° angle near plants. Cucumbers will climb the support and fruits will be easy to harvest.

Feed corn. Corn is a heavy feeder. Side-dress corn with a sprinkling of organic 5-10-10 fertilizer when plants are 4 to 6 inches tall. Side-dress them again when they tassel.

Hilling corn. Hill young corn seedlings when they are about 6 inches tall. Hilling means to draw up soil close to the base of the plant. Hilling anchors and supports shallow-rooted corn plants which are easily knocked about by wind. Use a hoe to draw soil from about a foot away up to the base of each plant. Be careful not to disturb shallow corn roots. Hilling can be done after the first side-dressing of corn with an all-purpose fertilizer. Hilling will also knock down or bury early weeds in the corn patch.

Feed peppers and eggplants. Draw a circle around pepper and eggplants with two or three fingers. Lightly sprinkle 5-10-10 organic fertilizer into the circle and cover with soil. Peppers and eggplants are slow growers; this will give them the nutrients they need to set fruit and reach harvest.

Pepper blossom drop. Pepper blossoms drop when hit by cold weather—even a chilly night. If hot weather returns, so will the blossoms. Give pepper blossoms and fruits a boost with Epsom salt spray (one teaspoon of Epsom salts dissolved in spray bottle of warm water). Spray the whole plant.

Pepper blossom fixer. To help pepper blossoms set fruit try this spray: mix one teaspoonful of Epsom salts in a spray bottle and fill it with lukewarm water; spray blossoms. Epsom salts are rich in magnesium which will help blossoms set fruit.

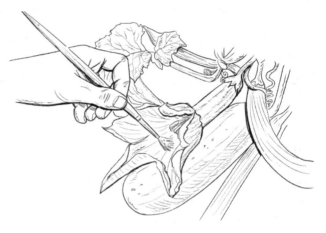

Hand pollination: use a small brush to transfer pollen from the male flower to the female flower.

Hand pollinate squash. Hand pollination is the manual transfer of pollen from the stamen of one plant to the pistil of another— that is from a male flower to a female flower. Members of the Cucurbit family—squash, melons, pumpkins, and cucumbers—often have pollination problems because male flowers commonly open days before female flowers and so often drop before pollinators such as bees can transfer pollen from male to female flowers. When female flowers are not pollinated, fruit will never appear. If fruit is not forming on your Cucurbit family plants, you can help. Rub a small brush or cotton swab, on the stamen of a male flower (it will be dusty with pollen) then rub the brush on the stigma of a female flower. Alternatively, you can remove the petals from a male flower and brush the stamen against the stigma of a female flower. Which flower is male and which is female? Female flowers will have a small bulge (a small immature fruit) where the stem meets the flower. Male flowers are shorter than female flowers and often appear in clusters.

Squash blossom blight is a fungal disease that can attack squash vines and flowers. Blossom blight is most common when the weather is wet and humid. Blossom blight will cause flowers to wilt and drop off the plant; before blossoms drop they can be covered with a white mold which can turn brown or purple. The disease can also infect young fruits causing a dark, wet rot. Immediately remove infected flowers or fruits and spray plants with a fungicide such as liquid copper (one fluid ounce per gallon of water) or a spray that contains the bacterium *Bacillus subtilis*. Repeat the fungicide every 10 days. Make sure plants are not crowded and have adequate air circulation and be sure to plant squash in compost-rich, well-drained soil.

Feed and water melons. Feed melons when they blossom. Give each plant a side-dressing of one tablespoon of 5-10-10 organic fertilizer. Keep the soil around melons just moist during the growing season. Don't let the soil go dry; melons need moisture to speed ripening.

Elevate melons. Elevate developing melons on a large tin can; this will expose the fruit to more sunlight throughout the day; the metal will also absorb solar heat and warm the melons all the way through. Melons that sit on the ground will stay cooler on the ground side and ripen more slowly.

Check potato tubers. Check the size of your potato tubers by pulling away soil from around the plant. Tubers big enough to eat can be lifted now. If the size is not right, just rebury the tubers and roots and pat the soil firm. Re-check tubes for size in two weeks.

Feed onions for big bulbs. Sprinkle a cupful of 5-10-10 organic fertilizer across every 10 feet of onion wide rows. Feed the green tops of onions beginning when tops are 6 to 8 inches tall. The taller the green tops grow, the larger the bulbs below will grow.

Side-dress winter squash before runner growth. Give winter a squash a side-dressing with one teaspoon of complete organic fertilizer before vines begin to run. This will give them energy to run and produce fruits.

Blanching celery. Blanch celery by mounding up soil a few inches around the base of each plant. The soil will block sunlight and keep the stalks white, tender, and mild tasting. Be careful to draw the soil from a foot or so away from the plants, celery is shallow rooted and easily overturned. For the best flavored celery, do not let the soil go dry—keep it just moist throughout the growing season.

Blanching leeks. To grow large, white, succulent leeks you must blanch the lower part of the stem or shank. Hilling up soil around the shank is one way to blanch leek stems, but hilling often leaves leeks gritty because soil and sand can easily slip between the whorls of overlapping leaves low on the plant. Leeks can be blanched and kept clean by growing them in tubes—paper tubes or tubes made of biodegradable material (cardboard toilet paper or paper towel tubes will work) or in recyclable plastic tubes such as thin-walled PVC tubing. Tubes will cuff and surround leek stems as they grow; the tubes block light (and soil) from the stem leaving the shank tender and white at harvest.

Cauliflower blanching. Each cauliflower plant produces one head. When a head starts to form, leaves around the head will spread revealing the white curds. As soon as this happens, bend the leave back across the curds to cover them. This will protect the curds from turning yellow, growing tough, and bolting to flower and seed. Bend the leaves until they snap, then lay them across the curds and tuck them in on the opposite side of the head. Check back every few days to be sure the crown and curds are covered as they develop.

Keep an eye on broccoli. Broccoli heads can grow quickly in warm weather and if the temperatures get into the 80s watch for heads to begin flowering. You want to harvest broccoli before florets open to bright yellow flowers. If heads start to separate and you see any hint of yellow, harvest immediately. As soon as buds begin to swell toward flowering, flavor will become sharp and less palatable. If the main head blooms, cut it off just under the center of the head right at the stem; the plant will produce lateral side shoots (small heads) that will be edible. Side-dress broccoli with a complete organic fertilizer or compost tea when heads are starting to form.

Brussels sprouts developing. Inspect your Brussels sprouts. Small sprouts develop above the juncture of the main upright stem and each side-leaf branch. These sprouts are edible as soon as they are the size of a large marble.

Why cabbages do not form heads. The cabbage is a cool-season crop; it doesn't like temperatures greater than 80°F and prefers to grow when temperatures are between 60 to 65°F. Very warm and hot temperatures will stress cabbage, preventing heads from forming. Temperatures greater than 75°F can cause cabbage to bolt that is switch from growing leaves to growing flowers and producing seeds. Other stresses that can cause cabbage not to head are overcrowding and lack of water. Be sure to thin cabbage to 18 inches apart and keep the soil moist. If the soil is not moist 4 inches below the surface, water right away.

Asparagus feeding. Small, thin spears leftover after the asparagus harvest should be nurtured; this will encourage strong plants for next season. Let spears left after the harvest grow tall, fernlike shoots. Feed plants with a high nitrogen organic fertilizer—blood meal, cottonseed meal, soybean meal, fish emulsion, or cow manure—and keep them well-watered. Let asparagus plants grow tall and bushy until they begin to set berries in the autumn, then you can cut them back for the winter and protect the bed with compost and straw mulch.

Watering and disease. Water at the base of plants during the summer to avoid splashing soil onto leaves. Fungal and bacterial diseases in the soil can be spread by splashing water. Place straw around the base of tomatoes, beans, cucumbers, melons, squash, and cucumbers. Bacterial blight of tomatoes and peppers and anthracnose of beans can be spread by splashing soil or by a gardener brushing against a diseased plant. Septoria leaf spot and early blight are common fungal diseases that attack tomatoes; both are spread by splashing soil. (Spots and yellowing lower leaves are symptomatic of Septoria leaf spot.) Read more about diseases at the end of this chapter.

Upkeep. Remove spent plants. Check the supports on tall and climbing plants.

PLANTING ZONE-BY-ZONE: Mid-Summer / July

Beginning with the warmest regions first, here is a seed starting and planting guide for mid-summer— July. It is safe to plant or do any of the tasks listed for regions cooler than yours.

USDA Zone 9-10—hot weather

- Direct seed pole beans, lima beans, cantaloupes, collards, sweet corn, okra, southern peas, watermelon, summer squash, and zucchini.

- Plant out tomato seedling for autumn harvest. Choose heat-tolerant cultivars, such as 'Heatwave.'

- Sow indoors seeds of eggplants, peppers, and tomatoes for the autumn reverse season garden if not already started.

- Sow cool-season crops indoors for autumn planting: broccoli, Brussels sprouts, cabbage, cauliflower.

- Plant rust resistant pole snap beans and pole lima beans until early autumn. Soil will be richer after harvesting because of nitrogen fixing nodules on roots.

- Sow cool-season crops indoors late summer planting; sow broccoli, cabbage, cauliflower for late autumn and winter harvest.

- Plant out late cauliflowers, winter cabbages, leeks, Swiss chard, and rutabagas.

- Set out more sweet potato slips.

- Prune tomatoes so that they don't become too heavy for stakes, cages, and trellises.

- Harvest runner and green beans as soon as they are ready; this will keep them producing.
- Cut back artichokes after bearing, to produce a crop next spring.
- Use an old sheet or shade cloth to protect peppers and tomatoes from sunburn.
- Mound soil around celery stems or wrap paper around the stems and lightly tie the stems together to blanch the stems.
- Pinch out the growing tips of runner beans when they reach the top of their support.
- Lift shallots if they have finished growing, and leave them on the surface for a few days to dry.
- Thin root vegetables sown earlier before they grow large enough to compete with each other.
- Prepare autumn and winter planting beds now. Add aged compost and well-rotted manure to beds and turn under two or three weeks before planting. Keep beds free of weeds before planting.
- Use small potatoes just harvested as seed for an autumn crop. Sprout seed potatoes under moist straw in a cool place ahead of planting.
- Order seed now for the autumn garden: purple top turnip, snap beans, curled mustard, leaf lettuce, long-root beets, 'Bermuda' onions, 'Chantenay' carrots.
- Harvest herbs regularly don't let the leaves become too old. Freeze leaves while they are still tender. Cut back bushy herbs.
- Take cuttings of perennial herbs to start new planting.
- Check supports on tall and climbing plants.
- Keep the soil evenly moist; letting the soil dry out will stress plants.
- Be sure garden is well mulched for hottest part of summer.
- Hoe regularly to keep down weeds.
- Side-dress crops with compost tea.
- Watch for early signs of pests and diseases. Caterpillars can devastate a cabbage crop if undetected.

- Spray outdoor tomatoes and potatoes with a fungicide to protect them from blight.
- Solarize empty beds that are infested with root-knot nematodes, or where diseases have been a problem.

USDA Zone 7-8

- Harvest runner and green beans as soon as they are ready. Freeze while they are still tender.
- Plant out late cauliflowers, winter cabbages, and leeks.
- Set out starts of Brussels sprouts, winter cabbages, and leeks.
- Sow seeds of globe beets, endive, Chinese cabbage, lettuce, round-seeded peas, radishes, rutabagas, spinach, Swiss chard, turnips.
- Sow seed of corn for a late harvest.
- Sow chervil and parsley seeds. Let dill, coriander, and fennel self-sow.
- Continue to thin vegetables sown earlier, before they grow large enough to compete with each other.
- Lift shallots and spread them out to dry; lift onions at the end of the month; leave both on the surface for a few days to dry.
- Continue to lift early potatoes.
- Give afternoon shade to leafy crops.
- Pinch out side-shoots of tomatoes, except bush varieties.
- Earth up or stake broccoli and Brussels sprouts.
- Mound soil around celery stem, and tie together.
- Cut back artichokes after bearing, to produce a crop next spring.
- Cut back bushy herbs.
- Continue to water and hoe the garden.
- Water vulnerable crops before they show signs of stress.
- Hoe regularly to keep down weeds.
- Be sure garden is well mulched for hottest part of summer.
- Spray outdoor tomatoes and potatoes with a fungicide to protect them from blight.

- Now's the time to solarize weed or nematode infested soil. Moisten empty planting beds then cover them with clear plastic for at least a month.
- Water vulnerable crops before they show signs of stress.
- Hoe regularly to keep down weeds.
- Mulch or give afternoon shade to leafy crops.

USDA Zone 3-6

- Late in month, direct-sow cool-season crops for autumn harvest; sow seed of, beets, carrots, chard, endive, Chinese-cabbage, lettuce, snap and snow peas, radish, spinach, turnips, for autumn harvest. Sow bush beans.
- Transplant cabbage family seedlings to garden: broccoli, cabbage, Brussels sprouts and cauliflower.
- Weed, water, and fertilize as needed.
- Remove spent plants.
- Turn compost pile.
- Check supports on tall and climbing plants.
- Watch for pests and signs of disease.
- Plant any sprouted potatoes for a late crop.
- Watch for early signs of pests and diseases.
- Ripen onions by lifting them gently and leaving them in place for a couple of weeks. Sow onions for an early crop next year.
- Mulch potatoes.
- Gather and dry basil, mint and other herbs before they flower.
- Side-dress crop with compost tea when ground is moist.
- Mulch if the weather is dry. Use aged compost, dry grass clippings, or clean hay.

MID-SUMMER HARVEST

Green beans harvest. Greens beans or snap beans are ready for picking soon after blossoms appear—about 45 days after sowing. Pick beans before the seeds in the pods grow big. If pods start to bulge, the plant will stop producing. Beans that are block planted will shade the soil and control weeds. Pick beans like peas; don't yank the pods off the plant—use two hands, one to hold the stem the other to pull the pod away or twist and snap the pods off the stem.

Summer squash harvest. Harvest summer squash when they are about the length of your hand or smaller. These squash will be tender and seedless and crunchy-firm. It is difficult to under- or over-cook small summer squash. Zucchini is best harvested small also, never longer than the length of your hand—smaller is tastier.

Onion and garlic harvest. Harvest onions and garlic after the tops start to yellow and die back. Cure onions for at least a week. Place them on a screen set off the ground with plenty of air circulation. When dry, cut the tops off keeping an inch of stem. Store onions cool and dry in net bags. Cure garlic by hanging bunches in a warm dry place out of the sun for two to three weeks.

Garlic scapes. When garlic plants produce seed they send up a long, thin stalk called a scape (in botanical jargon a scape is a stem without leaves). Most vegetables send up stalks that flower; garlic sends up a scape which produces small bulblets (seeds) at the tip—no flowers. When scapes first form they are curled; eventually they straighten and thicken. Curled scapes are tender and can be eaten much like you would chives; they can be chopped and eaten raw, steamed, or sautéed. The best time to harvest garlic scapes is just when they begin to curl. Removing scapes will help produce larger garlic bulbs.

Second and third harvest from one cabbage. To get a second and even third, fourth, and fifth harvest from one cabbage plant do the following: when you harvest the main cabbage head leave behind several leaves to grow on; don't cut the head off below the lowest leaves (if you cut below the lowest leaves the stub and roots will wither and die). Care for the leaves left on the stub like you would a whole cabbage: feed the stub compost tea and keep it watered. Small sprouts will soon form around the rim of the stub. The sprouts will grow into small baseball-size cabbages or sub-heads—as many as six new mini-heads. These heads will be pale, white and tender. They will be just right for salads and stir-fry.

Peas harvest. Garden peas are ready for picking when the pods become full, about two weeks after they blossom. Snow peas are ready for harvest as soon as they are large enough to eat—don't wait for the pods to fill. Hold the stem of the pea in one hand near the base of the pod and break off the pod with your other hand. Don't yank pods; you might break the stem. Peas start to lose sweetness as soon as they are picked, so don't pick more than you need each day.

Baby beets harvest. Beets the size of a marble along with their greens can be harvested and cooked together. One beet seed can produce as many as three plants, so thinning beets is important. Take up young beets for early eating leaving room for the remaining beet roots to grow to maturity.

Leafy harvest. Harvest the outside leaves of lettuce, spinach, kale, and collards leaving the inner crowns untouched to grow new leaves. Leaves no more than 6 inches long will be the most tender and sweet. Don't pick outside cabbage leaves, let them flop on the ground to stop soil moisture evaporation and weeds. Toss those leaves in the compost pile when you harvest cabbage heads.

Kohlrabi care and harvest. Kohlrabi is ready for harvest when the above ground bulbs are about 3 inches across. Don't let bulbs grow bigger or the flesh will be woody. Keep an eye out for cabbage worms as kohlrabi develops. Worms can attack the leaves and stunt the plant's growth. Dust plants with an insecticide that contains *Bacillus thuringiensis* (Bt)

Herb harvest. Harvest herbs at the peak of flavor and fragrance. Harvest herbs when the oils are most pungent usually when the plant is in bud and before it flowers. Herbs harvested in the morning will be most flavorful. Air dry herb sprigs and leaves by hanging them upside down in small bunches in a well-ventilated room out of direct sunlight. Herbs will dry in one to three weeks. Store herbs in an air-tight container.

HARVEST BY ZONE:
Mid-Summer / July

Crops coming to harvest this month were planted in spring.

- **USDA Zone 10:** amaranth, artichokes, basil, green beans, cantaloupes, chives, corn, cowpeas, cucumbers, edamame, eggplant, fava beans, garlic, melons, New Zealand spinach, okra, oregano, peas, peppers, rhubarb, southern peas, strawberries, summer squash, thyme, tomatillos, tomatoes, watermelon, zucchini.

- **USDA Zone 7-9:** arugula, artichokes, bush beans, beets, broccoli, cabbage, carrots, cauliflower, celery, collards, eggplant, fava beans, kale, lettuces, melons, potatoes, radishes, scallions, spinach, strawberries, Swiss chard, turnips.

- **USDA Zones 5-7:** green beans, beets, bok choy, broccoli, cabbage, carrots, chives, cilantro, corn, cucumbers, eggplant, fava beans, green onions, kale, kohlrabi, lettuce, melons, onions, parsley, peas, peppers, potatoes, radishes, radicchio, scallions, summer squash, strawberries, Swiss chard, tomatoes, zucchini.

- **USDA Zones 4-6:** arugula, Asian greens, beans, beets, broccoli, cabbage, cantaloupe, carrots, cauliflower, collards, corn, cucumbers, eggplant, garlic, green onions, kale, kohlrabi, lettuce, parsnips, potatoes, radishes, rutabaga, spinach, summer squash, tomatoes, turnips, watermelon.

SUMMER PESTS

Cabbage loopers are green caterpillars about 1½ inches long with white stripes down each side. They chew large irregular holes in the leaves of cabbage heads and broccoli and burrow into cabbage heads. They arch or loop their midsection as they move along. The adult looper is a brown night-flying moth with a silver chevron in the center of each wing. Row covers will exclude moths from laying eggs. Garlic or hot pepper spray will repel loopers. Handpicking loopers and their white, dome-shaped eggs on the undersides of leaves will control these pests.

The cabbage looper caterpillar gets its name from its looping motion. The adult is a brown night-flying moth.

Whiteflies are snow white insects about the size of a pinhead. They feed on the undersides of leaves, sucking juices leaving plants weak and leaves yellow or silvery. When disturbed they fly up in a cloud. Whitefly excrement is sticky and can host the growth of sooty mold—which further damages plants. Tomatoes, lettuce, melons, cucumbers, beans, and other crops are attacked by whiteflies—particularly in places where the air is still. Whiteflies can be active year round in greenhouses. Lacewing larvae and lady bug larvae eat whiteflies. Clean the garden of infested leaves; protect crops with row covers. Oil sprays will smother whiteflies.

Squash vine borers attack summer and winter squash in mid-summer. Wilting squash vines are a sign of squash vine borers burrowing and feeding on the inside of vines. A squash vine borer is a plump cream-colored caterpillar with a brown head. The adult is a wasp-like moth with a red or orange abdomen and metallic forewings and clear hindwings. When the larvae hatch they chew their way inside the vine and then feed for up to six weeks on the interior of the vine causing it to collapse. There is one generation each year in the north and two in warm southern regions. Handpick borers by slicing horizontally into the vine and removing the caterpillar; you can then re-root the vine by burying it. Row covers can exclude moths from laying eggs but may inhibit pollinators as well.

Japanese beetles feed mostly on beans, corn, and rhubarb; their grubs feed on plant roots. Adults are slightly larger than ¼ inch; they are metallic green with copper-brown wing covers. They attack beans and corn in early summer skeletonizing leaves. Place row covers over target plants early in the season to exclude the beetles; spray kaolin on plants to discourage feeding; handpick and destroy beetles early in the morning before they are active.

Corn earworm and the tomato fruitworm is the same pest. This caterpillar can be brown to yellowish tan with dark stripes down each side and a brown head. The adult is a pale tan moth with a dark spot at the center of each wing; the moth flies at night laying single, cream-colored eggs on corn silks and tomato and pepper leaves. These caterpillars eat kernels at the tips of corn ears and bore into the stem of tomato fruits. They also tunnel into bean pods and lettuce heads. Planting early corn varieties is one way to avoid corn earworm damage; the crop will mature before the caterpillars begin feeding. Vegetable oil dripped on corn silks will smother earworms. Handpicking is a good control. Spraying with spinosad and *Bacillus thuringiensis* will also control fruitworms.

Tomato hornworm damage. The tomato hornworm is a very large greenish caterpillar that can grow to 3 inches long and sometimes larger. It is the largest caterpillar in the vegetable garden (though they are smaller to start). The hornworm has a black horn on its back end and V-shaped white marks down its sides. The adult hornworm is the five-spotted hawk moth. Hornworms chew leaves; they leave only the midribs behind. They feed on all tomato-family crops. Handpicking hornworms is an effective control also spraying with *Bacillus thuringiensis* when worm are 2 inches long or smaller.

The tomato hornworm has two horns extending from its rear end. One hornworm can defoliate a plant in a day.

European corn borers are tan and white caterpillars about 1 inch long with brown spots. They chew small holes near the whorls of corn leaves and later tunnel into the husk of ears. Use the same controls as you would for corn earworms (see above).

Nematodes (also called roundworms or eelworms). A nematode is a very small even microscopic worm-like creature with a needle-like appendage coming out of its head. The needle is used to feed. There are both good and bad nematodes; both are parasites. Pest nematodes feed on plant roots, stems, and leaves and often spread disease. Beneficial nematodes enter the bodies of cutworms, root maggots, and Japanese beetles and feed on them until they die. Nematodes are slow moving; they usually infest one part of the garden and do not spread unless carried on tools or plant debris. Solarizing the soil can kill pest nematodes (and beneficial insects). Keep the garden clean and rotate crops. Most garden centers sell beneficial nematodes which you can release into the garden soil.

Bacillus thuringiensis, **Dipel and thuricide.** Dipel (brand name) is an insecticide that contains *Bacillus thuringiensis* (Bt). In the pest control form Bt is known generically as thuricide. Bt is a naturally occurring bacterium found in soils throughout the world; it is a biological pest control used to control leaf-feeding insects. It acts as a stomach poison by eating holes in the lining of an insect's stomach causing death in a few days. Bt is used to control cabbage loopers, tomato hornworms, bagworms, tent caterpillars, and gypsy moths. Use Bt at the first sight of tiny holes in the leaves of target plants.

BENEFICIAL INSECTS

Many insects help control pest insects and diseases in the garden; these helpers are called beneficial insects (about 90 percent of all insects are beneficial). Beneficial insects include the lacewing, lady beetle, and assassin bug. Beneficial insects prey on insect pests including aphids, mealybugs, and scales. The honeybee is also a beneficial insect; it helps pollinate plants. Beneficial insects should be welcomed in the garden. Planting flowers that provide nectar will attract beneficial insects; shallow dishes filled with water will give beneficial insects a safe place to drink. Be cautious using pesticides—both natural and synthetic; pesticides kill both pest and beneficial insects. Here are a few beneficial insects that help in the vegetable garden:

- **Ladybug:** preys on aphids, whiteflies, Colorado potato beetles.

- **Green lacewing:** larvae prey on aphids, whiteflies, leafhoppers, mealybugs.

- **Aphid midge:** larvae attack aphids and suck out body fluids.

- **Ground beetle:** preys on slugs, caterpillars, Colorado potato beetles, cutworms.

- **Minute pirate beetle:** preys on spider mites, aphids, thrips, and caterpillars.

- **Damsel bug:** preys on caterpillars, mites, aphids, cabbage worms,

- **Braconid wasp:** preys on caterpillars, aphids.

- **Trichogramma wasp:** feed on moth and butterfly larvae, including cabbage worms, tomato hornworms, and corn earworms.

- **Ichneumon wasps:** feed on cutworms, corn earworms, white grubs.

Dill and fennel are two common vegetable garden plants that will attract these beneficial insects to the garden.

VEGETABLE GARDEN DISEASES

Most vegetable garden diseases strike in spring and summer. Be on the lookout for diseases. It's best to remove diseased leaves, fruits, and plants before the diseases spreads. Here are the most common vegetable garden diseases:

Disease	Target plants	Damage	Control
Anthracnose (fungus)	Beans, cucumbers, eggplant, lettuce, melons, peas, peppers, potatoes, radishes, rhubarb, spinach, tomatoes, turnips	Small spots on leaves, stems, and fruit; spots grow larger, plant dies back	Plant resistant varieties, spray with compost tea, rotate crops
Bacterial blight	Beans, cabbage family, peas	Cabbage family: young plants are stunted—one side larger than the other; older plants lose leaves. Beans and peas: light or dark green spots on leaves dry and turn brown or bronze	Plant resistant varieties; spray with neem oil
Bacterial wilt	Carrots, cucumbers, eggplants, melons, pepper, potatoes, pumpkins, rhubarb, squash, sweet potatoes, tomatoes	Soft brown lesions appear on stems and grow until plant is girdled; stems develop brown streaks that become jelly-like	Use row covers to protect plants from cucumber beetles which spread disease; rotate crops on 4-year cycle
Clubroot (fungus)	Cabbage-family crops	Roots become swollen and lumpy; leaves wilted and yellowish	Plant resistant varieties; add compost to beds; raise pH to 7.2
Curly top (fungus)	Beans, beets, cabbage family, carrots, celery, cucumber, eggplant, melons, pumpkins, spinach, squash, Swiss chard, tomatoes	Leaves curl upward and become thick and leathery; bean leaves curl down	Use row covers to protect plants from leafhoppers which spread disease; control weeds
Damping-off (fungus)	All seedlings	Seedling stems rot before they break through surface of soil	Use sterile seed starting mix; water from below
Downey mildew (fungus)	Endive, lettuce, members of the beet, cabbage, onion, pea families	Leaf spots turn a fluffy white then violet-white mold spreads to both sides of leaf; rot starts	Plant resistant varieties; spray leaves with compost tea regularly; rotate crops; remove weeds that harbor disease
Early blight (fungus)	Carrots, onions, potatoes, tomatoes	Brown circular spots surrounded by rings commonly during period of warm, humid weather before fruits ripen	Plant resistant varieties; weed regularly; spray plants with compost tea; use row covers to exclude flea beetles which spread disease
Fusarium and Verticillium wilts (fungus)	Beans, cucumbers, melons, pumpkins, squash, sweet potatoes, tomatoes	Leaves turn yellow , then brow; stems turn brown and split	Plant resistant varieties; rotate crops; remove and destroy infected plants; add aged compost to planting beds

Disease	Target plants	Damage	Control
Gray Mold, also called Botrytis	Almost all plants, seedlings and mature plants	Airy, gray mold above a water-soaked brown, rotten area on leaves, stems, flowers, and fruit; kills seedlings but does not kill mature plants	Use clean seed-starting supplies; space plants so there is good air circulation; remove infected and dead leaves; spray plants with compost tea
Late blight (fungus)	Potatoes, tomatoes	Dark spots develop on leaves, often with strong foul odor; plants eventually rot and collapse	Plant certified disease-free seeds or transplants; rotate crops; spray plants with compost tea
Powdery mildew	Beans, peas, lettuce, cucumbers, melons, pumpkins, squash and other crops	Round white or gray spots and coating that can cover leaves, stems, and flowers; spores germinate on dry surfaces when humidity is high.	Plant in full sun where there is good air circulation; pick off infected leaves; spray plants with 1 part milk and 9 parts water or a baking soda spray.
Root rot	Most plants are susceptible	Plant wilts and lower leaves turn yellow; roots turn black or brown and become soft and foul-smelling; can be common in moist, wet soil during cool weather	Avoid overwatering; water with compost tea; add aged compost to soil; solarize soil; rotate crops
Rust (fungus)	Asparagus, beans, beets, carrots, chard, corn, onions, peanuts, peas, spinach	Red, yellow, or orange dots on undersides of leaves; on onion and asparagus foliage tips; leaves turn up; often strikes early or late in season during wet weather	Plant resistant varieties; spray plants with compost tea
Southern blight (fungus)	Almost all crops	White to pinkish growth at base of stem at soil line; leaves turn yellow and drop	Add aged compost to planting beds regularly; spray plants with compost tea; remove 6 inches of soil when removing infected plants
Tobacco mosaic virus	Tomato-family plants, beans, beets, cucumbers, melons, potatoes	Leaves turn yellow to pale green become mottled, deformed or stunted; plants becomes stunted; yield reduced	Plant resistant varieties; don't smoke near garden; avoid touching healthy plants after touching diseased plants—virus spreads on contact; clean tools and clothes after working with plants

August

Late Summer

August is a month of endings and beginnings in the vegetable garden. Yes, there are still several weeks of vacation time before school starts, but in nature change is about. Summer will begin to fade in many gardens during August giving way to autumn and cool weather. In warm summer regions there may be a month or more of summer growing to come. Wherever you live, now is the time to plan and plant the autumn and winter vegetable garden if you have not already begun.

August is also harvest time. Check crops nearing maturity daily. Your planting calendar along with seed packets that note the days to maturity for each crop will give you a very good estimate of when to begin harvest for each crop. Size, color, and skin sheen are good indicators of when a crop is near harvest. It's almost always better to pick early than late.

PREPARING FOR AUTUMN AND WINTER

Autumn and winter garden. To know when to plant the autumn and winter garden, follow these steps:

1. Check the seed packet for the number of days to maturity for the crop you plan to plant.

2. Mark the average date of the first frost in your area on the calendar.

3. Count backwards from the average first frost date the number of days to maturity for the crop you are planting.

4. Count backwards an additional 2 weeks and mark that planting date on your calendar. (The additional two weeks will allow for slower plant growth as day length decreases and temperatures cool as summer fades into autumn.)

One way to cut short the number of days a plant will need in the garden is to transplant out seedlings. Garden centers may still have warm-season seedlings available and very likely have cool-season seedlings on hand. These plants already have a 4 to 6 week head start over seeds you might sow today.

Days left in growing season. Use the number of days in your garden's growing season to determine which crops will do best this time of year as the days start to grow shorter and eventually cooler. You may have plenty of time for more warm-weather crops in your region (after all there are only 1 or 2 days of frost each year in San Diego, for instance), or time may be very short (there are on average just 60 frost-free days each year in Telluride, Colorado, with the average first frost date arriving about August 27).

Seeds that go into the ground now need time to germinate and grow. If the warm weather will be gone from your garden in 60 to 90 days, there may not be enough time for warm-weather crops to mature and produce a tasty harvest.

Check a frost date table (see frost dates Appendix 3, pages 169-180) to know the average first frost date where you live.

Planning to grow in a cold frame or plastic hoop tunnel. If you expect the first frost or hard freeze in September or October, the remainder of the outdoor growing season may already be too short to bring crops to harvest without protection. Plant vegetables for autumn and winter harvest in a cold frame or plastic hoop tunnel or have portable hoop tunnels or cold frames at the ready to set over plants when a frost or freeze threatens. (To learn more about cold frames and plastic hoop tunnels see Chapter 2—February and additional references cited in the Index.)

Crops for autumn and winter. Grow cool-season crops in autumn and winter unless you live in very southern regions where there is no winter frost or freeze. Cool-season crops are leafy greens and root crops such as beets, cabbage, carrots, lettuce, and spinach. These crops prefer cool temperatures. They use the shorter days of autumn to direct their energy into leaf and root formation and don't bother with flowering and seeding or fruiting. Cool-season crops can be planted in almost all gardens by the end of August—earlier in very cold-winter regions where summer is short. (See regional and zone-by-zone planting suggestions for August below.)

Reverse season gardening. Reverse season is a term used to describe planting warm-season crops in autumn and winter—reverse the time of year one might expect to plant warm-season crops. Reverse season gardens are planted in far southern regions of the United States—southern Florida, parts of the Gulf Coast, and southern California. In these regions, summers can get too hot to grow warm-season crops (temperatures averaging greater than 90°F). Warm-season crops in these regions can be planted in late summer to mature in late autumn or early winter (reverse the normal season) or they can be planted in mid- to late winter to mature in late spring. Cool-season crops are planted in mid-to late autumn to mature in late winter and early spring. (For more details on reverse season gardening see Appendix 4, pages 181-183.)

PLANTING ZONE-BY-ZONE:
August / Late Summer

Beginning with the warmest regions first, here is a seed starting and planting guide for late summer—August. It is safe to plant or do any of the tasks listed for regions cooler than yours.

USDA Zone10—hot weather

Reverse-season planting: set out bush beans, lima beans, cucumbers, eggplants, southern peas, peppers, tomatoes, and watermelon. Plant basil, string beans, beets, broccoli, carrots, Chinese cabbage, cauliflower, Swiss chard, sweet corn, dill, endive, kohlrabi, lettuce, okra, potatoes, rutabagas, summer squash, winter squash and pumpkins, spinach, and turnips. (More on reverse season gardening on pages 181-183.)

- Sow cool-weather crops indoors for planting out in 4 to 6 weeks.
- Take cuttings of perennial herbs to start new plants.
- Lay fresh mulch in garden.
- Watch for pests and signs of disease.

USDA Zone 9

Plant cabbage and Brussels sprouts to winter over. Also plant beets, bush beans, carrots, collards, kale, leaf lettuce, mustard, autumn peas, late potatoes, radishes, salsify, late spinach, and Swiss chard. Potatoes can go into the garden now.

Start winter vegetables in seedbeds or indoors for transplanting out in early autumn: broccoli, Brussels sprouts, cabbage and Chinese cabbage, cauliflower, chard, kale, leaf lettuce, Bermuda onions, autumn peas, radishes, rutabagas, salsify, spinach, winter squash, and turnips.

- Lift ripe onions gently; leave them in warm, dry place for two weeks.
- Sow onions for an early crop next year.
- Sow cabbages for spring use.
- Prune back okra by one-third to encourage side shoots to bear.
- Lay fresh mulch in garden.
- Side-dress plants with compost tea.
- Watch for pests and signs of disease.
- Take cuttings of perennial herbs to start new plants.

USDA Zone 6-8

Check the number of frost-free days left in your area. You may have time to set out transplants of broccoli, Brussels sprouts, cabbage, cauliflower. You also may have time to start from seed: beets, carrots, Chinese cabbage, endive, kale, leaf lettuce, mustard, onions, parsley, peas, radishes, rutabaga, salsify, spinach, Swiss chard, and turnips directly in the garden. You can also grow these crops in a plastic hoop tunnel or cold frame.

- Check the seed packets for "autumn" and "late" varieties; they are quicker maturing plants.
- Have season extending devices handy to protect crops when temperatures drop.
- Harvest self-blanching celery when large enough; it will not withstand frost.
- Blanch leeks and celery now; use plastic or paper tubes.
- Draw earth around late corn to prevent it from blowing over.

- Keep ground cultivated and weed free. Continue watering if a dry spell comes along.
- Build a cold frame.
- Sow a cover crop of rye or buckwheat to be turned under in late autumn or early spring.

USDA Zone 3-5

- Sow spinach, turnips, and cold-hardy lettuce for autumn harvest.
- Sow a cover crop of oats, rye or ryegrass.
- Top-dress strawberries with compost.
- At midmonth, pick off all tomato flowers so the plant's energy can be devoted to ripening fruit.
- Be ready to cover tomatoes, peppers and beans to protect against the first frost.
- Set out new strawberry plants.

HARVEST TIPS

Harvest Time. How do you know when it is time to harvest your crops? Here are a few indicators:

- **Color.** Many vegetables turn colors as they ripen–tomatoes and peppers for example turn from green to yellow to orange to red. Read the seed packet description to know when harvest will come.
- **Sheen.** Vegetables ready for picking commonly have a shiny, healthy look. If the skin of the vegetable is dull, the peak time for harvest may have passed. (Watermelon is one exception.)
- **Size.** Most vegetables are ready for harvest when they reach a useable size. To check the tenderness and flavor of a vegetable bite into it. Don't delay harvest simply to grow bigger crops–flavor will likely be sacrificed.

Harvest early in the day. Pick vegetables close to the time you want to use them. Pick vegetables in the morning if you can. They will be crisp and moist before the sun climbs high in the sky and the day heats up. Vegetables begin to dehydrate, shrivel, and lose crispness and flavor as sugars turn to starch after harvest. Keep vegetables in a cool, dark place until you are ready to prepare and serve them.

Harvest thinning. Pull up some beets and radishes when they are just large enough to eat. This will loosen the soil and give the roots still in the ground room to expand toward harvest.

Bean harvest. Green beans are most flavorful when picked young and pencil-thin both for eating fresh and preserving. Pick beans at least twice a week during the peak of the season, every other day is better. The more you pick the more plants will produce.

Pick pole and snap beans before the seeds have begun to fill out the pods. Pick snap beans when they are still able to snap when bent; pods will be tender, moist, and succulent. The time from sowing to harvest will vary with variety. Bush snap beans are usually ready for harvest in 8 weeks, pole snap beans in 9 weeks. Bush beans come to harvest over a 2 to 3 week period; pole beans take longer to reach the plump seed stage and will produce for 10 weeks or more as long as you keep picking. Pick pole beans every 2 to 3 days through the summer.

Picking shell beans when the beans inside the pods are fully formed (open one to see) but before the pods begin to deteriorate. Bush shell beans are usually ready for harvest 9 to 10 weeks after sowing.

Dry beans harvest. Dry beans should be left on the vine to dry before harvest. Wait until the foliage has yellowed and withered and pods have become papery before picking.

Lima bean harvest. Lima beans are commonly harvested when the pods are bulging and the outline of the seeds is pronounced (other beans that are harvested before the seeds are plump). Bush lima beans are usually ready 9 to 10 weeks after sowing, pole lima beans about 13 weeks after sowing. Southerners often pick lima beans when they are small and green and cook them up in butter and milk. (That is why lima beans are also called butter beans.) If pods are too hard to shell, steam them for a minute and they will soften up.

Red cabbage takes longer to reach harvest. Red cabbage varieties take 15 to 20 days longer to reach maturity than white cabbage. Red cabbage heads will be smaller and coarser than white varieties, but they also withstand harsh weather better and resist insect damage. They are a good choice for the autumn garden. Add red cabbage to autumn coleslaws and try red cabbage sautéed with apples, spices, and vinegar.

Smaller cabbage heads are tastier than larger heads. Cabbage is ready for harvest and most tasty when it is about the size of a softball or just larger—just right for one meal.

Blanch celery a week before harvest. Use a paper milk carton to blanch celery. Cut off the top and bottom of the carton so that it is open at both ends. Slip the carton around the plant and tie it snug with a string. (The old-fashioned way to blanch celery is to hill up soil around the stalks.) Harvest celery with a sharp knife; cut the plant off below the soil line. In mild-winter regions, you can harvest celery stalks individually cut-and-come-again as needed.

Cauliflower harvest. Keep an eye on cauliflower heads when the weather is warm. As soon as the flower clusters start to separate, cut the head no matter the size. It will be inedible within a day or so if you don't.

Corn ripeness test. Here's how to know sweet corn is ripe and ready for picking: pinch the top of the ear with your thumb and forefinger. If full and rounded when you pinch, the ear is ripe and ready for picking. If you feel the topmost kernels coming to a point when you pinch, the ear is not ready and the kernels need to fill out more. A ripe ear will be flat and slightly rounded; an unripe ear will be pointed. You don't need to pull back the leaves of the ear to test for ripeness.

Pick corn when the silks at the end of the ears turn brown and damp and the ears are full and firm. Kernels should be full, plump, and juicy. The top of the husk will be round and blunt, not pointed. Early varieties mature in about 75 days; late varieties mature in 85 to 95 days. Midsummer planted corn will require about 14 days extra to mature. To harvest corn, give the ear a sharp twist downward from the stalk.

Preserving sweetness of picked corn. Sweet corn just picked will be the sweetest flavored. If you can't cook and serve corn immediately after picking, do this: place the unhusked ears broken stalk side down in a pail of water; the stems should be just submerged. This will slow down the loss of moisture and sweetness. You can also preserve much of the flavor by placing ears in the refrigerator or a cool, moist place.

Cowpeas can be picked when they are young and succulent for use as green beans. To use cowpeas as green shell beans, pick them when they are nearly mature in size.

Cucumber harvest. Check cucumbers every other day and pick as soon as they are dark green and 4 to 6 inches long. Cucumbers can become bitter in hot, dry weather—so don't let them linger on the vine. Morning picked cucumbers will be sweeter and less bitter than afternoon picked cucumbers. Pickling cucumbers can be cut from the vine when they are 1½ to 3 inches long. Do not leave cucumber on the vine to turn yellow or orange. Cucumbers are usually ready for harvest about 60 days or more after sowing. Pick cucumbers regularly or the plant will stop producing.

Eggplant harvest. An eggplant is ready for harvest when it is about one-third its mature size—about 3 to 6 inches long and the skin is shiny, not dull. Dull fruit is overripe. Eggplant is usually harvested about 145 days after seeds have been sown, about 70 days after setting seedlings into the garden. Cut fruit from the plant with shears, the stems are tough. Sliced eggplant that contains brown seeds is past its peak.

Garlic harvest time. Garlic is ready for harvest 90 to 110 days after planting when the tops begin to yellow and droop. When leaves begin to yellow, stop watering and bend over the leaf tops to begin curing the bulb. Allow bulbs to dry in a shady place for several days until the skin becomes papery. Allow bulbs to completely dry then cut off the leaf stalks and trim the roots. Harvest garlic at any stage. Small bulbs are just as tasty as larger bulbs. You can eat the green tops as well; use them like chives as a flavoring.

Globe artichoke harvest. Artichokes are ready for harvest the second year after planting. Harvest artichoke buds when they are plump but before the bracts open. Harvest the large central globe first; afterwards, side-shoot globes can be picked. Buds are past harvest when they turn purple and the flowers become visible. Use a sharp knife to cut buds 5 to 6 inches down the stem.

Herb harvest. Basil, dill, sage, and summer savory can be harvested now. The ideal time to harvest herbs is between the times when flower buds first appear and before they are fully open. This is when the volatile oil content will be at its highest. The best time of day to harvest is early in the morning before the sun gets hot but after the dew has disappeared.

Horseradish root harvest. Lift horseradish roots after cool weather arrives in autumn. Several frosts will enhance the flavor of horseradish. Lift the roots by hand after loosening the soil with a spading fork. Horseradish requires an average of 120 days to reach maturity.

Kale cut-and-come-again. Pick the lower, larger, outside kale leaves first. The plant will keep producing new leaves from the center. Kale will produce through the winter.

Cut-and-come again harvesting of leafy crops: slice the leaves from the plant about an inch above the soil; new leaves will grow for another harvest.

Cut-and-come-again lettuce and spinach. To keep lettuce and spinach producing cut individual leaves one inch above the ground; this will force the plant to produce new leaves. Side-dress plants with compost tea to keep them productive.

Leeks harvest. Leeks can be harvested at any size though most gardeners wait until they are big and fat. Leeks require 100 or more days in the garden. You can lift some early thinning the row and giving the remaining plants room to fill out.

Prune to speed melon harvest. Once there are melons growing on the vine nip off the curled, fuzzy ends at the very end of the vine. These fuzzy curls are new growth that will unfurl to become new leaves, new flowers, and new fruit. Once two or three melons are growing on a vine, there is no need for more. A melon vine has only so much energy and there is only so much warm weather to mature fruit. Tip pruning allows existing fruits to reach maturity before the season ends.

Melon harvest tips. Cantaloupe is ready for harvest at the "slip" stage–when slight pressure at the point where the stem joins the melon causes the melon to slip off the vine. Casaba and honeydew melons are ripe when the skin turns yellow. Crenshaw and Persian melons are ready for harvest when they have a fruity scent. Watermelons are ripe when a rap on the fruit creates a dull sound.

Melons and water. Do not overwater cantaloupe and watermelons close to harvest. Reduce water just as melons reach mature size a week or two before expected harvest. Reducing water near harvest will concentrate sweetness and flavor. Once melons are maturing on the vine, pinch away any new blossoms. Pinching away blossoms will speed the ripening of melons on the plant. (Also pinch off blossoms on pumpkins and winter squash.)

New Zealand spinach. Cut New Zealand spinach leaves for harvest when they are 3- to 4-inches long. New Zealand spinach can be harvested cut-and-come-again. New Zealand spinach is not true spinach, it can grow to twice the size of true spinach, but its leaves and stems can be used in recipes that call for spinach.

Peanut harvest. Lift peanuts when the foliage yellows and the pods have filled out and the pods' veins begin to darken. This is usually before the first frost in autumn but could come after the first light frosts. Even after the foliage has died back, pods will continue to mature for several weeks Peanuts usually mature 110 to 120 days after planting.

Peppers harvest. Sweet peppers and hot peppers are edible at all stages of growth–whether immature or full size, whether green or red. Peppers reach maturity at 60 to 80 days from the time seedlings have been set out in the garden. Hot peppers should be picked fully ripe for drying or pickling. Cut fruit from the plant with a garden pruner rather than pull. All fruit should be picked before the first frost.

Potato lifting. Young potatoes–called new potatoes–can be harvested as early as 45 to 55 days after planting, usually about the time blossoms appear or a week or two later. Lift new potatoes as soon as they reach useable size. Early varieties are best for new potatoes. Late varieties–often used for storage–should be lifted about the time of the first autumn frost. Continue the harvest for 2 to 3 weeks after the tops have died back. Remove large tubers first allowing smaller ones time to grow. Lift potatoes in dry weather being careful not to bruise the skin.

Okra harvest. Pick okra when pods are 2 to 4 inches long— about 60 days after seeds are sown. Harvest comes just about five days after the flowers fade. Pick pods every 3 days and do not allow pods to mature on the plant. Be sure to use gloves to avoid getting stung by the prickly leaves which can leave your skin itchy. Regular picking will keep okra productive; pruning some of the lower leaves will also increase pod production. If the weather turns chilly and okra drops its blossoms, don't panic; if hot weather returns so will blossoms and pods. Keep okra fed with a side-dressing of compost tea every couple of weeks.

Onion harvest. Bulb onions depending upon variety are ready for harvest about 3 to 5 months after the seeds are sown or about three and a half months after sets or young plants have been set out. When leaves start to turn yellow, bend the stems to a nearly horizontal position to stop the growth of the bulb and allow it to ripen. Remove soil from around the top half of the bulb. When the leaves turn brown, lift the bulbs. Bunching or green onions or scallions can be harvested young as needed beginning just a few weeks after sowing. Scallions have the best flavor when harvested less than 10 inches long.

Root crop harvest. Always harvest the largest roots first—even if they are relatively small by supermarket standards. Lifting the largest roots first will give the smaller roots a place to grow and fill out. (The only vegetables that must grow to full size to be ripe for harvest are tomatoes, corn, melons, and winter squash.)

Shallots harvest. Shallots are ready for lifting when the tops turn brown and die back. When the tops die back, the bulbs will be as big as they are going to get. If you don't lift the bulbs, the plants will send up new green tops and the bulb will soften as the plant starts its new growth. (This is true for onions as well.) The start of new growth will leave a brown ring inside the bulb where the growth stopped and then started again. Dry harvested shallots for 2 to 3 days; the bulbs will harden and the roots will dry up. Let the bulbs cure for a couple of weeks in a warm, dry place out of the sun; the drier the bulb, the better it will store.

Onions and shallots for replanting. Save some onion and shallot bulbs for planting in autumn or next spring. Sort through harvested onions and shallots for bulbs that are firm and without nicks or bruises or disease. Size does not matter as long as the bulbs are well formed. Label and store these in a dry place until planting time.

Storing onions and shallots. Once onion and shallot bulbs have dried, they are best stored in a mesh bag in a cool, dark place where there is good air circulation. Onions and shallots that are hard and dry store best—up to 10 months.

Soybean harvest. Pick green shell soybeans to eat the shelled beans fresh when the seeds are just mature or nearly mature, from 70 to 100 days after sowing depending upon the variety. Pick green soybeans while the pods are plump and before they begin to wither. For storage as dry beans, pick the pods when they are dry but while the stems are still green.

Summer squash harvest. Summer squash is ready for harvest when fruits are tender and easily punctured with a fingernail, usually about 50 days after sowing. Pick summer squash when the skin yields to thumb pressure. Zucchini is best when about 7 inches long and 1½ to 2 inches thick. Scalloped summer squash is ready for picking when the fruit is 2 to 3 inches in diameter. Pattypan squash is best when about 3 to 4 inches across. Crookneck and straightneck squash is best when about 4 inches long. For best flavor harvest summer squash at no more than 6 to 8 inches long.

Squash too big. Summer squash and zucchini that grow to the diameter of a baseball bat are too big and too seedy to eat. Best to put the big ones in the compost pile. Try to pick and use summer squash as soon as they are about 6 inches long and about the diameter of a 50 cent piece.

Winter squash harvest. When the skin of a winter squash is hard and cannot be scratched by your thumbnail, it's ready for harvest. Winter squash is not winter hardy. It should come out of the garden before the first killing frost.

Swiss chard cut-and-come again. Cut chard leaves when they are 6 to 10 inches tall, about 40 to 60 days after sowing seeds. Cut outer leaves near the base of the plant with a sharp knife; the inner leaves will continue to grow and can be cut a few days later. Get rid of old or tough leaves to keep the plant producing new leaves.

Best vegetables for freezing. Smaller not larger vegetables out of the garden are the best choice for freezing. Use your larger specimens for fresh serving. Use the smaller specimens for freezing; they will remain firm when thawed and will be tastier than larger specimens.

TOMATO HARVEST

Tomatoes are ready for harvest when they have developed their full color; tomatoes ripen from the center of the fruit out. Pick tomatoes by gently lifting each tomato until the stem snaps. Tomatoes ripen best at about 70°F; tomatoes do not develop their natural red color in temperatures greater than 86°F; in hot regions, pick tomatoes when they are still pink and allow them to ripen fully indoors. Tomatoes can be ripened indoors in a paper bag; place a ripe apple in the bag with the tomatoes; a ripe apple will give off ethylene gas which will stimulate tomato ripening.

Sucker pruning tomatoes. Prune away larger suckers on staked or caged tomatoes to produce larger fruits—if you want larger fruits. If you live in a hot summer region, be careful not to prune away leaves that shade fruit below. Too much sun can leave tomatoes sunburned—also called sunscald.

Root-pruning tomatoes. To hasten the ripening of tomatoes—whether you are just in a hurry or you're running out of growing season—use a garden knife to cut a semicircle around the plant (semicircle, not a full circle). Cut two inches from the stem and about eight inches deep. This will sever some, but not all, of the roots. The plant will go into shock and use its final energy to ripen the tomatoes already on the plant.

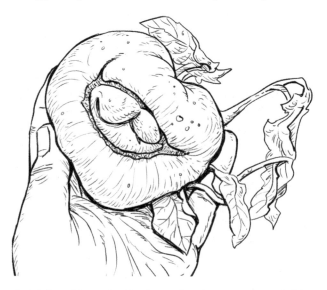

A cat-faced tomato: the irregular shape was caused by temperature shits or wet weather at blossom time.

Tomato problems and causes. Here are a few tomato problems you are likely to see this summer:

- **Cat-facing:** irregular, gnarled shapes and lines is caused by temperature shifts or wet weather at blossom time. Fruit is still edible.

- **Blossom-end rot:** rot at the blossom end of the fruit caused by irregular moisture uptake as fruit develops; irregular moisture uptake interrupts the delivery of calcium which is important for fruit development. Remember to keep the soil moist next season. Add calcium-rich fertilizer to planting holes.

- **Sunscald:** the skin looks papery and white; too much sun; be careful not to prune away leaves above developing fruit. Sunscald can be a problem for staked tomatoes; staked tomatoes are commonly pruned to just one or two main stems and have fewer leaves than caged tomatoes.

- **Split skin, cracking:** caused by irregular watering as fruits develop; keep the soil just moist so that plants do not take up water in fits and starts which can strain plant cells. Remove split tomatoes from plants right away; split tomatoes attract insect pests and will eventually rot.

Saving tomato seeds. To save seed from fleshy fruits such as tomatoes remove the seed and separate it from any surrounding pith or gelatinous material. Put the seed in a bowl of warm water and let it sit overnight. Viable seed will sink to the bottom; seed that is not viable will rise to the top. Dry the seed on a tray. Store the seed in a dry envelope in a cool place or in the refrigerator. Be sure to label the envelope with the name of the seed and the collection date.

HARVEST ZONE-BY-ZONE:
Late Summer / August

Plants coming to harvest now were planted in spring or early summer.

- **USDA Zone 10:** amaranth, basil, green beans, cantaloupes, chives, corn, cowpeas, cucumbers, edamame, eggplant, garlic, melons, New Zealand spinach, okra, oregano, peppers, southern peas, strawberries, summer squash, thyme, tomatillos, tomatoes, watermelon, zucchini.
- **USDA Zone 7-9:** green beans, cantaloupes, corn, cowpeas, cucumbers, edamame, eggplant, garlic, leeks, melons, New Zealand spinach, okra, onions, peppers, potatoes, scallions, summer squash, Swiss chard, tomatillos, tomatoes, watermelon, winter squash, zucchini.
- **USDA Zones 5-7:** Asian greens, basil, green beans, beets, bok choy, broccoli, carrots, celeriac, celery, chives, corn, cucumbers, eggplant, garlic, kale, kohlrabi, lettuce, melons, onions, parsley, peppers, potatoes, radishes, radicchio, scallions,

summer squash, Swiss chard, tomatoes, watermelons, zucchini.
- **USDA Zones 4-6:** arugula, Asian greens, basil, beans, beets, broccoli, cabbage, cantaloupe, carrots, cauliflower, collards, corn, cucumbers, dill, eggplant, fennel, garlic, kale, kohlrabi, lettuce, onions, parsnips, potatoes, radishes, rutabaga, shallots, spinach, summer squash, tomatoes, turnips, watermelon, winter squash, zucchini.

THINGS TO DO LATE SUMMER

Watering. Keep the soil evenly moist; this is important to keep vegetables green, healthy, and productive. A healthy plant is more resistant to insect pests and diseases.

Feeding plants. Give warm-season fruiting crops–eggplants, peppers, tomatoes, and squash–a side-dressing of compost tea or manure tea. Add a cup or two of well-rotted manure or compost to a gallon of water and let sit overnight before watering around plants.

Weeding. Keep after weeds in the garden. Go after weeds wherever and whenever they appear. One blooming weed can mean hundreds, even thousands of weed seeds. Hand pull weeds or cultivate lightly.

Warm-region successions. If you live where days will still be warm six weeks from now, direct sow bush beans and peas. Beans will get the daytime heat they need and peas will appreciate the evenings growing cooler into autumn. Plant varieties that will reach maturity in 50 days. Other succession plantings now are lettuce, spinach, beets, and carrots.

Brussels sprouts pruning. When buds begin to form just above each lateral leaf on Brussels sprouts, start pruning. Place your hand about a third of the way out on each lateral branch and press down sharply; the branches will snap right off. The loss of the lateral branches will cause the plant to direct its energy into the production of new buds higher up the plant. When sprouts are about marble size, give plants a side-dressing of compost tea. By the end of the season, Brussels sprouts can grow 3 to 4 feet tall. When you want to stop the upward growth of Brussels sprouts, simply snip off the uppermost leaf cluster—called the terminal leaves.

Cover crop planting time. As crops come out of the garden at the end of summer, sow a cover crop of buckwheat or ryegrass. Both will grow quickly and thickly and choke out weeds. You can cut these crops down just before the first frost and let them sit and decompose on planting beds through the winter. They will smother weeds, protect the soil, and keep earthworms warm through the winter.

Peas as green manure. Peas and beans can be turned under after harvest. The top growth and stubble will rot through the winter and feed the soil. Pea and bean green manure will add nitrogen to the soil. You can cut away and remove the top growth if you like or bury it if you are not planting in that spot until next season. Bury the top growth under about two inches of soil to speed decomposition, but don't bury it too deeply; it won't break down as quickly.

Cabbage cracking. Cabbage heads grow from the inside out. Fast-growing cabbage heads can split and crack—especially if they are given too much fertilizer or over-watered. To prevent cabbage splitting, take the cabbage in both hands and give it a half—180-degree turn. Half of the roots will be ripped and broken, cutting in half the supply of nutrients and moisture; this will slow down growth. If cracking continues, give the head another quarter turn.

Strawberries. Clean up strawberries once they have finished fruiting. Remove old leaves and unwanted runners. Runners can be detached from parent plants and transplanted or rooted in pots. Potted runner plants can be set out in the garden. Water all well. Replace worn out mulches. Keep watering ever-bearing strawberries; replenish their mulch as needed. In short season regions, have cloches ready to extend the season for late-fruiting plants.

Pinch tomato flowers. As the season comes to a close and days grow shorter pinch away new flowers on tomato plants. Flowers and new fruit forming in August will likely run out of season before they mature. Most tomatoes require 45 days from flower to ripe fruit. Pinching away flowers will allow plants to put energy into ripening fruit already on the plant.

Green tomatoes. Pick all tomatoes before the first frost. Green tomatoes may ripen off the plant indoors. Cut into one of the green tomatoes; if the seeds are surrounded by a clear gel, the tomato will likely ripen indoors; if not, it will not ripen at all. Often green tomatoes about the same size from the same plant will follow suit. Ripen green tomatoes indoors out of the sun. If possible take up the entire plant, remove the soil from around the roots and hang the plant upside down in the shed or garage. The warmer the spot, the more quickly the tomatoes will ripen. You can also ripen green tomatoes on the kitchen counter as long as they are not in direct sun. Tomatoes that have just begun to turn color on the plant will ripen indoors.

Herbs—freezing and drying. Cut herbs to freeze and dry for winter use, preferably before leaves become too old or plants begin to flower. Dry small quantities of herbs in an airy room away from direct sunlight and in the dark if possible. Tie the herbs in a bunch and hang them upside down; most will dry in about two weeks. To freeze herbs, package them without crowding in a freezer bag; you do not need to blanch them in advance. Frozen herbs will keep for a year or more without losing flavor.

Herbs for winter—division and cuttings. Pot up herbs for winter use, or take cuttings or divide perennial herbs to start new plants. Take cuttings of bay, lavender, mint, rosemary, rue, and sage; lift and divide clumps of chives—the roots can be gently pulled apart. To root rosemary and other perennial herbs: strip the leaves from the lower inch of the cutting and dip it in a rooting hormone (available at a garden center); stick the cutting in a small pot of seed starting mix or organic potting mix; place a clear plastic bag over the pot and cutting; mist the cutting until it is rooted in about two weeks.

Seed saving. You can collect and save seeds from open-pollinated plants. Seed from open-pollinated plants consistently produce plants that are very similar to the parent. Because the offspring from open-pollinated plants are similar to the parent the seed from these plants is called "stable." Hybrid plants—especially first-generation or F1 hybrids—are not stable; they produce seedlings unlike the parents. To collect seed from an open-pollinated plant place browning flowers or seedheads in a small bag. Close and seal the bag and label it with the plant's name. Place the bag in a warm dry place. In two to three weeks, the seeds will ripen and drop in the bag. Shake the bag to loosen any seeds that have not dropped. Separate the seeds from the seedheads. Store the seed in an envelope labeled with the plant name and collection date.

MORE PESTS AND DISEASES

Holes in vegetable leaves. Tomato hornworms, loopers, webworms, armyworms, cutworms, leaf rollers, and other caterpillars eat holes in vegetable and fruit leaves. *Bacillus thuringiensis* (Bt) a biological insecticide will kill these pests. It acts as a stomach poison that causes caterpillars to stop feeding within a few hours; death then follows in a few days. Apply Bt to leaves every 7 to 10 days until new caterpillars stop hatching. It can be applied up to the time of harvest. Dipel dust is one insecticide that contains Bt.

Hot pepper and garlic insect repellants. Garlic sprays can be used to repel aphids, caterpillars, flea beetles, leafhoppers, leafminer flies, maggot flies, spider mites, thrips, and whiteflies. Garlic extracts also kill mosquito larvae. Hot pepper sprays repel aphids, leafhoppers, mites, thrips, and whiteflies. You can make your own garlic or hot pepper spray in a blender. Combine two to six garlic cloves with one or two hot peppers (or 1 to 2 teaspoons of ground cayenne pepper) and 1 quart of water. Blend well then strain away the solid bits. Use a spray bottle to coat the top and undersides of leaves. Repeat after rainfall.

Mexican bean beetles chew on the leaves of all types of beans. They skeletonize the tender tissue between veins and sometimes feed on pods. Bean beetles are ¼ inch long they are light yellow when young and coppery bronze when mature with 8 black spots on each wing cover. The larvae are humpbacked yellow grubs with spines on their back. Bean beetles appear in late spring at about the time beans leaves are unfurling. Handpick bean beetles and check the undersides of leaves for yellow or yellow-orange eggs. Keep the garden clean of bean plant debris; coat plant leaves with kaolin clay to discourage feeding and egg-laying; spray insecticidal soap or oil or a pyrethroid insecticide.

Cucumber beetles eat the leaves of cucumbers, melons, winter squash, summer squash, watermelons, and corn. There are striped and spotted cucumber beetles. Both are about ¼ inch long. Striped beetles have three black stripes down the back; spotted beetles have 12 black spots on the wings. Cucumber beetles chew large holes between the veins of leaves; when they feed they also can spread bacterial wilt and cucumber mosaic virus from plant to plant. Later in the summer groups of cucumber beetles feed on cucumber and summer squash fruits leaving the fruits disfigured. Handpick beetles and destroy them or trap them with yellow sticky traps. The botanical pesticides rotenone or pyrethrum can also be used to kill cucumber beetles. (Plants that become infected with bacterial wilt should be removed from the garden and placed in the trash or buried away from the garden.)

Raccoon fence control. Fencing raccoons out of the garden is the only sure way to keep them at bay. Metal posts and chicken wire can be used to make a temporary, seasonal garden fence. Leave the top 2 feet of the fence unattached to the fence posts. When raccoons climb to the top, their weight will cause the unsecured top of the fence to fall backwards. Moth crystals also will give raccoons pause but may not keep them away for long.

Baking soda fungicide. Bicarbonate is a mild fungicide. Protect plants from fungal diseases such as powdery mildew by spraying leaves with a baking soda spray. Combine 1 teaspoon baking soda (sodium bicarbonate) with 1 drop liquid soap and 2 quarts water and mix well. An alternative formula is 1 tablespoon baking soda and 1 tablespoons mineral oil mixed in a gallon of water. Use a pump spray or backpack spray to apply. Be sure to spray both the top and undersides of leaves as well as plant stems.

September

Early Autumn

Second Spring

The weather will direct your efforts in the vegetable garden in early autumn—September. Frost may strike even the mildest of regions in early autumn.

Know the average first frost date for your area. This date will allow you to plan your garden activities and prepare for cold weather in advance. The average first frost date can vary from year to year but when the first frost comes your warm-weather crops will be done for the year unless you take steps to protect them and extend their season. Check the frost dates in Appendix 3 pages 169-180 to know the average first frost date near where you live.

From the date of the first frost, autumn and winter gardening needs to go under cover; use cloches (individual plastic or glass plant covers), plastic hoop tunnels, and cold frames to protect plants from chilly temperatures. (More on plastic hoop tunnels and cold frames on pages 27-29.)

Autumn brings what many gardeners refer to as "second spring". Temperatures during "second spring" are very similar to temperatures in spring. Nearly all of the cool-weather crops planted in spring can be planted again in "second spring".

In very warm winter regions (southern Florida and southern California) warm-season crops can be planted in autumn for winter harvest. Warm-weather southern regions are referred to as "reverse-season" regions because many warm-season crops are grown in winter. (See Appendix 4, pages 181-183, for more on reverse season planting.)

No growth time coming. No matter where you live, when nighttime temperatures drop below 50°F plant growth will slow and when temperatures drop below 40°F the garden will approach dormancy. When day light is less than 10 hours each day—in late autumn and winter, plant growth will all but stop until days begin to lengthen again in early spring. This is often referred to as the "no grow" time of year. Check the weather service near you for the date when day light drops below 10 hours each day in your area; crops in the ground then, should be near maturity in order to survive until the date when day light is again greater than 10 hours each day. Crops that are near maturity

during the "no grow" period can be harvested; leafy crops can be harvested "cut-and-come-again"—all but the bottom inch or two of each leaf is cut; they will generate new growth when daylight is greater than 10 hours each day.

SECOND SPRING

"Second spring" planting. Cool-season vegetables can be planted in early autumn in mild-winter or reverse season regions. Autumn planting of cool-weather crops is often referred to as "second spring." The same crops that thrive in spring will thrive in autumn. Plant now beets, broccoli, Brussels sprouts, carrots, cauliflower, celery, fava beans, kale, kohlrabi, leeks, both head and leaf lettuce, mustard greens, onions, parsley, peas, potatoes, radishes, rutabagas, spinach, Swiss chard, and turnips.

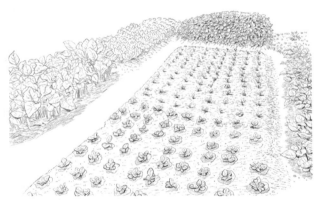

Second spring planting: while warm-season crops are still maturing on either side a new planting bed of leafy cool-season crops are planted for harvest in autumn—the second spring.

Plant broccoli, Brussels sprouts, cauliflower, and celery from transplants; plant potatoes from seed potatoes and onions from sets. Onions planted now will produce scallions. In mild winter regions; wait until early winter to plant onions for a large bulb harvest next summer.

Continue direct-seeding lettuce, endive, escarole, spinach. Be prepared to protect these crops should a hard frost be predicted. Use floating row covers (opaque garden fabric made of spun polypropylene) or a portable plastic hoop tunnel to protect leafy crops from frost. Sow new crops under a plastic hoop tunnel or in a cold frame. Protected leafy crops can grow into late autumn or early winter with protection. (For more on frost and freezing temperatures see page 132.)

Cold-hardy, frost-tolerant vegetables:
- Beets
- Brussels sprouts
- Cabbage
- Collards
- Kale
- Kohlrabi
- Parsnips
- Spinach
- Turnips

Vegetables that need cover from heavy frost or freeze (29° to 32°F):
- Broccoli
- Carrots
- Cauliflower
- Lettuce
- Peas
- Potatoes

Vegetables that can tolerate a light frost (about 32°F):
- Onions
- Garlic
- Leeks
- Shallots

Vegetables that are not frost tolerant:
- Beans
- Corn
- Cucumbers
- Eggplant
- Melons
- Okra
- Peppers
- Squash
- Tomatoes
- Watermelon

Cold frame and plastic hoop tunnel growing. A cold frame or plastic hoop tunnel can be used to extend the growing season, either in spring or autumn. Prepare the soil beneath the frame or hoop tunnel just as you would a planting bed. Sow seeds of lettuce, parsley, radishes and carrots for autumn and winter harvest. You can also grow spring cabbage, broccoli, broad beans, and kale from transplants. Be sure to ventilate the frame or hoop tunnel on warm days.

Quick frost protection. When freezing temperatures are expected, most vegetables still in the garden will benefit from protection. The simplest crop protection–a light blanket or overturned cardboard box–will protect plants by 1° or 2°F. A plastic or glass cloche (individual plant cover), plastic hoop tunnel, or simple cold frame can provide 3° or 4°F or more–often as much as 7°F or more–in additional temperature protection.

How to prepare a winter garden. As warm-season fruiting vegetable finish their run for the year remove them and prepare planting beds for winter crops. Here are 10 tips to prepare the winter vegetable garden:

1. Remove the remnants of the summer garden. This will ensure that summer pest insects and diseases do not overwinter in the garden.

2. Turn the soil to about 12 inches deep to aerate the garden and break up clods.

3. Add organic amendments to the planting beds—steer manure, chicken manure, and homemade or commercial compost.

4. Shape winter garden planting beds so that they are slightly raised at least 3 to 4 inches high and slightly sloped to the south for maximum sun exposure.

5. Prepare furrows or planting mounds. Make sure furrows run north and south so that crops get full exposure to the sun in the course of the day.

6. Sprinkle an all-purpose organic fertilizer across planting beds before planting.

7. Plant tall crops to the north and short crops to the south so that short crops are not shaded by taller crops.

8. Use only planting beds that get all-day sun. Plant near south-facing wooden fences, stone walls, or building; they absorb solar heat during the day and radiate it back into the garden at night.

9. Have portable plastic hoop tunnels or portable cold frames ready to set over crops when the first frost or freeze is forecast.

10. Add gravel, bark nuggets, straw or wooden planks in place to keep your feet out of the mud when rain and snow arrive.

PLANTING ZONE-BY-ZONE: Early Autumn / September

Beginning with the warmest regions first, here is a seed starting and planting guide for early autumn—September. It is safe to plant or do any of the tasks listed for regions cooler than yours.

USDA Zones 9-10—hot and dry weather can continue for several more weeks.

- In reverse-season gardens: set out transplants of tomatoes, peppers, and onions; direct-seed snap beans, sweet corn, cucumbers, melons, and squash as well as herbs.
- Sow seed of beets, bush beans, carrots, chard, Asian greens, endive, kale, leek, lettuce, mustard, early onions, parsnips, garden peas, potatoes, winter radishes, spinach, and turnips.
- Set out starts of cabbage, cauliflower, kale, kohlrabi, Romaine and leaf lettuce, late potatoes, salsify, and late spinach.
- Where frost is possible before plants mature prepare portable cold frames and plastic hoop tunnels to cover crops after the first frost.
- Clean up dropped leaves and other debris as summer harvest continues.
- Divide and transplant perennial herbs and flowers.
- Continue to weed, water, and fertilize as needed.
- Replenish mulches and soil amendments such as compost.
- Watch for pests and signs of disease.

USDA Zones 8-9—hot weather still possible:

- Sow bush snap beans, beets, cabbage (for spring use), cauliflower, celery, collards, endive, lettuce, mesclun, onions (for an early crop next year), parsley, potatoes, spinach, radishes, rutabagas, Swiss chard, and turnip. In frost-free regions such as southern Florida, continue to plant warm-season crops such as tomatoes.
- Set out transplants of broccoli, cabbage, kale and cauliflower.
- Direct-seed cold-hardy herbs such as parsley, chives and sage.
- Ripen onions and shallots by lifting them gently and leaving them in place for a couple of weeks.
- Clean up dropped leaves and other debris. Remove spent plants.

- Continue to water crops regularly.
- Hoe regularly to keep down weeds.
- Watch for pests and signs of disease.
- Use *Bacillus thuringiensis* spray if leaf-eating caterpillars appear on cabbage-family crops.

USDA Zone 6-7—weather will vary and can be unpredictable:

- Check the number of frost-free days left in your area. Check seed packets and choose "autumn" and "late" varieties; these are quicker maturing varieties.
- Set out starts of late cabbage, cauliflower, Brussels sprouts, broccoli.
- Plant cool-weather crops in cold frame or plastic hoop tunnel for winter harvest: beets, Asian greens, carrots, kale, kohlrabi, lettuce, smooth leaf mustard, winter radishes, spinach, Swiss chard, turnips.
- Plant next year's garlic.
- Divide rhubarb clumps now; leave one or two eyes per root.
- Sow chervil and parsley seeds outdoors for a spring crop.
- Harvest and store large green tomatoes in areas where first frost occurs this month. Harvest and store pumpkins and squash after frost kill the vines.
- Harvest carrots, potatoes, and beets, preferably when the soil is not wet.
- Plant green manure cover crop as soon as possible.
- Protect outdoor tomatoes with cloches or fleece to extend their season and ripen more fruit.
- Protect late cauliflowers from frost by bending surrounding leaves over the heads.
- Lift and store potatoes.
- Dig up sweet potatoes and peanuts while the weather is still warm; cure them before storing.
- Continue to earth up celery and leeks.
- Cut the dead tops off asparagus.
- Continue water as needed.
- Watch for pests and signs of disease.

- Prepare soil for autumn or spring planting. Start winter digging heavy soils.
- Sow cover crops.
- Pot up some herbs for winter use.
- Remove spent plants and crops debris.

USDA Zone 2-5—early frost possible.

- Frost is possible in some areas in early autumn. Check the number of frost-free days left in your area by counting back from the average first frost date for your region. You may have time to sow quick maturing crops without protection. Plant autumn salad greens such as spinach, winter lettuce, arugula, mâche (corn salad), mustard, and radishes. Use a cold frame or plastic hoop tunnel if time is short.
- Uproot tomato plants before the first frost. Hang plants upside down in a cool cellar or garage, where the fruit will ripen and be usable well into autumn.
- Collards, Brussels sprouts, and kale are better eating after the first frost. Strip lower leave of Brussels sprouts to encourage the sprouts to develop higher up.
- You can leave root crops in the ground until a serious freeze; parsnips taste best when exposed to frost.
- In the cold frame, sow parsley, lettuce, spinach, and chives. Parsley can be grown indoors during winter.
- Plant next year's garlic crop and divide multiplier onions.
- Clean the cold frame and line the interior with Styrofoam or place bales of hay around the exterior. If the cold frame is weather-proof and soil is prepared, sow or set transplants of lettuce, spinach, kale, parsley, radishes and carrots for late autumn and winter harvest.
- Keep the frame well ventilated on warm days.
- Sow a green manure cover crop in vegetable beds that are done for the season. Plant winter rye grass between vegetable rows.
- Prepare storage areas for roots crops.

- Harvest onion, turnips, carrots, and potatoes before month end; store winter squash at 50° to 60°F.
- Harvest and store parsnip, horseradish, and Jerusalem artichoke crops.
- Pick Brussels sprouts when the buttons firm up.
- Harvest leeks, trimming off roots and carefully disposing of any outer, rust-infested foliage.
- Protect late cauliflowers from frost by bending surround leaves over the head.
- Tidy up summer-flowering strawberries. Cut off old leaves and unwanted runners, remove straw, and control weeds.
- Remove spent plants. Clean up empty areas of garden.
- Turn the compost pile.
- Save seed from your best plants of heirloom beans, tomatoes, squash and melons.
- Cut back foliage of asparagus crowns planted in mid-spring. Mound soil over crowns.
- Gather leaves and pine needles to use for winter mulching.

EARLY AUTUMN PLANTING TIPS

Sow winter salad leaves now. Here are some vegetable leaves that are good in salads and stir-fries: beets, broccoli, carrot, cauliflower, kohlrabi, radish, and rutabaga. All of these are cool-season crops you can grow in a cold frame or plastic hoop tunnel this autumn and winter. Direct sow these crops in the garden or in a plastic hoop tunnel or cold frame now.

Plant Chinese cabbage. Time to sow Chinese cabbage, bok choy, mizuna, mibuna and other cool-season Asian vegetables. Chinese cabbage grows best when days are growing shorter and cooler. The same for bok choy, snow peas, mizuna, and mibuna. Sow these crops under a plastic hoop tunnel or cold frame in cold-winter regions. In warm-winter regions and reverse season regions these leafy crops can be grown in the garden.

Spring cabbage planting time. Plant spring cabbage in beds that have been amended with aged compost and manure. Where winters are wet, plant spring cabbages on mounds or ridges 9 inches high. Add a pinch of bone meal into each hole at transplanting. Set the plants with their bottom leaves at soil level, firming them in with your heel and then watering.

Herb planting. Sow parsley and chervil now for a spring crop. Divide and replant clumps of bergamot about one foot apart, preferably in rich soil. Take cuttings of bay, lavender, and rue and root them in sandy soil in a shaded frame or cloche.

EARLY AUTUMN HARVEST

Crops that must ripen in the garden. Beans, cucumbers, melons, zucchini and summer squash will not ripen or mature once they are picked; they must ripen and mature on the plant.

Ripening tomatoes on the vine. Strip away the lower leaves on tomato plants a day or two before harvesting red tomatoes; this will cause the fruits to ripen faster. If the fruits are still green or turning, let the leaves stay in place to prevent fruit sunburn. Pinch or cut away the top 6 inches of green leaves and stem as the season comes to a close. This will eliminate any new fruit development and let the plant put its strength into enlarging and ripening the fruit already on the plant.

Summer squash harvest. Don't let summer squash linger in the garden. Pick squash when just ripe: yellow summer squash is best when 4 to 5 inches long, scallop squash is best when 3 to 4 inches across, zucchini is best when about 6 inches long (smaller is better). Leave summer squash on the vine too long and it will become seedy. Pick summer squash regularly.

Watermelon and cantaloupe harvest. Watermelons are ready for picking when the curly section (tendrils) of the vine near the stem end turns brown and shrivels and when the section of rind touching the ground turns light yellow and rough. A dull thud when you rap the watermelon with your knuckle is another sign the melon is ripe. Cantaloupes are ripe when you gently slide your thumb from the melon to the vine and the vine easily separates. A ripe cantaloupe will have a strong sweet aroma around the stem end.

Give melons a helping stone. Place large stones or bricks wrapped in black plastic beneath developing melons as days grow shorter and cooler. The black-wrapped stones will absorb solar heat during the day and release it at night keeping melons toasty as they continue to ripen. Melons need light and heat to ripen.

Sweet potato harvest. Harvest sweet potatoes shortly after frost kill the vines; don't let them sit in the ground more than a couple of days after the vines start to wither otherwise the tubers will begin to rot. (You can actually start harvesting sweet potatoes as soon as they are big enough to eat. They gain most of their size in the last 30 days of growth.) Lift sweet potatoes carefully with a garden fork or spade. Do not bruise the skin at harvest. Dry sweet potatoes for two or three hours after lifting then spread them out on newspaper and allow them to dry in place where the temperature will remain about 80°F for 10 days to two weeks.

Carrot harvest. Begin the harvest by lifting fingerlings which will be most tasty eaten right away. Carrots generally are more flavorful smaller rather than larger. Lift larger carrots when the diameter at the shoulder is about the size of a quarter—not larger; deep green foliage is also a sign that carrots are ready for harvest. Give the carrot patch a good sprinkling of water the day before you plan to harvest. The softened soil will make it easier to lift the roots. Carrots harvested from dry soil often break in half.

If your carrots were stunted this year, keep the following in mind for next season: (1) carrots grow best in soil temperatures of 65°F—warmer or colder will stunt growth; (2) carrots like fertile, well-worked (fine tilth), compost-rich soil—amend your soil; carrots hate clay soil; (3) carrots don't like crowds—thin carrots early to 3 inches or more apart.

Protect carrot shoulders. Carrots maturing toward harvest will sometimes begin to work their way out of the ground. Keep carrot shoulders covered by mounding up soil. Check and mound regularly as harvest approaches. Carrot roots exposed to too much sun will turn green as they develop chlorophyll; their flavor will turn bitter.

Onion and shallot harvest. Onions (and shallots) are ready for harvest when one-third to one-half of the tops turn brown and fall over. When about 20 percent of the leafy tops turn brown you can hasten harvest by bending over the rest; the bulbs will be ready for lifting a week later. Let them cure in the sun or a warm, dry place for a week; don't store onions until the top and papery skins are dry and crinkly. Harvest shallots when the tops are yellow and shriveled. Store shallots and onions in mesh bag in a cool, dry, well-ventilated place. Eat thick-necked onions first; they do not store well.

Potato harvest. Potatoes are ready for harvest when the foliage begins to fade and some leaves turn brown. When leaves fade, potato plants stop manufacturing food to feed the growth of tubers. Use a garden fork to gently loosen the soil. Start digging tubers about a foot away from the plant and cautiously work inward. Lift the tubers by hand. Let potatoes dry out for an hour or so on top of the ground; cure them at 55°F for two weeks before storing. If the skin of a just harvested potato peels away when you push with your thumb, use the potato right away—it won't store well.

Corn on the table. Here's a few tasty ways to serve just picked corn: (1) butter the corn using a piece of bread slathered in butter—the bread is tasty too; (2) remove the outer husk, leave the inner husk intact, roast the corn in the oven at 375 degrees for 15 minutes—nutty flavor; (3) again remove the outer husk, leave the inner husk intact, soak the ears in water for 30 minutes; grill for 10 to 15 minutes turning periodically; serve with herb-flavored butter.

Fava bean harvest. Harvest fava beans before a hard frost. Dig up the whole plant and hang it upside down in a dry place out of the cold.

How to dry and store beans. Drying and storing pinto and kidney beans is not difficult. When the pods start to turn brown, pull up the whole plant roots and all. Hang the plant upside down in the garage or storage shed and allow the pods to dry some more. When the pods are completely dry pull or clip them off the plant and place them on a large

heavy cloth on the lawn or patio; fold the cloth over the pods and beat them with a flat stick. Cull the beans from the broken pods and put them in a jar or can. On a windy day (or use a fan) slowly pour the beans from the jar onto a cloth or clean surface again—the beans will fall and the chaff will blow away. Store beans in a paper or cloth bag in a cool, dry place and let them continue to dry.

Harvest Brussels sprouts from the bottom of the plant upwards. As you harvest from below new sprouts will grow above. Support upward growing plants with stakes.

Brussels sprouts—harvest low to high. Harvest Brussels sprouts from the sprouts lowest on the plant working your way up. To enlarge sprouts, strip off the next highest set of side branches; this will trigger faster development of the next set of sprouts and will also strengthen and enlarge the trunk.

Sprouts grow larger when leaves are pruned below. Prune leaves in the morning when they easily snap off. Brussels sprouts will be most tasty after they have been touched by a frost or two.

Root crops for winter harvest. Cold-tolerant root crops can stay in garden beds for winter harvest if protected by a thick layer of mulch. Root vegetables will draw moisture from the soil and stay firm. Carrots, leek, parsnips, and turnips can be left in the ground all winter in all gardens. Beets, celeriac, and winter radishes can be left in the ground where the soil does not freeze.

Lift rutabagas that are the size of an apple. This will allow smaller ones in the same row to grow on to size. Store rutabagas and other root crops in plastic bags with holes punched for air circulation. The bags will seal in the moisture and keep the roots clean until you are ready to use them. Rutabagas are milder tasting than turnips.

HARVEST BY ZONE:
Early Autumn / September

Most crops harvested now were planted in late spring or early summer.

- **USDA Zone 10:** amaranth, arugula, basil, green beans, cantaloupes, chives, corn, cowpeas, cucumbers, edamame, eggplant, garlic, melons, New Zealand spinach, okra, oregano, peas, peppers, southern peas, strawberries, summer squash, thyme, tomatillos, tomatoes, watermelon, zucchini.
- **USDA Zone 7-9:** arugula, Asian greens, asparagus beans, green beans, beets, broccoli, cabbage, cantaloupes, corn, cauliflower, celeriac, celery, Chinese cabbage, cowpeas, cucumbers, edamame, eggplant, kale, leeks, lettuce, lima beans, melons, New Zealand spinach, okra, peppers, potatoes, scallions, summer squash, Swiss chard, tomatillos, tomatoes, watermelon, winter squash, zucchini.
- **USDA Zones 5-7:** arugula, Asian greens, basil, green beans, beets, bok choy, broccoli, cabbage, carrots, celeriac, celery, chives, corn, cucumbers, eggplant, garlic, kale, kohlrabi, lettuce, melons, onions, parsnips, parsley, peppers, potatoes, pumpkins, radishes, radicchio, rutabagas, shallots, summer squash, Swiss chard, tomatoes, watermelons, zucchini.
- **USDA Zones 4-6:** arugula, Asian greens, basil, green beans, beets, broccoli, Brussels sprouts, cabbage, cantaloupe, carrots, cauliflower, celery, collards, cucumbers, dill, eggplant, endive, fennel, kale, kohlrabi, leeks, lettuce, melons, onions, peas, peppers, potatoes, pumpkins, radishes, rutabaga, shallots, spinach, summer squash, Swiss chard, tomatoes, turnips, watermelon, winter squash, zucchini.

STORING CROPS FOR WINTER

Ways to store crops. Here are the most common ways to store vegetables for winter use:

- **Freezing:** easy, fast, holds color, flavor and nutrients. Set freezer temperature at 0°F. For each 10° above zero, the storage life of the food will be cut in half. For example, to freeze whole or sliced tomatoes scald (blanch) the tomatoes for one minute (to stop enzyme action) then place the whole or sliced tomatoes on an oiled baking sheet and place it in the freezer for one day. When the tomatoes are frozen, transfer them to a plastic freezer bag and place in the freezer.
- **Drying:** simplest and most natural method of preserving food. Cut the vegetables into small pieces and spread those out in the sun; when dried place the food in a small container and store in a cool, dark place. Vegetables also can be dried in electric dehydrators and ovens.
- **Canning:** Home canned vegetables are just as or more flavorful than commercially canned vegetables. Most vegetables are low in acid so it is important to use a steam pressure canner. Low acid foods must be processed in a pressure canner to be free of botulism and other bacteria, mold, and yeast. You can use boiling-water canners for acid foods such as fruits and tomatoes. A pressure canner will require from 55 to 100 minutes to process jars loaded with vegetables. More time will be required if you are canning at high elevations.
- **Pickling:** Picking is simply adding vinegar and salt and often spices (and sometimes sugar) to vegetables and fruits. Cucumbers are the most commonly picked vegetables, but tomatoes, cabbage, beets, beans, corn, and carrots can also be pickled. Vegetables are first boiled to stop bacteria that cause spoilage then they are preserved in vinegar.
- **Cold storage (refrigerator, basement, or root cellar):** late season crops—root crops, winter squashes, pumpkins, onions, potatoes, and green tomatoes—can be stored in a refrigerator, cool basement, or root cellar at temperatures between 35° and 50°F.

Best storage methods for each crop. Here are the most flavorful ways to store each of the crops you grow:

- Beans: can, dry, freeze
- Beets: can, cold storage, freeze, pickle
- Broccoli: freeze
- Brussels sprouts: cold storage, freeze, pickle
- Cabbage: cold storage, freeze, kraut, pickle
- Carrots: can, cold storage, freeze, juice, pickle
- Cauliflower: freeze, pickle
- Celery: cold storage, dry pickle
- Corn: can, dry, freeze, pickle
- Cucumbers: pickle
- Eggplant: freeze, pickle
- Endive: cold storage
- Leeks: cold storage
- Okra: can, freeze, pickle
- Onions: can, cold storage, freeze, pickle
- Parsnips: cold storage
- Peas: can, dry, freeze
- Peppers: can, freeze, pickle
- Potatoes: cold storage
- Pumpkins: can, cold storage
- Potatoes: cold storage
- Pumpkins: can, cold storage
- Radishes: cold storage
- Rutabagas: cold storage
- Spinach: freeze
- Squash, summer: freeze, pickle
- Squash, winter: can, cold storage, freeze
- Sweet potatoes: cold storage
- Tomatoes: can, dry, freeze, juice, sauce

Vegetable storage time. Green tomatoes, sweet onions, celery, and cabbages will keep for 4 to 6 weeks in a cool (about 45°F), dark, dry place. Root crops will keep for two to four months (store beets, carrots, parsnips, rutabagas, and turnips in plastic bag with ventilation holes). Pumpkins will keep for three months. Onions, potatoes, and winter squash will keep for up to six months after curing. Check stored crops on a regular basis for signs of mold or rot; discard any spoiled vegetables.

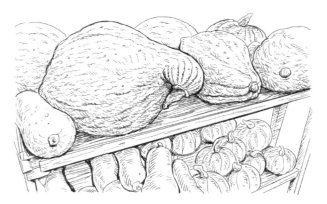

Winter squashes are set on open racks out of direct sunlight with plenty of air circulation to cure (the skin will thicken and harden for winter storage).

Root crops for storage. Allow any root crops you plan to store to dry off in the sun for an hour or so; excess soil will drop off as the roots dry. Don't wash vegetables for storage. Washing can bruise the skins.

Cure before storing. Some vegetables need to be cured before they can be stored. Curing simply means allowing the skin of the vegetable to dry and toughen so that it can be stored without rotting. Some thin skinned vegetables can rot if not cured. Curing happens by setting the vegetable in a dry, warm place for several days allowing the skin to dry and toughen. Do not wash vegetables before curing; cure only vegetables without blemishes or cuts.

Vegetables that must be cured before they are stored:

- **Garlic and onions:** cure between 70° and 85°F at 70 percent humidity for about two weeks, or until the necks are dry and tight.
- **Potatoes:** cure at 55° to 65°F and 95 percent humidity for two to three weeks.
- **Sweet potatoes:** cure at 85° to 90°F and 90 percent humidity for a week.
- **Winter squash:** cure at 80° to 85°F for two to three weeks at 70 percent humidity.
- **Shelled beans and peas:** dry thoroughly before putting in storage, usually several days to two weeks.

Curing onions for storage. Onions must be dry when they are stored. Let onions cure in the open garden or in a dry place for 2 to 3 days before you store them. You will know onions are dry enough for storing when the bottom-side roots turn brittle and break off easily. Once dry, cure onions for two to three weeks; place them in a mesh bag or braid the stems. Do not store onions with thick necks—use them right away. Onions with thick neck are near to producing a seedpod which drains the bulb's energy; these bulbs will not get hard or store well.

Basement and root cellar storage. Late harvest vegetables that can be stored in a basement or root cellar include cabbage, potatoes, winter squash, pumpkins, dry beans and legumes, green tomatoes, cabbage, and for a short while peppers. Apples and pears also store well. The storage space must have some degree of

An open wooden rack is used to store winter squashes, onions, and root crops in a cool basement, garage, or garden shed. Air circulation is important to prevent rot.

moisture (humidity) or vegetables will dry out over the winter; 60 degrees humidity is optimal. Storage spaces must also have some air circulation and ventilation. Here are a few storage tips:

- Late maturing and longer growing crops store best in a root cellar.
- Do not store bruised or blemished vegetables or fruits.
- Do not wash vegetables or fruits before storing.
- Store vegetables or fruits on slatted shelves, not on the floor.
- Allow space between each vegetable in storage; don't stack vegetables.
- Keep the temperatures between 35° and 50°F. Avoid spaces where the temperature fluctuates. Do not store vegetables in a space where temperatures drop below 33°F.
- Leave root crops such as parsnips, turnips, beets, and carrots in the ground until they reach maturity (check the number of days on the seed packet). Once harvested root crops are best stored in fresh-cut sawdust, sand, or dry leaves. Trim away the leafy tops before storing.
- Cure winter squash before storing. Your thumbnail should not be able to pierce the skin of a winter squash.
- Cure or dry potatoes before storing. Potato skins should not slip when a thumb is pushed across the skin.
- Cabbage heads for storing should be solid and heavy for their size. Wrap cabbages in several layers of newspaper to avoid strong odors.
- Hot peppers, onions, shallots, and garlic are best stored braided or strung with thread through the stems and hung on hooks or nails near the ceiling where they get the most ventilation.
- Green tomatoes that have reached mature size should be wrapped in newspaper and checked regularly for ripening.

Garbage can root cellar. If you don't have a root cellar, you can dig a deep hole and place a clean garbage can in it. Layer vegetables into the can separating each layer with a thick mulch of clean straw.

Parsnips will store in the garden under a layer of mulch until spring. Put a thick layer of straw or chopped leaves on top of the parsnip planting bed. Brush away the mulch if you want to harvest roots during the winter. Lift all of the roots in early spring before they sprout new tops; parsnips and other roots in the soil that sprout new top in spring will rot as the plant goes to seed.

EARLY AUTUMN THINGS TO DO

Feed late growers. If late sowings of vegetables do not seem to be growing as quickly as they should in order to be ready for harvesting before frost, give them a side-dressing of compost tea or liquid manure. Keep late crops well-watered so that they won't further slowdown in growth.

Watering. Keep the garden watered in autumn; crops depend on soil moisture to make their final growth and ripen.

Weeding. Continue weeding planting beds. Keep the garden clear of all weeds. Winter growing weeds such as chickweed and dead nettles germinate in cool autumn temperatures. Pull all weeds before they set seed and produce a new generation.

Pepper seed saving. Save the seed from overripe peppers. Those seeds will germinate better than seed from less mature fruit. Remember only seed saved from open-pollinated varieties will grow true next season.

Herbs indoors for winter. Time to think about bringing herbs indoors for the winter. In preparation, trim plants to a manageable indoor size, inspect them for bugs, and re-pot if necessary. Herbs will do just fine indoors over winter if they are in a sunny window or under strong light. Bring herbs indoors about three weeks before you turn on the heat so they can acclimatize to indoor conditions. If possible set them in a room where there's good air circulation and the temperature is between 55° and 70°F. Good indoor growers include basil, chervil, marjoram, mint, oregano, parsley, rosemary, lavender, chives, and sage.

Amend the soil. Add aged manure or aged compost to planting beds as soon as crops come out of the garden.

Winter mulch. Mulch vegetables with 1 to 2 feet of shredded leaves or straw to keep the ground from freezing solid. Make sure the mulch is pulled close to plant stems. Place pine boughs, newspapers, cardboard, or boards on top of mulch to keep it in place. Cover newspapers and cardboard with chicken wire weighted down with rocks or timbers. Where the ground does not freeze solid you can harvest all winter by pulling back mulch and lifting the crop. Where the soil freezes, mulch will keep the soil from heaving and roots can be harvested in spring when the ground thaws.

Cover crops that feed the soil. Vegetable garden cover crops are used to help protect the soil from weather and erosion when vegetables are not being grown. Some cover crops—beans, peas, clover, and alfalfa—also feed the soil; they "fix" nitrogen. (Grass cover crops such as annual rye and winter rye, do not feed the soil.) The roots of beans, peas, and other members of the legume family work in tandem with a symbiotic bacteria called rhizobia to turn nitrogen gas in the air into nitrogen in the soil; the conversion of a gas into a solid is called "nitrogen fixation." When you leave the roots of bean family cover crops in the soil at the end of winter, you are feeding the soil—and feeding next year's garden. Nitrogen fixation is an important biochemical processes; it will help you save money on fertilizers.

Fix poor compost pile decomposition. If grass clippings, kitchen vegetable scraps, fruit rinds, and eggshells don't seem to be decomposing in the compost pile—the pile may be too dry. Spray the pile lightly with dish soap or Murphy's Oil Soap (which has a potassium vegetable oil base and no phosphates). The tackiness of the soap will help moisture adhere to the compostables and help them decompose.

Cleanup. Begin garden cleanup as crops come out of the garden. Take out of the garden any debris that will allow pests and diseases to overwinter. Where there has been no disease or pest problem, green residue can be turned under.

Record keeping. Update your garden map and note the dates of the final harvest. These notes will come in handy next year. (See worksheet on page 163.)

October

Mid-Autumn

Extending the Season

Early October is the right time to begin thinking about the coming frost and cold weather. How will you extend the season if your summer crops are not yet ready for harvest? How do you protect young cool-season crops from an early frost or freeze? Many warm-weather crops and all cool-weather crops can withstand the first light frost with no protection but a second or third frost or freeze will severely damage or kill most unprotected vegetables.

Patches of frost can occur when temperatures fall below 36°F however the National Weather Service does not keep track of frost until temperatures hit the freezing mark of 32°F or colder; that's when frost becomes widespread. A "soft frost" happens when temperatures drop below freezing (32°F) for just an hour or two—usually just before dawn. Tender plants can be killed by a soft frost especially if the cold continues for more than an hour or two. A "hard frost" (also called a "light freeze") happens when temperatures are between 29° and 32°F for four consecutive hours. A "moderate freeze" happens when temperatures drop to between 25° to 28°F for four consecutive hours. A "severe freeze" happens when temperatures drop to 24°F and colder. A moderate to severe freeze will damage most plants and kill nearly all vegetables not protected.

Extending the season in autumn is different than extending the season in spring in that many plants now are near maturity and the polyethylene/plastic hoop tunnel or bell jar cloche that would keep a spring seedling safe might be too small for mature plants. But season extenders (if big enough) work the same in spring or autumn; they raise the temperature under cover by several degrees allowing plants to carry on without weather-related setbacks.

If you don't have a portable cold frame or plastic hoop tunnel on hand, now is the time to fashion one or purchase one ready-made. Take a look first at the crops you would like to protect. Choose a hoop tunnel or frame that is the right size to protect each crop. If you want to fashion and build your own, simply construct a frame over which you can place the polyethylene plastic sheeting (4 mm or thicker) or a spun polypropylene fabric row cover. (Some commercial garden fabrics will protect crops down to 20°F.) After the summer crops are in, you can easily use the same protection to keep autumn and winter crops going well into the middle and even late winter.

PLANTING ZONE-BY-ZONE: Mid-Autumn / October

Beginning with the warmest regions first, here is a seed starting and planting guide for mid-autumn—October. It is safe to plant or do any of the tasks listed for regions cooler than yours.

USDA Zone 10—cooling weather

- Pull spent plants out of the garden and put them in the compost pile. Dispose of diseased or pest infested plants in the trash.
- Fill empty spaces in the garden with Chinese cabbage, beets, cauliflower, collards, broccoli, kale, turnips, and spinach. Continue to weed, water, and fertilize as needed.
- Plant winter and spring lettuces.
- Plant bunching onions, regular onions and leeks and prepare a fertile spot for garlic.
- Plant spring cabbage.
- Thin and water autumn greens and root crops.
- Keep the roots of ripening tomato plants constantly moist so ripening fruits are less likely to crack after heavy rains.

The temperature inside a plastic hoop tunnel will be 5° to 20° warmer than the outside temperature. Thicker and heavier plastic or fabric provides the greatest protection where winters are very cold.

- Protect outdoor tomatoes from chill with cloches or fleece to extend their season and ripen more fruit.
- Even where there is little or no frost, when temperatures drop below 50°F plant growth will slow; when the temperatures drop to 40°F and lower, the garden will approach dormancy.
- Take cuttings of perennials herbs to start new plants.
- Watch for pests and signs of disease.

USDA Zones 8-9—early frost possible:

- Check the first frost date for your area. There may be time to sow or plant beets, broccoli, Brussels sprouts, cabbage, carrots, Chinese cabbage, collards, cress, endive, kale, kohlrabi, leek, Romaine and leaf lettuce, mustard, onion sets, parsley, parsnips, peas, potatoes, radishes, spinach and turnips.
- Add aged manure and aged compost to planting beds that will not be planted in the winter; turn these amendments under with a spading fork.
- Harvest carrots, potatoes, and beets, preferably when the soil is not wet.
- Harvest and store the bulk of the squash crop.
- Pick outdoor tomatoes, and ripen them in a warm spot indoors, away from the frost.
- Harvest sweet potatoes. Cure them and then store them.
- Lift parsley seedlings from around the parent plant, and plant them in containers.
- Lift onions to store.
- Place cloches over lettuces and other low-growing vegetables that will continue to grow with protection.
- Sow a crop of a green manure (such as mustard) in vacant ground.
- Continue to weed, water, and fertilize as needed.
- Watch for pests and signs of disease.

USDA Zones 6-7—early frost possible:

- Cool-season crops can be planted in the open garden if there are still enough days in your area before the first frost. Set out transplants: cabbage, cauliflower, Brussels sprouts, and broccoli, lettuce, radish, spinach, and turnips.
- Plant cool-season crops in a cold frame: beets, carrots, endive, kale, lettuce, mustard, radish, spinach, turnips, and onion sets.
- Plant garlic and multiplier onions.
- Thin early autumn plantings of carrots, beets and turnips when they are 3 to 4 inches tall.
- Harvest late summer vegetable crops; harvest early autumn crops.
- Harvest broccoli, cauliflower, cabbage, and kohlrabi as soon as they're ready or be prepared to cover them on cold nights. Dig up sweet potatoes and harvest pumpkins and winter squash before the first hard freeze. Cut the dead tops off asparagus.
- Place cloches over lettuces, spinach, and other low-growing vegetables.
- Cover broccoli and cauliflower on frosty nights.
- If you are not planting now, clean and close the garden for the season. Remove all garden refuse so insect pests and diseases cannot overwinter.
- Divide rhubarb clumps now.
- Divide and transplant perennial herbs.
- Thickly mulch root crops to be left in garden.
- Remove stakes and trellises; clean and store for next year.
- Clean and store stakes and cages.

USDA Zones 2-5

- For a winter crop of spinach, put cloches over late spinach sowing to protect them from frost.
- Grow in the cold frame celery, lettuce, Chinese cabbage.
- Use cloches to protect vulnerable vegetables.
- Leave root crops in the ground until a serious freeze. Parsnips, salsify, and Jerusalem artichokes can be left in the ground past the first few freezes; their flavor is improved by frost.
- Harvest remaining warm-season crops before the first frost: peppers, pumpkins, squashes, and tomatoes.

- Pull up tomato plants before frost; hang them by their roots from cellar or shed rafters and allow them to ripen.
- Plant cover crops.
- Plant annual rye or winter wheat in vacant beds to prevent weeds and provide green manure for next season.
- Mulch carrots heavily to keep them from freezing.
- Cover lettuce, spinach, and other greens with plastic on frosty nights.
- Turn and amend heavy soil.
- Pot up herbs for winter use.

MID-AUTUMN PLANTING TIPS

Grow greens indoors this winter. You can grow lettuce and other greens indoors under fluorescent lights this winter. Choose trays or containers about 3 to 4 inches deep. Sow seed and place under the lights. Keep the soil just moist by setting the containers in shallow trays so you can water from below as needed. Harvest cut-and-come-again.

Garlic autumn planting. Plump garlic cloves produce plump bulbs. Skinny cloves produce skinny bulbs. Plant garlic in sun-soaked, compost-rich, well-drained soil; set cloves 3 inches deep—deeper to

Plant garlic with the pointed end up. Plump cloves produce plump bulbs.

4 inches in cold-winter regions, 4 to 6 inches apart. Time garlic autumn planting so that plants have time to sprout before the first freeze. Sprouting indicates roots are established. (If the weather is already freezing—don't plant garlic, wait until next season.) As soon as autumn-planted garlic sprouts, put down winter mulch—at least 4 inches deep in cold regions. Clip back blooms in spring and let plants grow on until foliage dies back just before harvest next summer.

Planting peas in autumn. If you live in a mild winter region, plant peas now. Smooth, round pea seeds are very hardy and suitable for growing in cool to cold temperatures. Wrinkled-seed peas are a good choice for spring plants or growing under cover.

MID-AUTUMN HARVEST

Veggie and fruit storage. Carrots, parsnips, potatoes, and cabbage-family crops turn bitter when exposed to ethylene gas which is emitted by tomatoes, apples, peaches, plums, cantaloupes, and apricots. Store these crops apart in the refrigerator and root cellar.

Tomato ripening off the vine. Once tomatoes reach full size they begin to ripen from the inside out and the bottom up. Green tomatoes that are full size can be picked and ripened indoors. When autumn temperatures average 55°F or less, harvest all remaining tomatoes unless you can cover them with a plastic hoop tunnel or cold frame. Tomatoes that ripen at temperatures below 55°F will be mealy. Set harvested tomatoes in a warm, dark place and cover or wrap them in newspaper out of the light. Tomatoes will not ripen in the refrigerator; the cold will stop the ripening process. To make red tomatoes ripen faster place them in a paper bag with an apple or banana; the ethylene gas given off by the fruit will speed the tomato ripening process.

Potato harvest time comes two weeks after tops begin to wither and die back. If you want to hurry the harvest break the vines at ground level and the tubers will all mature at once. Lift potatoes with a garden fork being careful not to bruise them. Let them dry for about an hour then cure them in the dark at 38° to 40°F with relatively high humidity (potatoes exposed to too much light will turn green). Potatoes store well for two to three months—after that check the tubers often for spoilage; the tougher the skin, the longer potatoes store. (If you can rub the skin off with your thumb, the potatoes will not store well.)

Pumpkin harvest. Harvest pumpkins before the first freeze. Be sure to cut fruits from the vine (use a sharp knife or lopper). Leave 3 inches of stem attached. Wipe the fruit clean, cure until they are completely dry, and store at 50° to 55°F with good ventilation. Pumpkins with hard rinds store the longest. To store pumpkins (and winter squash) for a long time, wash them in a mild chlorine solution (1 cup of chlorine to 1 gallon of water); this will kill bacteria and keep the fruits from rotting. Store in a cool, dry, dark place and set a board or piece of cardboard under the fruit to prevent bottom rot.

Sweet potatoes can be harvested large or small. Harvest sweet potatoes when the first frost is near. If you leave them in the ground a day or two past the first frost they will spoil. Bruised sweet potatoes will also spoil so be careful lifting them from the soil. Before you store sweet potatoes, spread them out in the sun for a day and let the soil dry, then brush them off and set them in a hot (80°-90°F) humid spot out of direct sun for about 10 days to cure. Wrap each tuber in newspaper and place them in box to store at 55° to 65°F for up to 6 months.

Winter squash harvest. Winter squash will be ready for harvest when the skin is extremely hard, about 80 to 115 days after planting depending upon variety. Winter squash is ready for harvest when you cannot scratch or cut the skin with your fingernail. If you can, it's not ready. Acorn squash—unlike other winter squashes—does not store well, eat it soon after picking. Delay the harvest of winter squash until just before the first hard frost. A light frost or two will change starch to sugar and enhance flavor. Cut winter squash from the vine leaving a 2- to 3-inch stem on the squash. Allow winter squash to cure in the sun for a week or more, then store in a cool, dry place over the winter.

Beet harvest. Leave a half-inch to an inch of stem on harvested beets; they will store better and won't bleed so much during cooking. Beets with cut skin will bleed badly; don't snip off the root ends either. Store beets in a perforated plastic bag or a shallow box packed with moist sawdust.

Parsnip harvest. Spring planted parsnips are ready for harvest in early autumn, about four months after seeds are sown. The flavor of parsnip roots is enhanced by a few hard frosts. Parsnips will be very flavorful if left in the ground all winter. Harvest parsnips left in the ground over the winter before new growth begins in spring.

Jerusalem artichoke harvest. Lift tubers after the foliage has died back in autumn or early winter. Loosen the soil with a garden fork then pull the tuber from the ground. Jerusalem artichokes require about 120 days to mature.

Greens will not grow to full size in autumn. Don't expect loose-leaf lettuce or spinach to grow to full size in autumn—the days are too short. Autumn greens that grow 3 to 6-inch leaves are ready for harvest.

Kale is sweetened by frost. Kale will be more flavorful, even sweet, when touched by frost. You can harvest kale from under snow through the winter.

Cabbage harvest. Leave cabbage in the garden until you need it or until you are ready to put heads in winter storage. Cabbage left in the garden will stay fresh and crisp. If outer leaves are spoiled by wet weather or get attacked by slugs, just remove those leaves and toss the in the compost when you harvest.

HARVEST BY ZONE: Mid-Autumn / October

Crops coming to harvest now were planted in late spring, summer, or early autumn.

- **USDA Zone 10:** amaranth, arugula, Asian greens, basil, green beans, cantaloupes, corn, cowpeas, cucumbers, eggplant, garlic, melons, New Zealand spinach, okra, oregano, peas, peppers, potatoes, pumpkins, strawberries, summer squash, thyme, tomatoes, watermelon, zucchini.

- **USDA Zone 9:** arugula, Asian greens, asparagus beans, green beans, beets, bok choy, broccoli, cabbage, cantaloupes, carrots, cauliflower, celeriac, celery, Chinese cabbage, collards, cowpeas, cucumbers, edamame, eggplant, kale, leeks, lettuce, melons, mustards, New Zealand spinach, okra, peppers, potatoes, pumpkins, radishes, rutabagas, scallions, squash, Swiss chard, tomatoes, turnips, watermelon, winter squash, and zucchini.

- **USDA Zones 7-8:** arugula, Asian greens, beets, bok choy, broccoli, Brussels sprouts, cabbage, carrots, cauliflower, fava beans, green onions, kale, kohlrabi, leeks, lettuce, onions, parsnips, peppers, potatoes, pumpkins, radishes, radicchio, shallots, Swiss chard, tomatoes, winter squash. .

- **USDA Zones 4-6:** arugula, Asian greens, beets, broccoli, Brussels sprouts, cabbage, carrots, cauliflower, celery, collards, kale, kohlrabi, leeks, leeks, lettuce, onions, parsnips, peas, peppers, potatoes, pumpkins, radishes, rutabaga, shallots, spinach, Swiss chard, , turnips, winter squash.

MID-AUTUMN THINGS TO DO

Frost coming. If the temperature is dropping into the 30s at nightfall and the sky is cloudless, frost is likely. Clouds and wind will lessen the chance of a hard frost. Hang a lightweight piece of plastic from the eves or in a tree; if the plastic is fluttering, frost is unlikely.

Quick frost protection. Protect crops from an unexpected early frost as best and as quickly as you can. Here are some quick-use frost protectors: cardboard boxes, paper sacks, newspaper caps, old blankets, sheets of plastic, plywood A-frames, or trellis A-frames covered with plastic sheeting.

Bean frost savers. If frost is coming and bush snap or lima beans or peas are still in the garden, cover the plants with a sheet of plastic or a blanket. That protection will be enough to save the plants from an early frost. The leaves may be killed by the frost but the pods will be okay for harvest. You can also protect summer squash and eggplants this way.

Tomato frost protection. If an early frost is predicted take newspaper out to the garden in the evening and drape them over your tomato plants. Dew will make the paper cling to the fruit; that will be just enough to protect the tomatoes from frost damage.

Hay bale compost heap. Make a quick compost heap with four bales of hay. Place the bales to form an open square in the middle. Start tossing leaves, grass clipping, plant debris, food scraps, and cow or horse manure into the center. Decomposition will follow and in time the hay will begin to decompose as well. Throw a tarp over the top of the heap when heavy rain is predicted.

Worms aerate the soil. Cold temperatures drive earthworms deeper into the subsoil. If planting beds needs aeration, don't place mulch over the beds this winter. Cold surface temperatures will drive earthworms deeper; they will work the soil as they go. In spring add aged compost and manure to the planting beds and let spring rains carry the nutrients deep to the subsoil the worms have worked. As the soil warms in spring, worms will return to near the surface.

Dead plant stems. Plant stems left in the garden at the end of the season can carry disease over to the next season. Dispose of all stems, vines, and other garden debris. Never compost or turn under debris from diseased or insect-infested plants.

Remove and compost cornstalks. Remove spent cornstalks from the garden and compost them. Breaking and shredding the stalks will allow for faster decomposition. Cornstalks left in the garden can become winter shelter for pest insects and their eggs.

Weeds and diseased plant disposal. Weeds especially weeds that have flowered and diseased plants should be bagged and placed in the trash for disposal. Do not put weeds or diseased plants in the compost pile. A hot compost pile can kill most weed seed and burn diseased plants, but if that doesn't happen weed seeds and diseases will be spread with the compost in spring.

Clean stakes and cages. Clean plant stakes and tomato cages after harvest. Wipe them down with a 10 percent bleach solution. Leave the bleach on for about 5 minutes then rinse with clean water. Let stakes and cages dry completely before storing them for the winter. A bleach solution will kill most plant diseases including bacterial spot, bacterial canker, bacterial speck, fusarium wilt, and early blight.

Protect the cold frame. In cold-winter regions, protect the cold frame from freezing weather. Mound up soil around the base of the frame and mound up straw above that or place hay bales around the frame. Drape old rugs or blankets over the top of the frame on very cold nights. The south-facing side of a building is the best location for a cold frame.

Leaf mold bin. Collect autumn leaves and dump them in a bin that is about 4 feet by 4 feet. You can make your leaf bin out of chicken wire and 2-by-4s driven into the ground. Tamp down the leaves and sprinkle the pile with water; they will decompose in a couple of months. If possible, chop the leaves in

Leaf mold is simply leafy compost. Pack leaves into a wire cylinder or bin and let them decompose for a few months then spread the new compost across planting beds.

a shredder or run them over with the lawn mower before dumping them in the bin.

Herbs for winter use. Take cuttings of herbs to overwinter indoors or lift whole plants and pot them up to grow indoors. Lift and pot parsley and other herbs for growing indoors all winter. Use a potting mix. Sage, basil, and chives can be grown indoors in winter. Pot up roots of mint to grow indoors through winter.

Strawberry protection. Cover late-fruiting strawberries with cloches if the temperature dips below 20°F. Mulch strawberries but do not cover the crowns of strawberry plants. In warm-winter regions, set out new strawberry plants.

Asparagus beds. Cut ferny asparagus tops and put them on compost heap after the first heavy frost. Cover the planting bed and crowns with well-rotted manure or garden compost and thick mulch.

Rhubarb division. Divide rhubarb in late autumn. You may need a spade to divide the root. Rhubarb is a perennial and heavy feeder; top rhubarb crowns with an application of manure or compost and mulch.

Spring soil preparation. If you plan to expand your garden next spring, plow or break up the ground now, apply lime and manure (a week apart) if needed. The importance of autumn soil preparation cannot be over-estimated. Add manure or compost, spade deeply and allow the rough clods of earth to stand exposed. Frost snow, sun and rain during the winter have a beneficial action on the soil.

Improve clay and sandy soils in autumn. Soils with high clay or sand content can be improved with the addition of organic matter. Add shredded leaves, grass clippings, aged compost and manure to planting beds in autumn. Add several inches across the planting bed; you can't add too much. Organic matter needs time to decompose so if you are not planting this winter, add organic material to improve the soil. You can also sprinkle organic fertilizers across planting beds in autumn.

Don't save hybrid seed. Seed from hybrid plants will not grow true next season; it will revert to characteristics of one of its parents. Hybrid plants and seed are commonly labeled F1 on plant stakes and catalogues. You must buy hybrid seed new each year. Only open-pollinated seed (labeled OP) will grow true and is worth the effort to save.

Annual ryegrass cover crop. Annual rye grass grows quickly and is a good choice for an autumn cover crop. Like other annuals, annual rye grass will die when hit by the first frost. Leave dead rye grass in place through the winter. In the spring you will find the soil beneath, rich and crumbly. A mat of dead rye grass will protect earthworms through the winter.

HOW TO MAKE COMPOST

Spent plants from the garden as well as grass clippings, leaves, and any other organic matter are rich in plant nutrients. You can return nutrients to the garden by composting. Composting is simply natural decomposition. Composting can take place in a simple free-standing heap of garden waste, in a homemade wire-mesh container, or in a commercially made bin.

Types of compost bins. A home-made compost pile can be square or round. It can be made out of lumber, chicken wire, hardware cloth, concrete blocks, or bales of hay. You can use a wooden box leaving space between the side boards. You can use four wood frames covered with chicken wire and latched together to form a cube. You can use galvanized metal mesh or welded wire shaped as a cylinder and staked in place. You can use bricks omitting a few bricks on each side for aeration. You can use a steel drum with dozens of large holes punched in the side so that the external surface is about half and half holes to solid matter.

Size of compost bin. A compost bin or free-standing compost pile should be at minimum 3 feet in each dimension—that is 3 feet tall and 3 feet wide on each side; 4 feet in each dimension is better, and 5 feet in each dimension is best. Composting is accomplished most quickly when the pile runs "hot," when the ingredients of the pile, moisture, air, and the microorganisms in the pile combine to heat the interior of the pile to 130°F or more. Compost heat

A simple compost bin made from wood slats with space between each slat for air circulation. Create a bin at least 3 feet tall and square for quicker decomposition.

is produced as a by-product of the microbial breakdown of organic material. Heat produced depends on the size of the pile, its moisture content, aeration, and the ratio of carbon and nitrogen in the materials being composted. Large piles heat fastest.

Compost bin site. Site the compost bin or pile near the vegetable garden close to where the finished compost will be used. Choose a site in full sun or light shade sheltered from the wind. Place the compost bin or pile on bare soil so that excess water can drain away. Till or dig the soil underneath before you begin to fill the area. This will assist drainage and allow macro-organisms such as worms to enter the pile. Place the bin or pile with ample air circulation on all sides.

Materials to compost. The ideal compost pile will contain carbon-rich brown materials such as dried leaves, straw, and small wood chips and nitrogen-rich green refuse such as grass clipping, fresh leaves, and kitchen scraps. Carbon-rich refuse supplies energy to decomposers working in the pile–mostly microorganisms such as bacteria, fungi, and yeasts as well as macro-organisms such as worms and insects. Nitrogen-rich green refuse provides protein to the decomposers which allows them to grow and divide. Equal parts browns and greens will speed composting. Do not compost meat, poultry, fish, grease and fat, dairy products or dog or cat litter. These will attract scavengers–mice and vermin, dogs, cats, and raccoons.

Compost bin care. Keep the pile moist but not wet; this will aid decomposition. Moisten the pile with water every 2 weeks making sure the pile does not go dry. Make the top of the compost pile slightly concave so that water can penetrate, but cover the pile with a plastic tarp during heavy rains. Turn the compost once a month if you can; this will help aerate the materials and aid decomposition. Add nitrogen-rich cow manure, blood meal, and fresh grass clippings to the pile when composting tree leaves, straw, or sawdust; this will balance the carbon to nitrogen ratio which is important for decomposition.

Time to compost. Compost is ready to use when the starting materials have decomposed beyond recognition and become deep brown or black colored and crumbly textured. This process can take 3 to 6 months; quicker in warm weather, slower in cool weather. Finished compost is good for the garden; it both builds and feeds the soil. Spread your compost as garden mulch topdressing—2½ gallons of compost to each square yard of garden.

How to use compost. Use compost as a soil amendment by digging it into planting beds before planting or use it as a fertilizer side-dressing by placing it around growing crops. Make compost tea by placing a shovelful of aged compost into a burlap bag then setting it in a bucket of water to steep until the water is the color of tea. Use compost tea as a liquid fertilizer.

COVER CROPS

Cover crops and green manure. Cover crop and green manure crop are interchangeable terms to describe crops that feed, build, and protect the soil and attract and feed beneficial insects and soil microorganisms. Cover crops are planted to cover planting beds and enrich the soil. Cover crops for a home garden include annual ryegrass, buckwheat, crimson clover, fava beans, peas, and hairy vetch. When a cover crop is turned under to decay and to feed the soil it is called a green manure; green manures add humus to the soil. Sometimes cover crop/green manures fill in unplanted spaces in the garden—spaces left vacant between the harvest of one crop and the planting of another; cover crops that temporarily fill space are called catch crops.

Winter cover crops. Winter cover crops can be planted in late summer or autumn to grow or sit through winter; they then can be turned under in late winter or early spring when the soil is workable—about 4 to 6 weeks before spring crops are planted. Plant winter cover crops if there is still time for the seed to germinate and grow. Cool-weather cover crops include winter rye, vetch, Austrian winter peas, and burr clover. A cover crop will protect the soil from winter erosion and choke out weeds.

Cover crop benefits. Here are the benefits of planting a cover crop:

- Add nutrients and organic matter to the garden as a green manure. Green manure is similar to compost only it decomposes in the garden rather than in a compost pile.

- Retrieve nutrients deep in the soil and bring them to the surface. The roots of cover crops grow deep to nutrients and bring them to the surface; later when the cover crop is cut down and turned under those nutrients will remain in the topsoil.

- Block weeds from growing by covering planting beds not growing crops. A cover crop can be planted in any unused section of the garden, even around growing crops.

- Encourage beneficial insects—the flowers of many cover crops are food for beneficial insects.

- Encourage and feed beneficial soil microbes which break down organic matter in the soil; beneficial microbes, in turn, eat pathogen-causing fungi and bacteria.

- Protect the soil from erosion, especially during the rainy season and winter.

- Break up compacted topsoil and break through hardpan and compacted subsoil; many cover crops are deep rooted.

November

Late Autumn

Growing Into Winter

November is yet another busy month in the vegetable garden. Many gardeners would say November is the most important month. Now is the time to prepare the soil for next spring and then put the garden to bed for winter. Prepare the soil by removing all plant debris from planting beds and adding aged compost and manures whose nutrients will be carried deep into the soil by winter rains and snow. Garden cleanup is essential to insure insect pests and diseases do not overwinter in the garden and reemerge next spring.

Gardeners who have winter crops in the garden should move swiftly in November to get those crops under cover. Season-extending devices must be in place before the first hard freeze.

A row cover sits atop a row of Florence fennel. This spun poly fabric row cover "floats" upward with plant growth. Row covers are also used to cover hoop tunnels.

SEASON EXTENDERS

If you are growing into or through winter to spring, you should have season extending devices in place or at the ready now. Here are the most popular season extending devices for winter use:

Cold frame: A cold frame can be permanent or portable. It is an open-bottomed box that sits over the crops it protects. It has a translucent top which allows the sun to heat the frame interior. (See "How to Make a Cold Frame" in February.)

Hot bed: A hot bed is a cold frame heated by electric heating cables that run beneath the bottom of the frame's planting bed.

Hoop tunnel: A hoop tunnel is fashioned from PVC pipe or heavy gauge wire arched over the planting bed. The arches are covered with clear polyethylene/plastic. Hoop tunnels can vary in size from just a foot or two tall to a tunnel the size of a greenhouse which is called a hoophouse. See "How to Make a Plastic Tunnel" in February.)

Row covers: Row covers—spun polypropylene garden fabric—can extend the growing season by 3 to 4 weeks. The temperature under a row cover will be 1 to 3 degrees warmer than the outside temperature, just enough to protect plants from frost. In mild-winter regions, row covers may be enough to protect plants all through the winter. Here are the seasonal uses of row covers:

- **Autumn.** Use medium-weight row covers (also called plant blankets) in autumn to protect cold-sensitive crops such as tomatoes and peppers from early frosts or chilling winds. As daytime autumn temperatures continue to drop, medium-weight fabric can be replaced with heavyweight fabric; these fabrics should be supported by hoops or structures.

- **Winter.** In mild-winter regions medium- and heavyweight row covers can be used to extend the growing through the winter. Leaf and root cool-weather crops can be protected by row covers for harvest or storage through the winter. In cold-winter regions replace row covers with plastic sheeting in winter to create a cold frame or cold-weather plastic hoop tunnel.

Cloches and hotcaps: Cloches and hotcaps are small translucent plant covers that allow sunlight to warm the planting bed and air around individual plants. Light and solar heat is trapped in these covers to support plant growth. You can purchase cloches and hotcaps at a garden center or you can make your own using plastic jugs, heavy wax paper, and even plastic or paper bags.

LATE AUTUMN PLANTING

Plant corn salad (also called lamb's lettuce and mâche) in autumn. Corn salad is extremely cold tolerant. It can be planted in mid-autumn for over-wintering under a plastic hoop tunnel or cold frame. It can also be left unprotected in all regions except perhaps where the snow cover is very deep. There are two types of corn salad—large-seeded and small-seeded; small-seeded varieties grow best in winter (grow large seeded varieties in spring and autumn); plants can be harvested through the winter. Make successive sowing every 10 days.

Autumn lettuce and spinach sowing for spring harvest. You can direct seed lettuce and spinach in mid- to late autumn. If you want to harvest leafy greens through the winter grow them in a cold frame or under a plastic hoop tunnel. Sow seed so that there are six or seven leaves when the first heavy frost arrives. Before the leaves freeze, cover the plants with a thick layer of straw or chopped leaves or a portable plastic hoop tunnel. In early spring, pull the mulch back and cover the plant-ing bed with a plastic hoop tunnel; the overwin-tered leafy greens will emerge and give you an early spring harvest; cut the whole plants in spring before they bolt.

Kale and mustard under plastic hoop tunnels in autumn and winter. Kale and mustard are hardy plants that can withstand winter freezes when pro-tected by a plastic hoop tunnel. In mild regions kale can be grown outdoors without protection. Where snow is common grow kale and mustard under a hoop tunnel so that plants are not crushed by snow. Mulch heavily around plants so that the ground does not freeze.

Plant multiplier onions and top-setting onions in autumn. Autumn planting allows these crops to establish good root systems. Top-setting onions are also known as Egyptian or tree onions; they produce clusters of small bulbs at the tops of the stalks as well as underground. Multiplier onions are called potato onions; they form clusters of bulbs underground—shallots are multiplier onions.

Asparagus planting in autumn. Asparagus can be planted in the spring and the autumn. In autumn plant asparagus crowns 5 to 6 inches deep; add a sprinkling of bone meal or rock phosphate, cover with soil, and cover again with 12 inches of straw or chopped leaves to protect the roots from winter freezing.

The roots of an asparagus crown are spread out over a mound of soil at the bottom of a 6 inch trench. If you vary the height of each mound crowns are planted on by an inch the harvest of spears will be staggered and extended in spring.

Peas and annual ryegrass—autumn and winter cover crops. Peas and annual ryegrass can be planted in autumn; time planting so that these cover crops mature ahead of the first frost (it may already be too late in northern regions, but not in southern regions)—which will mark the end of their growth. These cover crops can lie down in winter protecting the soil and earthworms through winter. Turn these under in spring when the soil is workable. Summer and early autumn planted cover crops such as buckwheat can be turned under before the first hard freeze. (Buckwheat is your best cover crop choice for smothering weeds.)

PLANTING ZONE-BY-ZONE: Late Autumn / November

Beginning with the warmest regions first, here is a seed starting and planting guide for late-autumn—November. It is safe to plant or do any of the tasks listed for regions cooler than yours.

USDA Zone 10:

- Harvest squash, cucumbers and autumn tomatoes.

- Plant outdoors more cool-season vegetable seeds and transplants.
- Spray *Bacillus thuringiensis* (Bt) on cabbage-family crops as soon as you spot leaf-eating caterpillars.
- Water, fertilize, and thin crops sown earlier.
- Compost spent crops and weeds not gone to seed.
- Dig organic matter into soil or plant cover crops in empty parts of garden.
- Divide and transplant perennial herbs.

USDA Zone 8-9:

- Winter vegetables can be planted under a plastic hoop tunnel or in a cold frame: beets, broad beans, broccoli, Brussels sprouts, cabbage, carrots, cauliflower, celery, Chinese cabbage, collards, kale, kohlrabi, Romaine and leaf lettuce, mustard, onion sets, parsley, radish, spinach, Swiss chard and turnips.
- Plant garlic.
- Harvest beans, tomatoes, peppers and other tender crops before the first frost.
- Harvest and store parsnip, horseradish, and Jerusalem artichoke crops.
- Pick Brussels sprouts when the buttons firm up.
- Use a cloche or plastic hoop tunnel to protect vulnerable vegetables.
- Protect late cauliflowers from frost by bending surrounding leaves over the head.
- Water less frequently but deeply if the winter is dry.
- Remove vegetables and herbs killed by frost.
- Divide and transplant perennial herbs.
- Spread aged compost and manure over planting beds then turn the soil to the depth of a spade—12 inches.
- Seeds saved should be thoroughly dry, labeled, and stored in an air-tight jar. Store seeds in a cool, dry place.
- Lift rhubarb crown for forcing.
- Sow winter cover crops.

- Protect over-wintering root crops against frost by covering them with straw.
- Pot up some herbs for winter use.
- Inspect potatoes and other crops in storage; discard any showing signs of rotting or disease.

USDA Zone 6-7:

- Plant asparagus, cabbage, endive, kale, lettuce, radishes, onion sets, spinach, beets, Asian greens, lettuce, turnips, kohlrabi, mustard, parsley, and radishes in the cold frame. Plant winter spinach, kale, garlic, and onion sets.
- Harvest cold-weather sweetened carrots, Brussels sprouts, cabbage, cauliflower, kale, kohlrabi, leeks, bunching onions, parsnips, and rutabagas. Continue to thin lettuce and spinach.
- Start forcing rhubarb.
- Mulch strawberry beds with aged compost, do not cover crown of plants.
- Check for slug damage and take appropriate action.
- Store carrots, turnips, leeks, and parsnips in the garden under a one-foot-deep layer of mulch; harvest as needed all winter.
- Spread aged compost and manure across planting beds and turn them under.
- Pile autumn leaves on planting beds until it's time for early-spring planting.
- Test soil pH; apply lime if needed.

USDA Zone 2-5:

- Harvest crops that remain in the garden.
- Carrots, turnips, leeks, and parsnips can be left in the garden under a 12-inch layer of mulch; lift roots as needed all winter. Mark beds with tall stakes so you can find them after it snows.
- Remove vegetables and herbs killed by frost.
- Sow greens in the cold frame if the minimum temperature inside the frame can remain about 50°F during the day.
- Turn the compost pile.
- Store tomato cages and beans poles under cover.
- Store hoses and shut off garden faucets.

- Turn organic matter into soil before it freezes and cover with mulch.
- Update crop records and begin your seed order list for spring.

LATE AUTUMN THINGS TO DO

Crops that need protection from temperatures below 30°F: arugula, beet greens, bok choy, broccoli, Florence fennel, lettuce, mizuna, and mustard. These crops can withstand a light frost but should be protected from freezes and snow under a plastic hoop tunnel or cold frame.

Clean the garden at the end of the season. Garden cleanup is important. It brings the season to a close but more importantly, it prepares the garden for next season. Garden cleanup includes removing spent crops and plant debris eliminating winter shelter for pests and diseases. Here's a garden cleanup checklist:

- Remove plant remnants from the garden. Put diseased or pest plagued plant material and weeds in the trash. Spent plants can go in the compost pile.
- Row covers, cloches, and plastic hoop tunnels that won't be used through the winter can be hosed down and put in storage.
- Plant stakes, cages, pots, flats, and other containers can be cleaned of caked soil and scrubbed down with a bleach solution (1 part bleach to 9 parts water). Store them in a dry place through the winter.
- Clean and store tools. Rinse tools with soapy water to prevent the overwintering and spread of soil borne diseases. Dry tools thoroughly before they are stored for winter. Rub linseed oil on wooden parts to prevent cracking and rotting. Sharpen blades and rub a protective sheen of vegetable oil on metal parts. Sharpen spades, knives, and pruners.
- Coil and store hoses in a frost-free place and turn off outdoor faucets where freezing weather is common.

- Remove all annual and perennial weeds from the garden. Dig perennial weed roots out of the ground. Do not compost any weeds that have flowered.
- Mulch perennial vegetable planting beds. Put down a layer of aged compost and a second layer of straw or chopped leaves on strawberry, rhubarb, and asparagus beds. Remove the brown tops of these plants before mulching.
- Cover all empty beds with a blanket of compost and aged manure. You can also mulch empty beds with autumn leaves or straw.
- Turn aged compost, aged manure, leaf mold and other organic material into empty garden beds before the soil freezes.
- If you are not using the cold frame this winter, clean out the frame and line the inside with dry leaves, hay, or straw. Close the sash and cover it with straw, aged manure, or earth.
- Turn the compost pile with a fork and sprinkle with water to speed winter composting.
- Mark garden paths and planting beds with stakes. That way you will know where to shovel snow without harming beds.
- Erect a snow fence or windbreak on the windward side of exposed garden areas where there is no natural protection.
- Saved seed should be placed in airtight containers and labeled.
- Update your garden records and map so that you know what was planted this year and where; updated records will help you plan next season.
- Through winter note pooling water in the garden that might indicate poor drainage.
- In regions where autumn and winter are dry, give plants regular, deep water.

Remove asparagus ferny tops as soon as they turn yellow and before berries fall. The tops can be placed in the trash; they are not suitable for composting. Apply aged manure and compost to the planting beds.

Protect leeks and carrots from freezing soil and thaws. Cover leeks and carrots with a heavy mulch of straw or chopped leaves. You can even pack plastic trash bags with leaves and set them atop leek and carrot planting beds. The mulch will keep the soil temperature even; freezing and thawing through the winter will otherwise damage root crops.

Wood ashes collected this winter. If you burn wood through the winter, you can collect the ashes and use them in the garden. Wood ash contains about 5 percent potassium which is quickly released into the soil. Wood ashes will raise the soil pH; do don't add ashes until you have tested the pH and don't add wood ashes to alkaline soil. The best time to add wood ashes to garden soil is in late autumn, winter, and early spring; avoid adding ashes during the main growing season because ashes can burn sensitive plants.

AUTUMN SOIL CARE

Autumn is a good time to begin preparing the vegetable garden for spring planting.

Garden cleanup: remove all crop and plant debris from the garden at the end of the growing season. This will deprive insect pests and diseases from a place to overwinter.

Remove woody and diseased plant debris from the garden as soon as the harvest is complete–pull up tomato vines and beans and remove late cabbage, cauliflower, and broccoli stalks. Plant debris that is not diseased can be finely chopped and added to the compost pile or turned under to decompose in the garden during winter. Diseased plant refuse should be disposed of or burned.

If you are planning a new garden for spring, autumn is the time to remove sod and perennial weeds and turn the soil where the new garden will grow.

Spading, forking, and double digging will be easier in autumn before winter snows and spring rains waterlog the soil. The best time to cultivate is when the soil is damp but not soggy. If the soil is dry slightly moisten it the day before cultivating. An ideal soil has crumbly texture. Soil worked too soon in spring can become compacted. Heavy, clay soil and hard clods exposed to winter freezes and thaws will break apart more easily.

There are clear advantages to preparing the garden for spring planting in autumn:

- Compost and manure added in autumn has added time to decompose and release nutrients to the soil. Fertility and soil structure is improved.
- Turned soil is better able to absorb winter rains and melting snow.
- Insects are exposed to birds in autumn and cold temperatures in winter; pests will have less opportunity to over-winter in the garden.
- Less ground work will be required in spring; planting can begin as soon as the ground warms and the next harvest will come sooner.

Soil tests. Autumn is a good time to send a soil sample to the county extension or a private soil lab for testing. A soil test can determine the amount of organic matter in the soil, the soil pH, and the presence or lack of major and minor plant nutrients. The nearby cooperative extension service or a private laboratory can do a soil test for a fee. Home soil testing kits can be used but are usually not as accurate. A soil test usually requires several soil samples from around the garden—each about a handful of soil collected from 6 to 8 inches deep. The pH test will tell you if the soil is acidic, alkaline, or neutral. The uptake of many plant nutrients is directly affected by soil pH. Winter is the best time to adjust soil pH if necessary. The pH of acidic soil can be raised with occasional addition of lime. The pH of alkaline soil can be lowered with the addition of sulfur. Winter freezing and thawing will help break down lime and sulfur into the soil.

Compost, manure, and lime intended to adjust the soil pH are best added in autumn and allowed to decompose through winter. Add lime, phosphorus, and other soil amendments as prescribed by the soil test.

Once the planting beds are cleared, turned, and amended, plant green manure cover crops in autumn for turning in winter or early spring. Winter green manures–Austrian peas, crimson clover, hairy vetch, and winter rye–will improve soil fertility and structure and protect the garden from erosion.

Autumn mulch will protect the garden from winter frost and erosion but is not advised where the soil is in poor condition and would benefit from exposure to winter rains and snow.

HARVEST IN LATE AUTUMN

Crops that can withstand light frosts and snow. These crops will be just as tasty or tastier if hit by frost or snow: Brussels sprouts, cabbage, chard, endive, kale, radicchio, spinach.

Harvest root crops. Beets, carrots, daikons, parsnips, radishes, rutabagas, salsify, turnips, and, leeks (not a root) can remain in the garden in winter until you are ready to harvest them. Protect these crops from winter freezes by burying them beneath at least 12 inches of straw or chopped leaves. To harvest these crops in winter, pull back the mulch and lift what you need then replace the mulch. In very cold regions, you may want to add a thick floating row cover over the mulch; be sure to place stones or bricks around the cover to keep it from blowing away.

Overwintering crops for spring harvest. Here's a list of autumn-planted crops that can overwinter in the garden for harvest in early spring: leeks, winter lettuce, onions, parsley, and spinach. Plant these crops in autumn; if they don't reach maturity, don't worry. When early spring comes, they will finish their growth and be ready for an early spring harvest.

Brussels sprouts harvest time. Brussels sprout flavor is enhanced by a few good frosts; however, heavy freeze can turn these small cabbages to mush. So time your harvest or protect plants if a deep freeze is predicted. Brussels sprouts ripen slowing from the bottom of the stem up. Cut sprouts when they are about ¾ inch in diameter, not more than 1½ inch in diameter. Brussels sprouts are shallow rooted mound up soil around the base of each plant as it grows taller.

HARVEST BY ZONE:
Late Autumn / November

These crops were planted in late summer and autumn.

- **USDA Zone 10:** arugula, Asian greens, beans, broccoli, carrots, cucumbers, garlic, lettuce, oregano, peas, potatoes, strawberries, thyme, tomatillos, tomatoes, watermelon, zucchini.

- **USDA Zone 9:** arugula, Asian greens, beets, bok choy, broccoli, Brussels sprouts, cabbage, carrots, cauliflower, celeriac, celery, Chinese cabbage, cilantro, collards, kale, leeks, lettuce, mustards, parsnips, radishes, rutabagas, scallions, Swiss chard, turnips, winter squash.

- **USDA Zones 7-8:** arugula, Asian greens, beets, bok choy, broccoli, Brussels sprouts, cabbage, carrots, cauliflower, green onions, kale, kohlrabi, leeks, lettuce, onions, parsnips, radishes, radicchio, shallots, spinach, Swiss chard, winter squash.

- **USDA Zones 4-6:** arugula, Asian greens, beets, broccoli, Brussels sprouts, cabbage, carrots, cauliflower, celeriac, chives, fennel, kale, kohlrabi, lettuce, onions, parsley , radicchio, radishes rutabaga, scallions, shallots, spinach, Swiss chard, turnips.

CROP ROTATION FOR NEXT SEASON

Winter is the time to plan where to plant each crop next season. Consider rotating your crops. Crop rotation means moving vegetables around the garden

147

so that crops from the same plant family do not grow in the same spot year after year. Crop rotation helps maintain soil fertility and health. By rotating crops from one spot to another each season—or even in the same season, you can preserve and even boost nutrients in the soil. Some crops are heavy feeders; some are light feeders and add nutrients to the soil.

Crop rotation by nutrient uptake. A simple crop rotation would take into consideration plant nutrient requirements: plant heavy feeders in a dedicated planting bed the first year, followed by light feeders in the same bed the second year, followed by soil builders the third year. This rotation presumes there are separate planting areas big enough for all of the crops you want to plant in each of the three rotation groups. Here are the groupings:

- **Heavy feeders:** tomatoes, broccoli, cabbage, corn, eggplant, beets, lettuce, and other leafy crops.
- **Light feeders:** garlic, onions, peppers, potatoes, radishes, rutabagas, sweet potatoes, Swiss chard, and turnips.
- **Soil builders:** peas, beans, and cover crops such as vetch and clover.

Crop rotation by harvest groups. Crop rotation by harvest groups is a simple rotation strategy: rotate (1) leafy crops, (2) root crops, and (3) fruiting crops. Harvest group rotation is not a precise crop rotation method (for example, peppers are light feeders and tomatoes are heavy feeders, but both are fruiting crops—but it is an easy way to group plants and to remember the rotation from one year to the next.

Into this mix you can add cover crops such as peas or vetch and beans to follow fruiting crops. Because fruiting crops are almost all summer crops—tomatoes, peppers, squash, melons, eggplants, they can be replaced with a winter cover crop such as winter rye or fava beans. In spring, the cover crop is turned under and leafy crops can be planted to continue the rotation. This rotation would look like this:

1. **Fruiting vegetables:** corn, eggplants, peppers, tomatoes.
2. **Legumes and cover crops:** beans, clover, fava beans, peas, vetch, and winter rye.

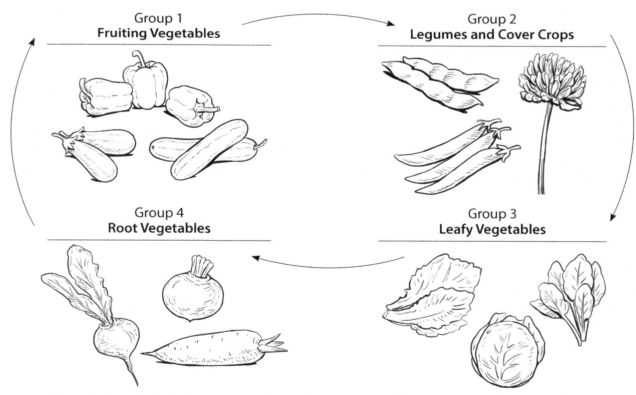

Group 1
Fruiting Vegetables

Group 2
Legumes and Cover Crops

Group 4
Root Vegetables

Group 3
Leafy Vegetables

Crop rotation: plant similar crops together each year; move each group to a new location each year.
This illustrates a simple four-year rotation.

3. **Leafy vegetables:** cabbage, lettuce, spinach, Swiss chard.

4. **Root vegetables:** beets onions, parsnips, potatoes, radishes, rutabagas, turnips.

Crop rotation by plant family. Crop rotation by plant family is perhaps the most traditional way to rotate crops though it can be difficult in a small garden of just one or two beds. Using the plant family rotation, crops from the same family are not planted in the same spot more often than every three years. Crop rotation by family not only maintains soil fertility but also is the best way to avoid attacks by pests and diseases; specific pests and diseases tend to attack plants from the same family. By rotating plant families, pests are not easily able to find the plants they want to attack. The notable vegetable plant families are:

- **Squash family** (heavy feeders): cucumber, zucchini, summer and winter squash, melons.

- **Cabbage family** (heavy feeders): arugula, broccoli, Brussels sprouts, cabbage, collards, kale.

- **Tomato family** (heavy feeders) tomatoes, peppers, eggplants, potatoes.

- **Bean family** (soil enrichers): beans, peas, soybean, peanut, and other legumes.

- **Lettuce family** (heavy feeders): lettuce, artichoke, cardoon, chamomile, tarragon.

- **Carrot family** (mostly light feeders): carrots, parsnips, celery, parsley, fennel, dill, chervil

- **Onion family** (light feeders): onions, shallots, leeks, garlic, chives.

- **Spinach family** (medium feeders): beets, spinach, Swiss chard.

Rotation by plant family will take some planning; you can match up light feeders to rotate with heavy feeders and separate the two with the soil builders.

December

Early Winter

Looking Ahead

Winter arrives on December 21—the shortest day of the year. There is never a shortage of things to do in the garden, even in winter.

Winter vegetables protected by season extending devices will continue to live through winter cold even though there will be little to no growth during the days when there is less than 10 hours of daylight (growth will resume when daylight increase to greater than 10 hours). If snow has fallen on your winter vegetable garden, do not despair. Snow is akin to an insulating blanket and the cool-season vegetables that are near maturity beneath can still be harvested.

A killing hard frost or freeze will do more damage than snow to the unprotected vegetable garden in winter. Protect crops from freezing temperatures with plastic hoop tunnels or cold frame. Mulch of loose mounds of straw or fallen leaves also will protect plants from freezing temperatures.

If temperatures are in the high 20s or low 30s, cabbage, Swiss chard, head lettuce, carrots, turnips, and Brussels sprouts can still be harvested–even from under a blanket of snow. Scallions and autumn leeks can be harvested also–the leeks will be about the size of scallions. Onions can stay in the garden under a protective layer of mulch as long as the soil does not freeze.

COLD FRAME TUNE-UP

Check the seal between the lid and top of your cold frame to make sure it is tight. The frame edge can be lined with weather stripping or a strip of used carpet under pad to ensure cold air does not enter the frame. (For more on cold frames see "How to Make a Cold Frame" in February and check for other references in the Index.)

Where temperatures are very cold, a piece of plastic sheeting can be stretched over single layer lids made of glass, plastic, or Plexiglas. Double layers of glass– or an added layer of plastic sheeting–will provide the greatest insulation.

The height of a cold frame should be just taller than the height of the tallest crop that you are growing in the frame. Stackable cold frame units will serve this purpose. Stackable frame units 6 to 8 inches tall can be set one atop the other to raise the frame up. A cabbage plant may require four 8-inch tall units to total 32 inches tall which should clear the largest mature cabbage. Place the sloping frame unit–sloping toward the South–on top. You can secure stacking frame units with pegs that fit into the unit below. Plastic sheeting, a tarp, or old carpet can be stretched around the inside of the frame to insulate and keep wind and cold from coming through the gaps. A low frame 6 to 8 inches tall is all that is needed for lettuce, spinach, and root crops.

EARLY WINTER PLANTING

No grow time: When daylight is less than 10 hours each day, plants in the garden will stop growing. If protected from cold they will not die, but they will not actively grow where there is less than 10 hours of sunlight; they will enter a period of dormancy. This is true for all plants including vegetables and herbs. The no-grow period can last two to three months depending on where you live (check the weather service for sunrise and sunset where you live). Leave crops in place and protect them from the cold; when daylight hours are again greater than 10 hours, vegetables will resume growth toward maturity and harvest. (Spring cabbage, for example, is planted in late summer or early autumn. It grows to near maturity but then stops growth and sits near dormant during the winter no-grow time; then in early spring as daylight increases the cabbage resumes growth, reaches maturity, and is harvested in spring.)

Garlic can be planted from autumn to early spring where the ground is workable. Garlic planted in autumn and early winter will be harvested the next mid-summer. Plant softneck garlic if you live where winters are mild. Plant hardneck garlic where winters are cold and where springs are cool and wet. Be sure to plant garlic at least 4 to 6 weeks before the ground freezes; this will allow for the development of a strong root system. Garlic leaves can be chopped and used like chives.

Pixie tomatoes. Grow pixie tomatoes indoors this winter in a pot in a sunny window or under grow lights. Pixies are very sweet, meaty, juicy, and flavorful—perfect for salads and garnishes. They are ready for harvest 55 days after transplanting.

Sow cress seed indoors. Grow cress indoors in a flat or shallow pot for sprouts. Fill the flat with seed-starter mix or organic potting soil, sprinkle the seeds across the soil, and then lightly cover the seed with seed-started mix or vermiculite. Seed will germinate in 2 to 6 days and be ready for harvest at 2 to 3 inches tall in two weeks. Cress has a peppery tang. Add cress to salads, sandwiches, and vegetables dishes.

Growing herbs indoors in winter. Grow culinary herbs in a sunny window for winter use. Herbs easy to grow indoors include: anise, basil, bergamot, borage, caraway, chamomile, chervil, chives, coriander, dill, lemon balm, lemon grass, marjoram, parsley, peppermint, rosemary, sage, summer savory, and thyme. Annual herbs can be started from seed. Sow seed in 3- to 4-inch pots so they will have room to grow through the winter. To grow herbs indoors in winter you will need:

- **Light:** Herbs require plenty of light. Grow them in sunny window or under fluorescent lights; set the lights 6 to 8 inches above the plants.

Crop rotation: each square represents a planting bed. This is a simple four-year rotation.

- **Temperature:** Herbs want daytime temperatures between 60° and 70°F with cooler temperatures of 50° to 65°F at night.
- **Water:** Keep the soil just moist. Don't overwater. If humidity is low, spray plants with a light mist at least once a day.

Overwintering herbs outdoors: Mints, oregano, and tarragon are hardy perennial herbs that can survive outdoors in winter if protected. Use plant blankets or burlap covered frames to protect perennial herbs. Small herbs can be covered with straw or dry leaves when the soil freezes. You can even cover herbs with evergreen boughs. Bay, rosemary, lavender, pineapple sage, and lemon verbena are tender perennial herbs that will take some frost but their roots will be killed off outdoors if the temperature dips below 15°F. In cold-winter regions, these herbs should be potted up and brought indoors for the winter.

PLANTING ZONE-BY-ZONE:
Early Winter / December

Beginning with the warmest regions first, here is a seed starting and planting guide for early winter—December. It is safe to plant or do any of the tasks listed for regions cooler than yours.

USDA Zone 10: mild to cool weather likely, frost possible

- Sow in the open garden: beets, Bermuda onions, broccoli, Brussels sprouts, carrots, cabbage, collards, endive, Asian greens, kale, kohlrabi, leeks, lettuce, mustard, green onions, parsley, English peas, parsley, potatoes, radishes, salsify, spinach, Swiss chard, and turnips.
- Sow tender annual and vegetable seeds indoors that require 12 weeks or more indoors such as tomatoes, peppers, and eggplants.
- Plant perennial vegetables: asparagus, artichokes, horseradish, and rhubarb.
- Make new strawberry beds.
- Check crops and water if needed.
- Turn aged compost into planting beds after harvests and before planting.

153

USDA Zone 9: cool to cold temperatures, frost possible

- Harvest vegetable crops from garden and cold frame; harvest leeks, turnip, rutabagas, kohlrabi, and parsnip.
- Plant cool-weather crops such as lettuce and cabbage-family crops in garden or cold frame; crops grow slowly during winter's short days.
- Sow tender vegetable seeds indoors that require 12 weeks or more indoors.
- Start forcing rhubarb.
- Harvest herb leaves and seeds.
- Divide and transplant perennial herbs.
- Clean up empty planting beds and add aged compost and manure or plant cover crops.
- Update garden records; determine crop locations for coming season; begin preparing seed and plant orders for spring.
- Test garden soil. Apply lime if the test shows it is necessary.

USDA Zone 7-8: cold weather, freezing weather possible

- Plant perennial vegetables and herbs: asparagus, horseradish, rhubarb, strawberry, sage, mint, rosemary.
- Place cloches over spring cabbages and winter lettuces.
- Sow in the cold frame Bermuda onions seed, cabbage, cauliflower, broccoli, head lettuce, mustard, radish, and spinach.
- Finish planting garlic and onion sets.
- Harvest parsnips, salsify, leeks, Brussels sprouts, kale, and Swiss chard as needed.
- Mulch Jerusalem artichokes, carrots, parsnips and other root crops that are still in the garden.
- Start forcing rhubarb.
- Clear the garden of any plant remnants and debris.
- Spread mulch over beds where early spring crops will grow.
- Check windbreaks, mulches, and other winter protection.

- Turn compost pile. Cover the pile with a tarp to prevent nutrients from leaching away during winter rains
- Test your soil. Apply lime if necessary.
- Spread aged compost and leaf mulch across vacant garden beds.
- Update garden designs; begin preparing seed and plant orders for spring.

USDA Zone 3-6: cold and freezing temperatures, snow likely

- Lift root crops stored in garden under mulch as needed—parsnips, turnips, rutabagas.
- Harvest Brussels sprouts, cabbage, and leeks as needed. These crops can overwinter under snow—or protect them under a plastic hoop tunnel.
- Grow spinach and greens through the winter under a plastic hoop tunnel or cold frame.
- Harvest crops from cold frame.
- Ventilate cold frame on warn days.
- Check windbreaks, mulches, and other winter protection.
- After the ground freezes lay heavy mulch on planting beds. Clean hay, leaves, pine needles, and straw can be used to protect planting beds through the winter. Chop or shred leaves if you use them to mulch; whole leaves will mat when wet. Be sure asparagus crown and rhubarbs are protected by mulch.
- Update garden designs; begin preparing seed and plant orders for spring.

EARLY WINTER THINGS TO DO

Late season soil care. Spading, forking, and double digging will be easier while the ground is relatively dry and before winter snows and spring rains waterlog the soil. The best time to cultivate is when the soil is damp but not soggy. An ideal soil has crumbly texture. Soil worked too soon in spring can become compacted. Heavy, clay soil and hard clods exposed to winter freezes and thaws will break apart more easily. There are clear advantages to preparing the garden for spring planting before spring:

- Compost and manure added in autumn and winter has added time to decompose and release nutrients to the soil. Fertility and soil structure is improved.

- Turned soil is better able to absorb winter rains and melting snow.

- When the soil is turned, insects are exposed to birds and cold temperatures; pests will have less opportunity to over-winter in the garden.

- Less ground work will be required in spring; planting can begin as soon as the ground warms and the next harvest will come sooner.

Soil tests. Early winter is a good time to send a soil sample to the county extension for testing. Compost, manure, and lime intended to adjust the soil pH are best added in autumn and allowed to decompose through winter. Add lime, phosphorus, and other soil amendments as prescribed by the soil test.

Winter mulching will protect planting beds from the impact of rain, snow, freezing, and prevent the loss of soil nutrients. Mulch for winter can be straw, chopped leaves, aged compost, or a cover crop. Clearing the garden of debris and weeds and putting mulch in place before winter freezes will make getting the garden re-started in spring easier. Before setting down mulch, do the following:

- Remove annual weeds from the garden; don't let weeds flower or drop seed.

Protect fallow planting beds from winter rains and freezes by laying a thick layer of straw, chopped leaves, or aged compost across the beds.

- Dig out perennial weeds; remove taproots and all creeping roots.

- If insects have been a problem the past season, turn the soil 6 to 8 inches deep and leave it uncovered for two weeks then turn the soil one more time. This will expose pest insect larvae (potato beetles, flea beetles, wireworms, June bugs, grasshoppers, onion maggots, and brassica root maggots) to birds and the killing cold. Mulch after two or three weeks.

- When spring arrives, pull the mulch back about two weeks before planting to allow the soil to warm. Loosen the top 4 inches of soil and rake the bed smooth before planting.

Protect leeks, shallots, garlic, and strawberry roots through the winter with mulch. Place a thick layer of straw or leaves on top of the planting bed before the ground freezes. Be sure to mark the corners of the beds with stakes before winter snows come.

Asparagus and rhubarb winter care. Asparagus and rhubarb have perennial roots but their leafy tops die back in the winter. Cut off and clear away the dead leafy tops in winter. When the ferny tops of asparagus turn brown and brittle cut them back and put them in the trash so that asparagus beetle eggs do not overwinter. Test the soil pH; it should be 6.5 to 7.0. Add lime to raise the pH or sulfur to lower it. Spread an inch or aged compost and well-rotted manure over the planting bed then put a 6-inch layer of chopped leaves or straw on top of that to protect the roots from freezing weather.

Container gardens. Move tender container plants indoors or into cold frames for winter. Half-hardy container plants can go into the cold frame; sink clay pots with plants into the ground. Shallow containers should be sheltered away from frost and freezing weather. Set containers up on low supports so that they drain freely. Check these plants regularly. Remove spent plants from containers and compost; clean containers and store for winter. In mild regions, move container plants away from eves into sheltered positions. Begin to plan container vegetable planting for next year; order seeds as necessary.

Parsnips can be stored in the ground over the winter. Cover the planting bed with at least 12 inches of straw or shredded leaves. Do this before the ground freezes. Next cover the insulating layer of straw or leaves with a thick floating row cover and be sure to place stones or bricks in place to keep the cover from blowing away. As you need parsnips in the winter, pull back the cover and insulating straw then use a garden or hand fork to lift the roots; don't pull the roots, they may snap in two.

Autumn leaves in compost pile. Be sure to shred autumn leaves before adding them to the compost pile. Unshredded leaves are slow to decompose because they mat together keeping oxygen and moisture out. Dry leaves have a high carbon-to-nitrogen ratio so add grass clippings to the compost pile with the leaves or sprinkle a high nitrogen organic fertilizer atop the leaves.

Keeping compost warm. Heat up the winter compost pile by adding a thin layer of "hot" chicken manure. Also place a sheet of black plastic on top of the pile on sunny days. Keep turning the pile and it will heat up.

Use sand to de-ice walkways. Use sand, not salt, to keep walkways passable after a freeze. Salt can damage plant roots next season. Sand can be rinsed down and into the garden with no damage.

Vegetable gardener's gift list. Tools most vegetable gardeners need include: spade, hoe, rake, spading fork, pruning shears, gardening gloves, hand trowel, sprayer, wheelbarrow, watering can, cold frame, shredder, seed starting supplies, grow lamp.

Holly berries. If there are few berries on holly now, it will be a mild winter. If there are lots of berries, it will be a cold, harsh winter.

Snow—not to worry. If snow has fallen on your winter vegetable garden, do not despair. Snow is akin to an insulating blanket and the cool-season vegetables beneath can still be harvested. A killing frost or freeze will do the most damage to your vegetable garden in winter–not snow. Protect crops from freezing temperatures with mulch, plastic hoop tunnels, or cold frame. Loose straw or fallen leaves will protect plants from freezing temperatures also.

Garden records and map. Winter is a good time to update your garden records from last season and review your garden design. What worked and what can be improved next season. Garden records should keep track of sowing, transplanting, blooming, and harvest dates for each crops. Planting and harvest dates can be used for planning succession crops. Plan the spring and summer garden on paper. Sketch a base plan. Consider the location of house, garage, shed, fences, walls, and large trees that will cast shadows across the garden. If this is your first garden, monitor your planting area and map where the snow melts first, these will be good spots for planting early crops. Consider the light, water, and nutrient needs of each crop and crop family. Plant crops with similar needs or crops from the same families close together. Make a garden map to keep track of just what was planted where; this map will be invaluable should your garden labels become misplaced or illegible. These records will help you plan your garden in following years.

Plan ahead—succession and intercropping for next season. Plan succession crops for next season by charting the entire growing season on paper. Consider days from sowing to germination, growing days to maturity, and the number of days in the harvest period for each crop. Add these together to plot how many days each crop will spend in the garden. Then you can plan successions; for example, warm-weather bush lima beans can follow cool-weather peas; cool-weather lettuce and spinach can follow beans. That is a simple succession plan from spring to autumn. Intercropping matches a fast-growing small crop with a slow-maturing crop: an example, quick-growing radishes planted between slow-maturing carrots, or shade tolerant peas planted under corn. Succession and intercropping will allow you to get the most out of your garden and the growing season.

WINTER HARVEST

Cool season crops planted early in autumn will come to harvest in the next several weeks. If crops have slowed down–don't fret. Once daylight drops to less than 10 hours, cool-weather vegetables slip into a no growth mode. Growth will resume when the light each days increases in January and February.

If temperatures are in the high 20s or low 30sF, cabbage, chard, lettuce, carrots, turnips, and Brussels sprouts can still be harvested–even from under a blanket of snow. Scallions and autumn leeks can be harvested also. Onions can stay in the garden under a protective layer of mulch.

Dig and harvest root crops stored in garden under mulch as needed. Root crops such as carrots, parsnips, and salsify that come out of the garden can be stored in a cool basement until you need them. If the ground does not freeze Jerusalem artichokes, carrots, parsnips, rutabaga, turnips, and other root crops can spend winter underground.

Brussels sprouts, cabbage, chard, collards, and kale harvested now will keep for weeks if stored in a cool basement or root cellar. To enjoy spinach, winter lettuces, and spring cabbage all winter, cover the plants with a plastic hoop tunnel or cloche. Bend the leaves of cauliflower over the curds to protect them from frost damage.

Asparagus harvest. Asparagus is not ready for harvest until spears are about 8 inches tall when they can be snapped off at soil level. Two-year-old roots can be harvested for 2 or 3 weeks; three-year-old roots can be harvested for 3 to 4 weeks; older asparagus beds can be harvested for 6 to 8 weeks. Don't cut spears smaller around than your little finger.

Broccoli harvest. Broccoli and other cabbage family member seedlings should be thinned to 18 to 24 inches apart to ensure full growth. Keep an eye on broccoli florets as they develop. You'll want to harvest them when they are full but before they become heavy and floppy. Once the main floret is cut, smaller florets will develop in leaf axils for further harvest.

Swiss chard harvest. Swiss chard leaves can be cut when they are about 6 inches long and still young. Cut just what you can eat and come back later for more. Chard will keep producing as long as you avoid lifting the roots.

Fennel harvest. Florence fennel is ready for harvest when bulbs are about 2 inches across at the base.

Don't let fennel get much bigger or it will bolt and set seed.

Turnip and kohlrabi harvest. Harvest the kohlrabi above soil bulb when it is 2 to 3 inches in diameter. Turnips are best harvested at about the same size. Lift the bulbs gently or cut them off just above the soil to avoid pulling up neighboring bulbs. Don't let bulbs grow much larger or they will become woody.

Lettuce harvest. Lettuce must be protected from freezing temperatures; keep the plastic hoop tunnel handy when temperatures dip. Leaf lettuce can be harvested cut-and-come-again, just like chard. Cut the leaves you can eat just above the base and let the plant grow on. Head lettuce is ready for harvest when the head is firm. Keep excessive rain from head lettuce or it will swell up and the head will split.

Peas harvest. Pick snow pears before pods begin to bulge; pick snap peas before pods fully develop; pick shelling peas when the pods are plump and still bright green–and tender. Begin the pea harvest soon after the first blossoms appear–the first pods for picking will be low on the plant. Continue to pick peas every day until the harvest is finished.

Crops that can survive under snow (but not sustained freezing temperatures or ice) include asparagus, rhubarb, beets, broccoli, Brussels sprouts, cabbage, carrots, cauliflower, cress, rutabaga, spinach, endive, horseradish, kohlrabi, kale, leek lettuce, onions, parsley, parsnips, radishes, and turnips. The best time

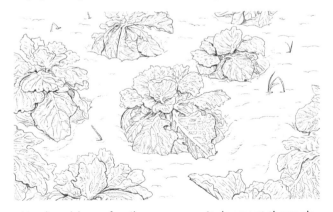

Hardy cabbage family crops can sit dormant through the winter under a layer of snow. Snow will actually protect these crops from freezing temperatures. Growth of these nearly mature cabbage plants will resume in spring for an early year harvest.

for harvesting cold-weather crops from under snow is when temperatures are in the high 20s or low 30s, especially if you are uncovering only a portion of the crop for harvest and leaving the rest for later harvest. If freezing weather threatens to freeze the soil, all crops should be lifted from the garden.

HARVEST ZONE-BY-ZONE:
Early Winter / December

The crops coming to harvest now were planted in autumn.

- **USDA Zone 9-10:** arugula, Asian greens, asparagus, beets, bok choy, broccoli, Brussels sprouts, cabbage, carrots, cauliflower, celeriac, celery, Chinese cabbage, chives, cilantro, collards, fennel, garlic, kale, kohlrabi, leeks, lettuce, mustards, oregano, parsley, parsnips, peas, radishes, radicchio, rutabaga, salsify, spinach, thyme, turnips.

- **USDA Zones 7-8:** arugula, Asian greens, beets, bok choy, broccoli, Brussels sprouts, cabbage, carrots, cauliflower, kale, kohlrabi, leeks, lettuce, mustards, parsnips, radishes, radicchio, rutabaga, salsify, spinach, turnips.

- **USDA Zones 4-6:** grow under cover: arugula, Asian greens, beets, broccoli, Brussels sprouts, cabbage, carrots, , kale, kohlrabi, lettuce, onions, parsley , radicchio, rutabaga, spinach, Swiss chard, thyme, turnips.

Appendix 1

Worksheets
to Plan the Season

Get-Started Worksheet:

Location of my garden: ....

Hardiness zone: ....

Last average frost date in spring: ....

First average frost date in autumn: ....

Number of days in the growing days: ....

Advanced Climate and Hardiness Worksheet:

- My garden USDA Hardiness Zone: _____.

- Last hard frost* in spring: average date: _____; actual date: _____.
  Season extending protection is required for starting seeds and seedlings before the first soft frost..

- Last soft frost* in spring: average date: _____; actual date: _____.
  Main planting and growing season is underway.

- First soft frost* in autumn: average date: _____; actual date: _____.
  Main growing season comes to an end. Many crops will require season extending protection from this point.

- First hard frost* in autumn: average date: _____; actual date: _____.
  The growing season is over unless crops are grown under the protection of a cold frame or plastic hoop tunnel.

- Days in natural growing season (count the number of days between the last soft frost in spring to the first soft frost in autumn): _____.

- No growth period: Date when daylight drops below 10 hours each day until date when daylight is greater than 10 hours each day: _____.

- Date nighttime low is above 60°F in spring: _____.
  Warm-season crops can be grown without protection from this date until nighttime temperatures fall below 60°F.

- Date nighttime temperatures fall below 60°F in autumn: _____.
  Warm season crops must be protected with season extending devices after this date.

- Number of days when temperature is greater than 95°F: _____.
  Vegetables slow growth when temperatures are greater than 86°F and stop growth when temperatures are greater than 95°F; growth will resume when temperatures moderate.

---

*Frost: gardeners often speak of "soft frost" and "hard frost".

- A soft frost happens when temperatures drop just a few degrees below freezing (32°F), usually 28° to 32°F for less than 4 consecutive hours.
- A hard frost happens when the temperature falls below freezing for more than 4 consecutive hours.
- A "hard freeze" or "killing freeze" happens when temperatures fall below 25°F for 4 consecutive hours; few cool-season vegetables can survive a killing freeze.

The frost dates in Appendix 3, pages 169-180, are soft frost dates. Most cool-season vegetables can survive a soft frost; some can survive a hard frost; few can survive a hard freeze. Warm-season (summer) vegetables commonly require day and night temperatures greater than 60°F to thrive.

Planting Schedule Worksheet:

Year: ....

Expected Last Frost Date: ....

Crop/ variety	Date to start indoors	Scheduled date to set out transplants or start seed in the garden	Actual date started indoors	Actual date transplants set out or seeds sown in garden

Garden Record: Year

Vegetable/Variety	Days to maturity	Date Seed Started Indoors	Date Seed Started Outdoors	Date Transplants Set in Garden	Harvest Start Date	Days in Harvest	Total Days in Garden

Succession Crop Planner

This chart will help you plan succession crops. In the first column note the total number of days in the growing season. Then list the first crop to be planted followed by each succession crop and the number days each crop will be in the garden. The total number of days for all of the succession crops should not be greater than the total days in the garden season—unless you plant to protect crops using season extending devices.

Total days in garden season	Spring-planted cool-season crop variety	Total days in garden	Late spring-planted warm-season crop variety	Total days in garden	Summer-planted warm-season crop variety	Total days in garden	Fall-planted cool-season crop variety	Total days in garden

Appendix 2

Planting and Harvest Charts

Planting and Harvest Planning Chart

Vegetable	Days to Harvest	Plants Needed per Person Each Season	Number of Plants per Square Foot	Harvest from One Sowing Lasts
Artichoke	2 years	1	3-4 sq. ft. per plant	5 weeks
Asparagus	2 years	20	1-2	5 weeks
Beans, green	45-75	12-15	9-12	Bush 4-6 weeks Pole 8 weeks
Beans, Lima	65-95	12-15	4	4 weeks
Beets	50-70	30	36 for baby beets	8 weeks
Broccoli	75	2	1	10 weeks
Brussels sprouts	90	1-3	1-2	8 weeks
Cabbage	65-100	3-4	1-2	8 weeks
Carrots	60-85	30-40	40-60 for baby carrots	8 weeks
Cardoon	110-150	1	1-2	5 weeks
Cauliflower	60-75	2-3	1-2	2 weeks
Celery	90-135	2-3	4	8 weeks
Chinese cabbage	70-75	1-2	1-2	8 weeks
Collards	60	3-5	1	8 weeks
Chard, Swiss	60	10	6	20 weeks
Chives	90	1	16	20 weeks
Corn, sweet	75-105	10-15	4	10 days
Cucumbers	55-75	2-3	4-5	5 weeks
Dandelion	75-90	2-3	4	2 weeks
Eggplant*	75-85	1-2	1	8 weeks
Endive/Escarole	90-100	4-8	2	6 weeks
Florence fennel	85	1	4	3 weeks
Garlic	90	8-16	16	6 weeks
Horseradish	6-8 mo.	2	2-4	6 weeks
Kale	70	4-6	4	8 weeks
Kohlrabi	60	5-6	6-9	3 weeks

Vegetable	Days to Harvest	Plants Needed per Person Each Season	Number of Plants per Square Foot	Harvest from One Sowing Lasts
Leeks	90-120	6-10	4-36	8 weeks
Lettuce, leaf & Romaine	35-90	10-20	4	6 weeks
Muskmelon	80-100	2-4	1 spreading	4 weeks
Mustard	35	4-6	6-16	4 weeks
Okra	65-70	1-2	1-3	4 weeks
Onions, green	25-45	20-30	16-16	6 weeks
Onions, mature bulb	90-100	10-20	4-8	12 weeks
Parsley	90-140	1	4	16 weeks
Parsnip	100-130	10-15	9-16	Fall and Winter
Peas	55-85	30-50	16-36	2-4 weeks
Peppers*	60-85	1-3	1	8 weeks
Potatoes	90-110	10-20	3-9	4 weeks
Pumpkin	70-85	1	1 spreading	4 weeks
Radish	25-40	30-60	36	1-4 weeks
Rhubarb	75	1	1-3	4 weeks
Rutabaga	80-90	10-15	2-4	6 weeks
Salsify	140	10	16	Fall and winter
Sorrel	60	1	2	5 months
Spinach	40-50	5-15	4-8	3 weeks
New Zealand spinach	55	5	1	14 weeks
Squash, summer	50-65	1-2 per type	1 spreading	12 weeks
Squash, winter	80-105	1-2 per type	1 spreading	12 weeks
Tomatoes*	60-85	1-2	1-3 sq. ft. per plant	12-16 weeks
Turnips	40-75	10-20	8-16	2 weeks
Watermelon	85-95	1	1 spreading	4 weeks

*Days to harvest from transplanting

Weeks Needed to Grow to Transplant Size

Crop	Number of days to germination	Weeks to grow to transplant size	Total days to maturity from seed depending on variety
Artichokes	7-14	4-6	1 year
Asparagus	7-21	1 year	3 years
Broccoli	3-10	5-7	60-80 from transplant
Brussels sprouts	3-10	4-6	80-90 from transplant
Cabbage	4-10	5-7	55-65 from transplant
Cauliflower	4-10	5-7	55-65 from transplant
Celery	9-21	10-12	90-120 from transplant
Collards	4-10	4-6	65-85 from transplant
Cucumber	6-10	4	55-65
Eggplant	7-14	6-9	75-95 from transplant
Kale	3-10	4-6	55-80
Kohlrabi	3-10	4-6	60-70
Leeks	7-12	10-12	80-90 from transplants
Lettuce, head	4-10	3-5	55-80
Lettuce, leaf	4-10	3-5	45-60
Muskmelon	4-8	3-4	75-100
Onions, seed	7-12	8	100-165
Parsley	14-28	8	85-90
Peppers	10-20	6-8	60-80 from transplant
Tomatillo			
Tomato	6-14	5-7	55-90 from transplant

Appendix 3

Frost Dates,
Length of Growing Season,
Hardiness Zones

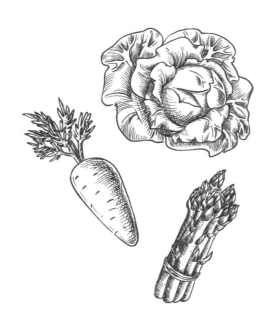

Frost Dates, Length of Growing Season, Hardness Zones

Frost Dates: Here are the first and last average frost dates and the number of days in the growing season for selected cities and towns in the United States and Canadian Provinces. These cities and towns represent diverse climate and growing regions for each state and province—that is north, south, east, west, costal, mountain, or plain.

The dates and growing season days listed here are estimates or averages based on a compilation of information from the United States Department of Agriculture and several other sources. This information should be used only as estimated guidelines; these are averages based on temperatures recorded over the past decade or so. Climate, weather, and growing season days in your region can change from year to year. For more information on growing season days and average temperatures in your town or region contact your Cooperative Extension Service, a master gardener group, or nearby nursery or garden center.

Length of Growing Season: The growing days or growing season is the number of days between the last frost in spring and the first frost in autumn.

Hardiness Zones: Hardiness zones are geographic areas with similar climatic conditions relevant to plant growth and survival. The most widely used hardiness zone format was developed by the United States Department of Agriculture (USDA). This system is based on a scale of annual extreme minimum temperatures. The zones number 1 (the coldest) which is in the far north to zone 13 (the warmest) in the tropical south. In the continental United States, the coldest hardiness zone is Zone 4 in the upper Midwest and Plains states and the warmest zone is Zone 11 in southern parts of Florida and California. Zone-ratings are generally regional but not always; elevation can sometimes factor into zone designations. High elevations in southern regions may experience winter cold that will put a specific location into a hardiness zone commonly found much further north.

Each USDA zone is divided into a northern and southern sub-zones—labelled "a" and "b". . The northern part of the zone is labeled "a" and the southern part is labelled "b". It is interesting to note that over the past few decades, warm zone designations have creeped north. For example, Santa Rosa, California was a few decades ago part of zone 8, now it is part of zone 9a-9b; the winters there are growing warmer and warmer; this is true for most regions of the country.

Number of days when temperature is greater than 86°F: The American Horticultural Society has developed a Plant Heat Zone Map which is somewhat similar to the USDA Hardiness Zone map but instead of designating regions by extreme low temperatures it measure the average number of days each summer when the temperature is greater than 86°F (the temperature at which some, but not all, plants experience cellular damage). These zones, like the hardiness zones, are generally distributed by latitude and topography; southern regions have more average days greater than 86°F than northern regions. You should factor hot weather into vegetable plant growth; most plants will stop growing and enter a period of near dormancy when temperatures rise greater than 86°F. Crop maturation will be slowed by hot temperatures causing the number of days to maturity and harvest to be greater. Note: Far southern regions of the United States where there are long, hot summers and nearly frostless winters are often referred to by gardeners as "reverse season" regions where warm-season crops are grown in the spring and autumn and cool-season crops are grown in winter. For more on Reverse Season gardening see pages 181-183.

State and City	Average date of last frost (Based on 32°F at 50 percent probability)	Average date of first frost	Length of growing season—days	USDA Zone	Average extreme minimum	Days per year on average greater than 86°F
Alabama						
Birmingham	Apr 3	Nov 5	215	7b-8a	5° to 10°F	91-120
Huntsville	Apr 3	Nov 2	212	7a-7b	0° to 5°F	91-120
Mobile	Mar 6	Nov 29	267	8b	15° to 20°F	91-120
Montgomery	Mar 24	Nov 6	226	8a-8b	10° to 15°F	91-120
Thomasville	Mar 21	Nov 14	237	8a	10° to 15°F	91-120
Alaska						
Anchorage	May 4	Sep 22	140	4b-5a	-25° to -20°F	—
Barrow	Jul 28	Aug 8	10	2a	-45°F to -40°F	—
Cordova	Apr 14	Oct 24	192	7a	0° to 5°F	—
Fairbanks	May 20	Sep 1	103	2a	-45°F to -40°F	—
Arizona						
Flagstaff	Jun 11	Sep 23	103	6a	-10° to -5°F	60-90
Phoenix	Jan 20	Dec 27	340	9a-9b	20° to 25°F	151-180
Tucson	Feb 5	Dec 7	304	9b	25° to 30°F	151-180
Winslow	May 5	Oct 13	160	6b-7a	-5° to 0°F	91-120
Yuma	Jan 15	Dec 18	336	10a	30° to 35°F	181-210
Arkansas						
Fort Smith	Apr 5	Oct 31	208	7b	0° to 5°F	91-120
Jonesboro	Apr 8	Oct 25	199	7a	0° to 5°F	91-120
Little Rock	Mar 28	Nov 7	223	7b	0° to 5°F	91-120
Pine Bluff	Mar 26	Nov 8	226	8a	10° to 15°F	91-120
California						
Bakersfield	Feb 4	Dec 3	300	9b-10a	25° to 30°F	121-150
Blythe	Feb 5	Dec 9	315	9b-10a	25° to 30°F	181-210
Eureka	Mar 2	Dec 4	276	9b	25° to 30°F	1-7
Fresno	Feb 13	Dec 1	290	9b	25° to 30°F	121-150
Los Angeles	infrequent	frost		10a-10b	30° to 35°F	7-14
Marysville	Feb 3	Dec 5	304	9b	25° to 30°F	91-120
Merced	Mar 14	Nov 17	247	9a-9b	20° to 25°F	121-150
Palm Springs	Jan 17	Dec 17	333	9a-9b	20° to 25°F	181-210
Red Bluff	Mar 9	Nov 23	258	9a-9b	20° to 25°F	91-120
Riverside	Jan 30	Dec 13	316	9b	25° to 30°F	91-120
Sacramento	Feb 21	Nov 26	277	9b	25° to 30°F	61-90
San Diego	infrequent	frost	365	10a-10b	30° to 35°F	1-7
San Francisco	infrequent	frost		10a-10b	30° to 35°F	1-7

State and City	Average date of last frost (Based on 32°F at 50 percent probability)	Average date of first frost	Length of growing season—days	USDA Zone	Average extreme minimum	Days per year on average greater than 86°F
San Jose	Jan 11	Dec 31	336	9b-10a	25° to 30°F	14-30
Santa Barbara	Jan 28	Dec 8	313	10a	30° to 35°F	14-30
Santa Rosa	Feb 26	Nov 26	272	9b	25° to 30°F	14-30
Colorado						
Boulder	May 9	Oct 1	144	5b-6a	-15° to -10°F	1-7
Denver	May 4	Oct 5	153	5b-6a	-15° to -10°F	1-7
Durango	May 27	Sep 23	118	6a-6b	-10° to -5°F	14-30
Fort Collins	May 5	Oct 1	148	5b	-15° to -10°F	7-14
Grand Junction	May 2	Oct 12	162	6b-7a	-5° to 0°F	61-90
Connecticut						
Bridgeport	Apr 12	Oct 28	198	7a	0° to 5°F	14-30
Danbury	May 4	Oct 7	155	6a-6b	-10° to -5°F	30-45
Hartford	May	Oct 8	159	6b	-5° to 0°F	30-45
Stamford	Apr 30	Oct 11	163	6b-7a	-5° to 0°F	14-30
Delaware						
Dover	Apr 11	Oct 29	200	7a	0° to 5°F	15-30
Laurel	Apr 22	Oct 18	178	7a	0° to 5°F	15-30
Milford	Apr 17	Oct 20	185	7a	0° to 5°F	31-45
Wilmington	Apr 12	Nov 1	202	7a	0° to 5°F	1-7
Florida						
Jacksonville	Feb 17	Dec 10	295	8b	15° to 20°F	91-120
Miami	infrequent	frost	365	11a	40° to 45°F	91-120
Orlando	Jan 29	Jan 1	336	9b	25° to 30°F	151-180
Tallahassee	Mar 29	Nov 9	224	8b	15° to 20°F	121-150
Tampa	Jan 17	Dec 27	333	9b-10a	25° to 30°F	121-150
Georgia						
Atlanta	Mar 29	Nov 13	228	7b-8a	0° to 5°F	61-90
Macon	Apr 1	Nov 2	214	8a	10° to 15°F	91-120
Savannah	Mar 15	Nov 20	249	8b	15° to 20°F	91-120
Tifton	Mar 18	Nov 14	240	8b	15° to 20°F	121-150
Hawaii						
Hilo	infrequent	frost	365	11b-12a	45° to 50°F	14-30
Honolulu	Infrequent	frost	365	11b-12a	45° to 50°F	14-30
Idaho						
Boise	May 7	Oct 7	152	6b-7a	-5° to 0°F	46-60

State and City	Average date of last frost (Based on 32°F at 50 percent probability)	Average date of first frost	Length of growing season—days	USDA Zone	Average extreme minimum	Days per year on average greater than 86°F
Coeur d'Alene	May 1	Oct 8	159	6b	-5° to 0°F	15-30
Idaho Falls	May 25	Sep 18	115	5a-5b	-20° to -15°F	31-45
Orofino	Apr 29	Oct 10	163	6a	-10° to -5F	61-90
Illinois						
Cairo	Apr 10	Oct 26	198	7a	0° to 5°F	61-90
Chicago	Apr 18	Oct 29	193	5b-6a	-15° to -10°F	14-30
Peoria	Apr 24	Oct 13	173	5b	-15° to -10°F	8-14
Springfield	Apr 23	Oct 9	168	5b-6a	-15° to -10°F	15-30
Indiana						
Bloomington	Apr 23	Oct 17	176	6a	-10° to -5°F	31-45
Evansville	Apr 8	Oct 31	205	6b	-5° to 0°F	91-120
Fort Wayne	May 1	Oct 9	160	5b-6a	-15° to -10°F	14-30
Indianapolis	Apr 25	Oct 14	171	5b-6a	-15° to -10°F	14-30
Iowa						
Cedar Rapids	Apr 30	Oct 5	157	5a	-20° to -15°F	
Des Moines	Apr 23	Oct 11	170	5a	-20° to -15°F	30-45
Mason City	May 6	Sep 27	143	5a	-20° to -15°F	14-30
Sioux City	May 3	Sep 28	147	4b	-25° to -20°F	45-60
Kansas						
Colby	May 5	Oct 3	150	5b	-15° to -10°F	60-90
Concordia	Apr 24	Oct 11	169	6a	-10° to -5°F	60-90
Topeka	Apr 19	Oct 11	174	6a	-10° to -5°F	60-90
Wichita	Apr 12	Oct 26	196	6b	-5° to 0°F	90-120
Kentucky						
Corbin	Apr 22	Oct 16	176	6a	-10° to -5°F	45-60
Lexington	Apr 20	Oct 21	183	6b	-5° to 0°F	45-60
Louisville	Apr 10	Oct 30	202	7a	0° to 5°F	60-90
Paducah	Apr 10	Oct 27	199	6b	-5° to 0°F	60-90
Louisiana						
Baton Rouge	Mar 8	Nov 23	259	8b	15° to 20°F	
Lake Charles	Mar 1	Dec 1	274	9a	20° to 25°F	120-150
New Orleans	Feb 17	Dec 12	297	8b	15° to 20°F	120-150
Shreveport	Mar 16	Nov 14	242	8b	15° to 20°F	120-150
Maine						
Bangor	May 11	Sep 30	141	5a	-20° to -15°F	7-14

State and City	Average date of last frost (Based on 32°F at 50 percent probability)	Average date of first frost	Length of growing season—days	USDA Zone	Average extreme minimum	Days per year on average greater than 86°F
Fort Kent	May 31	Sep 16	107	3b	-35° to -30°F	7-14
Jackman	May 29	Sep 19	112	4a	-30° to -25°F	1-7
Portland	May 5	Oct 5	152	4b	-25° to -20°F	7-14
Maryland						
Baltimore	Mar 27	Nov 17	234	7b-81	5°F to 10°F	45-60
Cumberland	Apr 20	Oct 16	178	6a-6b	-10° to -5°F	45-60
Salisbury	Apr 10	Nov 1	204	7b	5°F to 10°F	60-90
Massachusetts						
Amherst	May 13	Sep 30	139	5a	-20° to -15°F	7-14
Boston	Apr 10	Nov 3	206	6b-7a	-5° to 0°F	14-30
Hyannis	Apr 30	Oct 18	170	7a	0° to 5°F	14-30
Pittsfield	May 14	Sep 30	138	5a-5b	-20° to -15°F	7-14
Worcester	Apr 28	Oct 13	167	5b-6a	-15° to -10°F	30-45
Michigan						
Detroit	Apr 23	Oct 23	182	6a-6b	-10° to -5°F	30-45
Grand Rapids	May 5	Oct 8	156	5b	-15° to -10°F	7-14
Houghton	May 28	Sep 25	119	5a-5b	-20° to -15°F	1-7
Lansing	May 9	Oct 4	147	5b	-15° to -10°F	14-30
Traverse City	May 27	Oct 1	126	5b	-15° to -10°F	7-14
Minnesota						
Duluth	May 25	Sep 22	119	4a-4b	-30° to -25°F	1-7
Mankato	May 6	Sep 29	145	4b	-25° to -20°F	30-45
Minneapolis	Apr 29	Oct 8	161	4b-5a	-25° to -20°F	30-45
Moorhead	May 10	Sep 28	140	4a	-30° to -25°F	30-45
Mississippi						
Biloxi	Mar 1	Dec 4	277	8b	15° to 20°F	90-120
Jackson	Mar 19	Nov 11	236	8a	10° to 15°F	120-150
Tupelo	Apr 5	Oct 29	206	7b	0° to 5°F	90-120
Vicksburg	Mar 28	Nov 7	223	8a	10° to 15°F	120-150
Missouri						
Jefferson City	Apr 14	Oct 21	189	6a	-10° to -5°F	60-90
Kansas City	Apr 11	Oct 28	199	6a-6b	-10° to -5°F	60-90
Saint Joseph	Apr 22	Oct 6	166	5b-6a	-15° to -10°F	60-90
St Louis	Apr 15	Oct 18	185	6b	-5° to 0°F	60-90
Springfield	Apr 20	Oct 17	179	6b	-5° to 0°F	60-90

State and City	Average date of last frost (Based on 32°F at 50 percent probability)	Average date of first frost	Length of growing season—days	USDA Zone	Average extreme minimum	Days per year on average greater than 86°F
Montana						
Billings	May 14	Sep 25	133	4b-5a	-25° to -20°F	30-45
Bozeman	Jun 6	Sep 12	97	4b	-25° to -20°F	14-30
Great Falls	May 25	Sep 17	114	4a	-30° to -25°F	14-30
Helena	May 19	Sep 20	123	4a-4b	-30° to -25°F	7-14
Nebraska						
Chadron	May 22	Sep 19	119	4b	-25° to -20°F	45-60
North Platte	May 6	Sep 30	146	5a	-20° to -15°F	60-90
Ogallala	May 7	Sep 30	145	5b	-15° to -10°F	60-90
Omaha	Apr 27	Oct 5	160	5b	-15° to -10°F	60-90
Nevada						
Carson City	May 28	Sep 26	120	6b-7a	-5° to 0°F	45-60
Las Vegas	Feb 15	Nov 27	284	9a	20° to 25°F	150-180
Reno	May 9	Oct 15	158	7a	0° to 5°F	45-60
Winnemucca	Jun 27	Sep 18	113	6a-6b	-10° to -5°F	60-90
New Hampshire						
Berlin	May 20	Sep 24	126	4b	-25° to -20°F	1-7
Concord	May 19	Sep 24	127	5a-5b	-20° to -15°F	14-30
Grafton	Jun 3	Sep 7	95	4b	-25° to -20°F	14-30
New Jersey						
Cape May	Apr 9	Nov 3	207	7b	0° to 5°F	30-45
New Brunswick	Apr 24	Oct 16	174	6b-7a	-5° to 0°F	30-45
Toms River	Apr 19	Oct 16	179	6b-7a	-5° to 0°F	45-60
New Mexico						
Albuquerque	Apr 15	Oct 30	197	7b	5°F to 10°F	45-60
Roswell	Apr 10	Oct 29	201	7a-7b	0° to 5°F	90-120
Ruidoso	May 18	Oct 1	135	6b	-5F to 0°F	
Santa Fe	May 20	Oct 1	133	5b-6a	-15° to -10°F	14-30
New York						
Albany	May 4	Oct 5	153	5b-6a	-15° to -10°F	14-30
Binghamton	May 5	Oct 4	151	5b-6a	-15° to -10°F	7-14
Bridgehampton	Apr 26	Oct 17	173	7a	0° to 5°F	
Buffalo	May 7	Oct 6	151	6a	-10° to -5°F	7-14
Lake Placid	Jun 6	Sep 9	94	4a	-30° to -25°F	

State and City	Average date of last frost (Based on 32°F at 50 percent probability)	Average date of first frost	Length of growing season—days	USDA Zone	Average extreme minimum	Days per year on average greater than 86°F
North Carolina						
Asheville	Apr 16	Oct 22	188	6b	-5° to 0°F	45-60
Charlotte	Apr 11	Oct 28	199	7b-8a	5° to 10°F	60-90
Fayetteville	Apr 8	Nov 3	208	8a	10° to 15°F	90-120
Raleigh	Apr 8	Oct 29	203	7b-8a	5° to 10°F	90-120
Wilmington	Mar 27	Nov 13	230	8a	10° to 15°F	60-90
North Dakota						
Bismarck	May 19	Sep 19	122	4a	-30° to -25°F	30-45
Fargo	May 10	Sep 28	140	4a	-30° to -25°F	14-30
Minot	May 15	Sep 24	131	4a	-30° to -25°F	
Williston	May 27	Sep 14	109	4a	-30° to -25°F	45-60
Ohio						
Cincinnati	Apr 23	Oct 16	175	6a	-10° to -5°F	30-45
Cleveland	Apr 13	Nov 4	204	5b-6b	-15° to -10°F	14-30
Columbus	Apr 29	Oct 8	161	6a	-10° to -5°F	30-45
Toledo	Apr 23	Oct 24	183	6b	-5° to 0°F	
Youngstown	May 8	Oct 10	154	6a	-10° to -5°F	
Oklahoma						
Lawton	Apr 3	Nov 1	211	7b	0° to 5°F	90-120
Miami	Apr 12	Oct 21	191	6a	-10° to -5°F	60-90
Oklahoma City	Apr 3	Nov 3	213	7a	0° to 5°F	90-120
Tulsa	Apr 4	Nov 1	210	7a	0° to 5°F	90-120
Oregon						
Bend	Year round frost possible			6b	-5° to 0°F	45-60
Eugene	Apr 29	Oct 14	167	8a	10° to 15°F	14-30
Medford	May 5	Oct 3	150	8a	10° to 15°F	30-45
Portland	Mar 11	Nov 22	255	8b	15° to 20°F	14-30
Salem	Apr 28	Oct 19	173	8a	10° to 15°F	14-30
Pennsylvania						
Erie	May 1	Oct 26	177	6b	-5° to 0°F	14-30
Harrisburg	May 15	Oct 20	187	7a	0° to 5°F	45-60
Philadelphia	Apr 5	Nov 11	219	7a-7b	0° to 5°F	30-45
Pittsburgh	Apr 23	Oct 19	178	6b	-5° to 0°F	14-30
Scranton	May 2	Oct 7	157	6a	-10° to -5°F	14-30

State and City	Average date of last frost (Based on 32°F at 50 percent probability)	Average date of first frost	Length of growing season—days	USDA Zone	Average extreme minimum	Days per year on average greater than 86°F
Rhode Island						
Kingston	May 12	Oct 2	142	6b	-5° to 0°F	14-30
Newport	Apr 23	Nov 4	194	6b	-5° to 0°F	14-30
Providence	Apr 19	Oct 19	182	6a	-10° to -5°F	14-30
South Carolina						
Charleston	Feb 19	Dec 15	298	8b-9a	15° to 20°F	60-90
Columbia	Mar 23	Nov 14	235	8a	10° to 15°F	90-120
Greenville	Apr 3	Nov 5	215	8a	10° to 15°F	60-90
Myrtle Beach	Mar 31	Nov 5	218	8b	15° to 20°F	90-120
South Dakota						
Huron	May 10	Sep 25	137	4b	-25° to -20°F	60-90
Pierre	May 8	Sep 26	140	4b	-25° to -20°F	14-30
Rapid City	May 7	Oct 1	146	5a	-20° to -15°F	30-45
Sioux Falls	May 9	Sept 24	137	4b	-25° to -20°F	60-90
Tennessee						
Knoxville	Apr 18	Oct 24	188	6b	-5° to 0°F	45-60
Memphis	Mar 27	Nov 8	225	7b-8a	0° to 5°F	90-120
Nashville	Apr 12	Oct 28	198	7a	0° to 5°F	60-90
Sewanee	Apr 16	Oct 26	192	7a	0° to 5°F	
Texas						
Amarillo	Apr 21	Oct 18	179	7a	0° to 5°F	90-120
Austin	Mar 1	Nov 30	273	8b	15° to 20°F	120-150
Brownsville	Jan 25	Dec 30	355	9b	25° to 30°F	180-210
Corpus Christi	Feb 17	Dec 8	293	9b	25° to 30°F	150-180
Dallas	Mar 12	Nov 22	254	8a-8b	10° to 15°F	120-150
El Paso	Mar 25	Nov 8	227	8a-8b	10° to 15°F	120-150
Houston	Feb 17	Dec 10	295	9a	20° to 25°F	150-180
Utah						
Blanding	May 4	Oct 14	162	6b-7a	-5° to 0°F	60-90
Logan	May 17	Sep 26	131	5b-6a	-15° to -10°F	60-90
Salt Lake City	Apr 20	Oct 31	193	6b	-5° to 0°F	60-90
Vernal	May 15	Sept 28	135	5b	-15° to -10°F	45-60
Vermont						
Burlington	May 10	Oct 3	145	4b	-25° to -20°F	7-14

State and City	Average date of last frost (Based on 32°F at 50 percent probability)	Average date of first frost	Length of growing season—days	USDA Zone	Average extreme minimum	Days per year on average greater than 86°F
Chelsea	Jun 2	Sep 12	101	4a	-30° to -25°F	14-30
Montpelier	May 21	Sep 24	125	4a	-30° to -25°F	14-30
Virginia						
Alexandria	Apr 2	Nov 10	221	7a-7b	0° to 5°F	60-90
Norfolk	Mar 20	Nov 27	251	8a	10° to 15°F	30-45
Richmond	Apr 10	Oct 30	202	7a-7b	0° to 5°F	60-90
Roanoke	Apr 15	Oct 21	188	6b-7a	-5° to 0°F	45-60
Washington						
Olympia	May 4	Oct 6	154	8a-8b	10° to 15°F	7-14
Seattle	Mar 17	Nov 16	243	8b	15° to 20°F	7-14
Spokane	May 10	Oct 4	146	6a-6b	-10° to -5°F	45-60
Walla Walla	Apr 8	Oct 21	195	6b	-5° to 0°F	45-60
West Virginia						
Charleston	Apr 23	Oct 18	177	6b	-5° to 0°F	30-45
Lewisburg	May 14	Sep 28	136	6a	-10° to -5°F	14-30
Martinsburg	Apr 28	Oct 9	163	6b	-5° to 0°F	14-30
Parkersburg	Apr 23	Oct 20	179	6b	-5° to 0°F	45-60
Wisconsin						
Eau Claire	May 12	Sep 28	138	4a	-30° to -25°F	14-30
Green Bay	May 11	Sep 29	140	4b	-25° to -20°F	14-30
Madison	Apr 28	Oct 8	162	5a	-20° to -15°F	45-60
Milwaukee	Apr 29	Oct 17	170	5b	-15° to -10°F	30-45
Wyoming						
Casper	May 31	Sep 16	107	4b-5a	-25° to -20°F	45-60
Cheyenne	May 18	Sep 24	128	5a	-20° to -15°F	45-60
Rock Springs	Jun 6	Sep 13	98	5a	-20° to -15°F	14-30
Sheridan	May 31	Sep 17	108	4a	-30° to -25°F	45-60

State and City	Average date of last frost (Based on 32°F at 50 percent probability)	Average date of first frost	Length of growing season—days	USDA Zone	Average extreme minimum	Days per year on average greater than 86°F
Canada						
Alberta						
Calgary	May 29	Sep 6	99	4a	-30° to -25°F	
Edmonton	May 15	Sep 16	123	3b	-35° to -30°F	
Lethbridge	May 25	Sep 11	108	4b	-25° to -20°F	
Medicine Hat	May 18	Sep 14	118	4b	-25° to -20°F	
Red Deer	May 24	Sep 10	108	4a	-30° to -25°F	
British Columbia						
Chilliwack	Apr 19	Oct 28	191	8b	15° to 20°F	
Nanaimo	May 4	Oct 15	163	8b	15° to 20°F	
Vancouver	Apr 21	Oct 19	180	8b	15° to 20°F	
Victoria	Apr 14	Nov 9	208	9a	20° to 25°F	
New Brunswick						
Bathhurst	May 30	Sep 21	113	4b	-25° to -20°F	
Edmundston	May 21	Sep 1	122	4a	-30° to -25°F	
Saint John	Apr 30	Oct 13	165	5b	-15° to -10°F	
Nova Scotia						
Halifax	May 8	Oct 20	164	6b	-5° to 0°F	
Kentville	May 26	Sep 26	122	6a	-10° to -5°F	
Truro	Jun 7	Sep 19	103	5b	-15° to -10°F	
Ontario						
Hamilton	May 3	Oct 11	160	6b	-5° to 0°F	
Ottawa	May 13	Sep 26	135	5b	-15° to -10°F	
Windsor	Apr 28	Oct 18	168	7a	0° to 5°F	
Quebec						
Montreal	Apr 25	Oct 11	168	6a	-10° to -5°F	
Quebec City	May 12	Sep 28	138	5a	-20° to -15°F	
Sherbrooke	May 27	Sep 20	115	5a	-20° to -15°F	
Trois-Rivieres	May 19	Sep 25	128	5a	-20° to -15°F	
Saskatchewan						
Moose Jaw	May 24	Sep 12	110	3b	-35° to -30°F	
Prince Albert	Jun 7	Sep 4	88	3a	-40° to -45°F	
Regina	Jun 1	Sep 1	91	3b	-35° to -30°F	
Saskatoon	May 15	Sept 19	126	3b	-35° to -30°F	
Swift Current	May 23	Sept 13	112	4a	-30° to -25°F	

European Hardiness Zones

City	Zone	City	Zone
Alicante, Spain	10a	Almeria, Spain	10b
Amsterdam, The Netherlands	8b	Antwerp, Belgium	8
Barcelona, Spain	10a	Belfast, Northern Ireland	9
Berlin, Germany	7b	Bratislava, Slovakia	7b
Birmingham, England	9a	Bucharest, Romania	6b
Cadiz, Spain	10a	Cardiff, Wales	9
Belgrade, Serbia	8a	Copenhagen, Denmark	8a
Dublin, Ireland	9a	Dűsseldorf, Germany	8
Edinburgh, Scotland	8b	Gdańsk, Poland	7
Glasgow, Scotland	8b	Hamburg, Germany	8a
Helsinki, Finland	6a	Istanbul, Turkey	8b
Kaliningrad, Russia	6	Kiev, Ukraine	6a
Krakow, Poland	6	Lisbon, Portugal	10b
Ljubljana, Slovenia	7b	London, England	9b
Madrid, Spain	8b	Málaga, Spain	10a
Marseille, France	9a	Milan, Italy	8b
Minsk, Belarus	5b	Moscow, Russia	5a
Munich, Germany	7b	Murmansk, Russia	5
Nicosia, Cyprus	10b	Oslo, Norway	6a
Simferopol, Ukraine	7a	Palma, Spain	10a
Prague, Czech Republic	7a	Reykjavik, Iceland	8a
Riga, Latvia	6a	Rome, Italy	9b
Rovaniemi, Finland	4	Saint Petersburg, Russia	5b
Sarajevo, Bosnia and Herzegovina	7b	Santander, Spain	10a
Sicily (Catania, Italy)	10b	Simrishamn, Sweden	8a
Sochi, Russia	9	Sofia, Bulgaria	7a
Stockholm, Sweden	6b	Strasbourg, France	7
Tallinn, Estonia	6b	Trabzon, Turkey	9
Tbilisi, Georgia	8	Tuapse, Russia	8
Tôrshavn, Faroe Islands	7-8	Tromsø, Norway	7
Trondheim, Norway	6	Umeâ, Sweden	5
Valencia, Spain	10a	Valletta, Malta	11a
Vienna, Austria	8a	Vilnius, Lithuania	6
Vorkuta, Russia	2	Warsaw, Poland	6b
Wroclaw, Poland	7a	Zagreb, Croatia	8a
Zurich, Switzerland	8a	Zaragoza, Spain	9a

Appendix 4

Reverse Season
Gardening

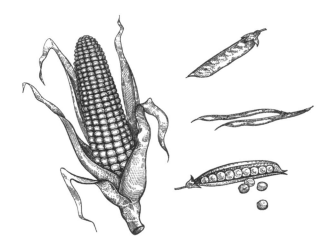

Reverse Season Vegetable Gardening

Sun Belt and reverse-season gardens. A reverse season garden is one that comes to harvest before the heat and drought of summer. Many gardens in the Sun Belt (most of Florida, the Deep South, Texas, parts of the Southwest, and parts of Southern California) are reverse-season gardens. In the Sun Belt where there is little or no frost and long, hot summers choose varieties that can be sown indoors or directly in the garden from mid to late winter. Gardens in these regions often have "two springs"—one in late spring and the other in autumn; not even all warm-season crops can withstand the summer heat in some Sun Belt regions.

Sun Belt garden planning. Where summers are long and hot—like most places in the Sun Belt—adjust your spring and autumn planting calendars according to when the last frost comes in spring (or even late winter) and when the first frost comes in autumn (or early winter). If you live in a very mild winter region, your autumn and spring may run together and might best be simply called the cool season. Summer may be the time when no crops grow in the vegetable garden where you live—temperatures are simply too hot. Here are a few suggestions for Sun Belt vegetable gardeners:

- Plant cool-season crops so that they come to harvest before temperatures average greater than 75°F.
- Plant cool-season crops again in late summer or autumn so that they come to harvest when temperatures on average fall below 75°F and the sun is setting lower in the sky.
- Time spring (or late winter) planting of warm-season, fruiting crops so that they come to harvest before temperatures average 90°F or greater.
- Choose crop varieties with days to maturity that fit the window of temperature and growing opportunity. For example, a 55-day to harvest Early Girl tomato can be planted in early spring to reach harvest before temperatures on average are greater than 90°F.
- Plant in wide rows so that plants form a shady canopy over the soil; this will slow soil moisture evaporation and keep roots cool.
- Use windbreaks to protect crops from hot winds that sap plants and soil of moisture.
- Limit the planting of thirsty plants during the heat of the year; celery, corn, potatoes, melons, cucumbers, and squash demand uninterrupted moisture. If you plant these crops in hot weather regions, mulch the soil to stem soil moisture evaporation.
- Avoid side-dressing plants with fertilizer during the warmest time of the year; fertilizers can cause roots to grow close to the surface and become dependent on regular watering. Use aged-compost as a side dressing.
- Add aged compost to planting beds twice a year. Aged compost holds soil moisture around deep plant roots.

Reverse Season Planting Schedule:

Warm-Season Crops:

Crop	Gulf Coast & Southwest	Southern Florida	Southern California
Beans, lima	Mar-Apr	Oct-Apr	Apr-July
Beans, pole	Mar-Apr	Jan-Feb	Apr-July
Beans, snap	Mar-Apr	Oct-Mar	Mar-July
Corn, sweet	Mar-Apr	Jan-Feb	Mar-July
Cucumber	Mar-Apr	Jan-Feb	Apr-June
Eggplant*	Mar-Apr	Dec-Feb	Apr-June
Okra	Mar-May	Feb-Mar	Apr-June
Peas, southern	Mar-May	Feb-Mar	
Peppers	Mar-Apr	Jan-Feb	Apr-May
Pumpkin	Apr	Mar	June
Squash, summer	Mar-Apr	Jan-Feb	Apr-June
Squash, winter	Mar-Apr	Jan-Feb	Apr-June
Tomatoes	Mar-Apr	Oct-Mar	Mar-June

*transplants

Cool-Season Crops:

Crop	Gulf Coast & Southwest	Southern Florida	Southern California
Beets	Oct.-Feb.	Oct.-Feb.	All year
Broccoli*	Sept.-Jan.	Oct.-Jan.	Sept.-Feb.
Cabbage*	Oct-Jan	Oct.-Jan.	Sept.-Mar.
Carrots	Oct-Mar	Oct.-Feb.	Sept.-Jun.
Collards	Sept-Dec	Sept-Jan	Sept-Mar
Lettuce	Sept-Feb	Sept-Jan	All year
Mustard	Sept-Feb	Sept-Mar	Oct.-Mar
Onions	Oct-Feb	Sept-Mar	All year
Parsley	Dec-Jan	Sept-Jan	Oct.-Mar
Peas	Sept-Feb	Sept-Feb	Oct.-Mar
Radishes	Sept-Feb	Oct-Mar	All year
Spinach	Oct-Jan	Oct-Nov	Oct.-Feb.
Turnips	Sept-Feb	Oct-Feb	All year

*transplants

Appendix 5

Recommended Vegetable Varieties

Vegetable Varieties – Dependable Growers:

Crop	Favorites ("op" following variety name denotes open-pollinated plant)
Artichoke	• 'Green Globe': ready for harvest usually the second summer after seeding. • 'Imperial Star': produces the first season, 180 days from seed to harvest. • 'Violetto' has purplish, elongated buds.
Asparagus	• 'Martha Washington' and 'Mary Washington' are old-time varieties. • All-male varieties produce larger spears; they include 'Jersey Giant', 'Jersey Knight', 'Jersey Supreme', 'Greenwich', and 'UC 157'.
Beans	**Pole Snap:** • 'Blue Lake' (60 days) oval dark green pods, op • 'Kentucky Wonder' (70 days) 7-inch stringless pods, op • 'Kentucky Wonder Wax' (61 days) butter yellow pods, op • 'Romano' (75 days) flat, stringless pods, op • 'Scarlet Runner' (75 days) intense flavor, colorful flowers, op **Bush Snap:** • 'Bountiful' (55 days) flavorful, wide pods, op • 'Commodore' (60 days) AAS winner, compact plant, op • 'Contender' (49 days) stringless, tender pods, op • 'Tenderette' (58 days) stringless delicious pods, op • 'Tongues of Fire' (90 days) flame red steaks, good baked, op **Dry Beans:** • 'Dragon's Tongue' (60 days) tender, sweet, speckled, op • 'French Navy' (100 days) dry, stores well, op • 'Great Northern' (95 days) white, flat, kidney shape, op • 'Jacob's Cattle' (83 days) mottled, soup bean, op • 'Pinto' (95 days) high protein, Mexican dishes, op • 'Vermont Cranberry' (90 days) robust flavor, shell or dry, op
Beans, Lima	• 'Fordhook' 242 (75 days) AAS winner, heat-resistant, op • 'Henderson's Bush' (67 days) dwarf plant, big yield, op • 'Jackson Wonder' (66 days) good fresh or dried, op
Beets	• 'Albion' (50 days) white globe, spinach-like greens, op • 'Chioggia' (54 days) red and white rings, Italian heirloom, op • 'Crosby's Egyptian' (60 days—35 for greens) pickle or boil, op • 'Cylindra' (60 days) long, carrot-like, uniform slices, op • 'Detroit Dark Red' (55 days) round, dark red, AAS Selection, op • 'Early Wonder' (55 days) canner, grown for greens as well, op • 'Green Top Bunching' (55 days) bright red roots, tasty greens, op • 'Ruby Queen' (52 days) semi-round, dark red, AAS Selection, op
Broccoli	• 'Arcadia' (63 days) cold tolerant, good side shoot yield, hybrid • 'Belstar' (75 days) grows in warm winters, hybrid • 'DeCicco' (50-85 days) extended harvest choice, op • 'Green Comet' (55 days) AAS selections, spring plant, op • 'Premium Crop' (58 days) AAS winner, long harvest, hybrid • 'Waltham 29' (75 days) favorite for autumn harvest; op

Crop	Favorites ("op" following variety name denotes open-pollinated plant)
Brussels sprouts	• 'Catskill' (100 days) dwarf variety best for autumn growing, op • 'Diablo' (110 days) produces uniform, sweet sprouts, hybrid • 'Jade Cross' (90 days) early maturing, heat tolerant, hybrid • 'Long Island Improved' (90 days) short stalks, best for autumn growing, op
Cabbage	• 'Charleston Wakefield' (80 days) good grower in southeast, op • 'Danish Ballhead' (105) large, solid heads to 5 pounds, op • 'Early Flat Dutch' (85 days) heat tolerant, 6 pound heads, op • 'Early Jersey Wakefield' (63 days) early harvest, 3 pounds, op • 'Late Flat Dutch' (110 days) blue-green winter storage, op • 'Red Acre' (76 days) red-purple head, early harvest, op
Carrot	**Short (2 to 4 inches):** • 'Little Finger' (60 days) op • 'Minicor' (55 days) op • 'Minipak' (60-65 days) • 'Ox Heart' (75 days) op **Half-long (5 to 6 inches):** • 'Danvers Half-Long' (75 days) op • 'Gold King' (70 days) • 'Royal Chantenay' (70 days) op **Cylindircal (6 to 7 inches):** • 'Nantes Coreless' (68 days) • 'Royal Cross Hybrid' (70 days) • 'Tuchon Pioneer' (75 days) op **Standard (7 to 9 inches):** • 'Gold Pak' (75 days) • 'Imperator' (75 days) op • 'Spartan Bonus' (77 days) • 'Tendersweet' (75 days)
Cauliflower	Days to harvest after transplanting are given. • 'Early Snowball' (60 days) crisp, tender, 6-inches across, op • 'Self-Blanche' (70 days) 9-inch white head, op • 'Snow Crown' (50 days) white crown, tolerates frost, hybrid • 'Super Snowball' (55 days) firm, white heads to 8 inches, op
Celery	• 'Tango' (80 days) tender, flavorful stalks, op • 'Utah 52-70' (120 days) , crispy, foot-long stalks, op • 'Ventura' (80 days) disease tolerant, strong tender stalk, op
Chinese cabbage	• 'Michihili' (75 days) tender, use for stir fries, op • 'Rubicon' (52 days) sweet, tangy, blanched interior, hybrid
Collards	• 'Champion' (60 days) deep green leaves, cold tolerant, op • 'Georgia Blue Stem' (80 days) heat- and cold-resistant, succulent, op • 'Vates' (75 days) summer grower for autumn harvest, op

Crop	Favorites ("op" following variety name denotes open-pollinated plant)
Corn	• 'Bodacious' (75 days) yellow kernels, great flavor, hybrid • 'Country Gentleman' (90 days) white kernels, 7-inch ears, op • 'Golden Bantam' (83 days) yellow kernels, AAS winner, op • 'Golden Jubilee' (105 days) tender, yellow kernels, old hybrid • 'How Sweet It Is' (87 days) bi-color kernels, 7-inch ears, hybrid • 'Honey and Cream' (78 days) creamy bi-color, hybrid • 'Kandy Korn' (89 days) golden kernels, long season, hybrid • 'Peaches & Cream' (70 days) sugar enhanced, bi-color, hybrid • 'Silver Queen' (94 days) best white corn, 8-inch ears, hybrid • 'Sugar Buns' (72 days) juicy sweet yellow kernels, hybrid
Cucumber	**Slicing:** • 'Diva' (58 days), All-America winter, thin, no-peel skin, hybrid • 'Marketmore' 76 (76 days) favorite, straight slicer to 8 inches, op • 'Straight Eight' (60 days) heirloom, All-America selection, op • 'Tendergreen Burpless' (63 days) 6-8 inches, dark green, op **Pickling:** • 'Boston Pickling' (52 days) smooth fruit to 3 inches, op • 'Bush Pickle' (45 days) compact grower, fruit to 4 inches, hybrid • 'National Pickling' (52 days) 3 inch gherkins or 4 inches to slice, op **Container varieties:** 'Spacemaster' (60 days) bush type, dark green 8-inch fruit, op **Others:** 'Armenian' (70 days) fruit more than 12 inches 'Lemon' (64 days) yellow, 3 inches round, op 'Suyo Long' (61 days) Chinese origin, deep green to 15 inches, op 'White Wonder' (60 days) ivory white, 8-10 inches, op
Eggplant	Days to harvest after transplanting: **Bell-shaped eggplant:** • 'Black Beauty' (80 days) purple-black, 6-inch bell-shape standard, op • 'Florida Market' (85 days), old standard, purple bell-shaped, op **Long, cylindrical eggplant:** • 'Dusky' (61 days) 6-inch purple, short season, hybrid • 'Long Purple' (75 days) 12-inch long purple, op **Colorful eggplants:** • 'Casper' (70 days) white to 5 inches, wild mushroom flavor, op • 'Listada de Gandia' (75 days) white with purple stirpes, tender, op • 'Rosa Bianca' (75 days) round to 5 inches, light pink lavender, op
Garlic	• **Softneck garlic:** Soft, pliable neck at maturity is the strongest-flavored garlic and less winter hardy than hardneck. Varieties include: 'California White' (120 days), 'Red Toch' and 'Inchelium Red' (90-240 days)'. • **Harneck, also called Rocambole, and Spanish garlic:** Stiff central stem or neck which curls at the top forming a 360° coil, mild flavor, commonly left in the ground nearly a year before harvest. Varieties include: 'Brown Tempest', 'German Porcelain', 'Killarney Red', and 'Red German'; all are 240 days, autumn planted for summer harvest. • **Elephant garlic:** Not true garlic, a type of leek. Gets its name from fist-size bulbs weighing ½ pound or more. Mild flavor.

Crop	Favorites ("op" following variety name denotes open-pollinated plant)
Kale	• 'Blue Curled Scotch' (60 days) blue-green leaves, winter crop, op • 'Lacinato', also called 'Toscano' (65 days) crinkled green leaves, op • 'Red Russian' (60 days) leaves gray-green with purple veins, op • 'Winterbor' (60 days) compact clusters, very hardy, hybrid
Kohlrabi	• 'Early Purple Vienna' (60 days) standard, white flesh, op • 'Early White Vienna' (55 days) quick-maturing standard, op
Leeks	• 'American Flag' (120 days) cold tolerant, over-winter variety, op • 'Giant Musselburgh' (150 days) winter hardy favorite, op • 'King Richard' (75 days) early maturing for summer harvest, op
Lettuce	• 'Black-Seeded Simpson' (45 days) loose leaf, easy to grow, op • 'Buttercrunch' (75 days) butterhead, AAS winner, op • 'Cosmo' (55 days) tall savoy romaine, op • 'Little Gem' (50 days) tasty butterhead romaine, op • 'Lollo Rossa' (53 days) looseleaf, frilled red leaves, op • 'Marvel of Four Seasons' (55 days) butterhead, all seasons, op • 'Red Sails' (45 days) loose leaf, slow to bolt, AAS winner, op • 'Salad Bowl' (50 days) loose leaf, heat tolerant, AAS select, op • 'Sierra' (50 days) crisphead, red-tinged leaves, op • 'Tom Thumb' (60 days) butterhead, small heads, op • 'Winter Density' (58 days) butter-romaine, upright, op
Melons	**True Cantaloupe:** • 'Charentais' (85 days) small, super sweet French melon, op • 'Savor' (75 days) classic sweet French melon, hybrid **Muskmelon:** • 'Ambrosia' (86 days) sweet and juicy, lots of flesh, hybrid • 'Honey Bun' (73 days) sweet, 5 inches across, hybrid **Casaba:** • 'Casaba Golden Beauty' (105 days) spicy sweet white flesh, op • 'Sungold Casaba' (95 days) sweet flesh, early harvest, op **Crenshaw:** • 'Burpee's Early Hybrid' (90 days) pink fleshed, all regions **Honeydew:** • 'Earlidew' (80 days) creamy green flesh, hybrid • 'Golden Honeymoon' (92 days) green flesh, gold rind, op **Persian:** • 'Galia Diplomat' (80 days) aromatic green flesh, hybrid • 'Ha'ogen Israeli' (85 days) green flesh, fragrant, op • 'Small Persian' (115 days) orange flesh, op
Okra	• 'Blondy' (50 days) 6-inch pods, dwarf plant, AAS winner, op • 'Burgundy' (60 days) 6-inch pods, high yield, op • 'Clemson Spineless' (55 days) very popular, AAS winner, op • 'Perkins Long Pod' (60 days) 4-inch pods, high yield, op

Crop	Favorites ("op" following variety name denotes open-pollinated plant)
Onion	Onions are sensitive to day length. Long-day onions are best suited for northern regions where summer days are longest. Short-day onions are suited for southern regions where summer days are not as long as those in the north. American and Spanish onions are long day onions. Bermuda onions are short day onions. **Red:** • 'Desert Sunrise' (100 days) spicy, stores well, short day, hybrid • 'Red Baron' (65 days) purple-red bunching, hybrid • 'Red Long of Tropea' (90 days) mild flavor, op • 'Red Grano' (115 days) crisp mild flavor, short day, op • 'Ruby Red' (120 days) aromatic, stores well, long day, op • 'Southport Red Globe' (120 days) stores well, long day, op **Yellow or White:** • 'Alisa Craig' (110 days) large, round white, mild, long day, op • 'Candy' (100 days) sweet large yellow, intermediate day, hybrid • 'Copra' (104 days) yellow, best storage, long day, hybrid • 'Early Yellow Globe' (114 days) fresh eating, op • 'Evergreen Hardy White' (65 days) cold tolerant bunching, op • 'Southport White Globe' (110 days) versatile white, long day, op • 'Yellow Sweet Spanish' (110 days) sweet flavor, long day, op • 'Yellow Granex'—'Vidalia' (125 days) sweet, short day, hybrid • 'Walla Walla' (110-300 days) super sweet, long day, op • 'White Bermuda' (90 days) small white soup or pickle onions, op • 'White Ebenezer' (85 days) long-day white, eat raw, op
Parsnip	• 'All-American' (105 days) sweet, tender, small root, op • 'Harris Early Model' (120 days) snow white flesh, great flavor, op • 'Hollow Crown Improved' (135 days) smooth, sweet standard, op
Peas	**Short vines:** • 'Little Marvel' (62 days) sugary pods, small bush and pods, op • 'Sugar Ann' (52 days) 2-foot bush, 3-inch pods, AAS winner, op • 'Sugar Bon' (57 days) dwarf plant, large yield, op • 'Wando' (70 days) sweet, 8-inch pods, grows in all regions, op **Tall vines:** • 'Sugar Snap' (68 days) sweet 3-inch pods, AAS winner, op • 'Tall Telephone' also called 'Alderman' (75 days) sweet climber, op **Snow peas:** • 'Dwarf Gray Sugar' (65 days) compact plant, thrives in cool, op • 'Mammoth Melting Sugar' (69 days) long pod, best in cool weather, op • 'Oregon Sugar Pod' (65 days) tender, large pod snow pea, op

Crop	Favorites ("op" following variety name denotes open-pollinated plant)
Peppers, Hot	Hot peppers are rated by their heat–called Scoville heat units (SHU). The greater the SHU the hotter the pepper. Days to harvest after transplanting are given. **Mildly Hot (500 SHU plus):** • 'Anaheim' (80 days) used in Mexican food, op • 'Pepperoncini' (70 days) good yield even in cool regions, op **Medium Hot (1,000 SKU plus):** • 'Pablano' or 'Ancho' (100 days) called Ancho when dried, op • 'Hungarian Wax' (65 days) sweet hot pepper, op **Hot (2,500 SHU plus):** • 'Jalapeño' (75 days) pleasant hot pepper, op • 'Serrano' (80 days) not overpowering hot, op • 'Long Red Cayenne' (90 days) very hot, used in sauces, op • 'Tabasco' (80 days) very hot, smoky flavor, op • 'Thai Chile' (90 days) fiery hot, hybrid **Very Hot (100,000 SHU plus):** • 'Chiltepin' (95 days) pea size, very hot, op • 'Jamaican Hot' (95 days) fruity hot flavor, op • 'Habanero' (90 days) intense heat, op **Extremely Hot:** • 'Scotch Bonnet' (120 days) smoky hot flavor, op • 'Bhut Jolokia' also called 'Ghost Pepper' (100 days) hottest, op
Peppers, Sweet	Days to harvest after transplanting are given. **Blocky sweet peppers:** • 'Ace' (55 days) high yield, tolerates cool weather, hybrid • 'Bell Boy' (75 days) glossy, blocky, AAS winner, hybrid • 'Bull Nose' (75 days) delicious for salads, op • 'California Wonder' (73 days) stuffing pepper, op • 'Chocolate Bell' (75 days) sweet flavor, deep color, op • 'Emerald Giant' (74 days) sweet, heavy yield, op • 'Yankee Bell' (80 days) sweet, grows in northern regions, op • 'Yolo Wonder' (73 days) thick wall, heavy yield, op **Long sweet peppers and others:** • 'Cubanelle' (62 days) mild, rich flavor, long, op • 'Gypsy' (65 days) sweet yellow cone shape, AAS selection, hybrid • 'Jimmy Nardello' (90 days) mild Italian, frying pepper op • 'Pimento' (65-80 days) mild cherry, op • 'Sweet Banana' (80 days) sweet, mild, AAS winner, op

Crop	Favorites ("op" following variety name denotes open-pollinated plant)
Potatoes	**Russet**, also called Idaho, baking potato: • 'Burbank' (80 days) • 'Butte' (130 days) • 'Norkotah' **Fingerling**: • 'French Fingerling' (100 days) • 'Purple Peruvian' • 'Red Thumb' • 'Russian Banana' (120 days) **Yellow**: round to slightly oblong, thin, yellowish skin, and buttery yellow flesh; boil, steam, mash, roast, and grill. • 'Yukon Gold' (100 days) op • 'Yellow Finn' (85 days) op • 'German Butterball' (110 days) op **Round white**: medium-sized, light tan to freckled brown skin, waxy to creamy textured flesh; boil, roast, fry, and mash. • 'Katahdin' • 'Kennebec' (80 days) • 'Superior' (90 days) **Round red** also called boiling potato: medium-sized, dense, crisp white flesh; boil, roast, grill. • 'Norland' (85 days) op • 'Pontiac' (80 days) op • 'Red Gold' (65 days) op **Others to grow:** • 'All Blue' (130 days) blue skin, op • 'Caribe' (70 days) purple skin • 'Carola' (late season) yellow flesh
Pumpkin	• 'Atlantic Giant' (125 days) up to 200 pounds, op • 'Big Max' (120 days) up to 100 pounds, op • 'Connecticut Field' (120 days) 15-25 pounds, op • 'Howden' (115 days) up to 25 pounds, op • 'Jack O'Lantern' (115 days) 10-20 pounds, op • 'Sugar Pie' (100 days) 4-5 pounds, op
Radish	• 'Champion' (25 days) crisp, round, scarlet, AAS winner, op • 'Cherry Belle' (22 days) mild flavor, op • 'Easter Egg' (30 days) multicolored, crisp crunchy, op • 'French Breakfast' (28 days) long and cylindrical heirloom, op • 'Miyashige' (50 days) long, white daikon, autumn harvest, op • 'Round Black Spanish' (55 days) black skin white flesh, late harvest, op
Rutabaga	• 'American Purple Top' (90 days) large root, sweet flavor, op • 'Champion Purple Top' (80 days) mild, sweet, op • 'Laurentian' (90 days) good flavor, stores well, op
Spinach	• 'America' (52 days) crumpled leaves, bolt resistant, op • 'Bloomsdale Long Standing' (43 days) market favorite, op • 'Noble Giant' (45 days) large, thick leaves, op • Malabar spinach (70 days) summer climber, spinach substitute • New Zealand spinach (70 days) hot weather spinach substitute

Crop	Favorites ("op" following variety name denotes open-pollinated plant)
Summer Squash	**Patty pan scallop:** • 'Benning's Green Tint' (55 days) light green skin, op • 'Peter Pan' (50 days) productive, excellent flavor, AAS winner, hybrid • 'Sunburst' (52 days) buttery flavor, AAS winner, hybrid • 'Scallopini' (52 days) sweet, meaty AAS-winner, hybrid • 'Early White Bush' (55 days) tender, high yield, op **Yellow straight- and crook-necked:** • 'Early Prolific Straighneck' (55 days) excellent flavor, AAS winner, hybrid • 'Sundance' (52 days) creamy flesh, very good flavor, hybrid • 'Early Golden Summer Crookneck' also called 'Yellow Crookneck' (55 days) mild flavor, very productive, op • 'Dixie' (45 days) delicious, small crooked neck, hybrid **Zucchini type:** • 'Aristocrat' (53 days) slender green, AAS winner, hybrid • 'Ambassador' (51 days) tender, compact bush, high yield, hybrid • 'Burpee Fordhook' (57 days) vigorous bush, AAS winner, op • 'Cocozelle' (55 days) pale greenish-white skin, dark green stripes, op • 'Costata Romanesco' (52 days) ribbed, Italian heirloom, op • 'Dark Green' (50 days) 6-8 inches, reliable, op • 'Gold Rush' (52 days) long, golden yellow, AAS winner, hybrid • 'Greyzini' (55 days) grayish-green, mottled fruit, AAS winner, hybrid • 'Ronde de Nice' (50 days) round green, op
Winter Squash	**Acorn squash:** • 'Table King' (80 days) yellow orange flesh, excellent flavor, op • 'Table Queen' (85 days) tender, moderately sweet, op **Buttercup squash:** • 'Buttercup' (105 days) deep orange flesh, sweet flavor, op • 'Emerald' (90 days) orange-yellow sweet flesh, short vine, op • 'Sweet Mama' (100 days) sweet, nutty, AAS selection, hybrid **Butternut squash:** • 'Early Butternut' (80 days) good flavor, bush, AAS winner, hybrid • 'Waltham Butternut' (100 days) sweet, AAS winner, op **Hubbard squash:** • 'Baby Blue Hubbard' (90 days) dry, sweet, flat round fruit, op • 'Blue Hubbard' (120 days) large globular, dry sweet flesh, op **Spaghetti squash:** • 'Spaghetti' (100 days) stranded flesh for baking, op • 'Tivoli Spaghetti' (100 days) noodle-like flesh, bush, hybrid **Other winter squash:** • 'Delicata' (92 days) sweet, rich, cylindrical, deep orange, op • 'Golden Cushaw' (115 days) bulbous, salmon flesh, op • 'Golden Delicious' (100 days) orange-yellow flesh, heart-shaped, op • 'Kabocha' (105 days) rich sweet, fiberless flesh, hybrid • 'Pink Banana' (105 days) sweet for pies, large cylindrical, op • 'Red Kuri' (95 days) sweet, rich, globular shape. op • 'Sweet Dumpling' (100 days) sweet tender, striped globe, op • 'Turk's Turban' (110 days) tender, juicy, turban shaped, op

Crop	Favorites ("op" following variety name denotes open-pollinated plant)
Swiss Chard	• 'Bright Lights' (55 days) vivid red and yellow leaves, op • 'Fordhook' (60 days) AAS winner, dark green white ribs, op • 'Lucullus' (60 days) white stalks, op • 'Ruby Red' (55 days) bright red stalks, green leaves, op
Tomatillo	• 'Purple' (83 days) sweet, cherry size, purple skin, op • 'Rio Grande Verde' (83 days) large fruit, rich flavor, op
Tomato	Days to harvest after transplanting are given. **Salad tomatoes** (hold shape when sliced): • 'Black Krim' (80 days) reddish brown-purple, bold flavor, op, ID • 'Brandywine' (80 days) exceptional rich flavor, Amish heirloom, op, ID • 'Costoluto Fiorentino' (80 days) terrific tomato taste, Italian heirloom, op, ID • 'Delicious' (77 days) meaty, excellent flavor, op, ID • 'German Pink' (85 days) meaty, almost seedless, German heirloom, op, ID • 'Green Grape' (80 days) sweet, juicy, op, ID • 'Marglobe' (75 days) thick wall, sweet flesh, hybrid, D • 'Marmande' (70 days) rich flavor, French heirloom, op, SD • 'Oregon Spring' (60 days) excellent flavor, grow in cool regions, hybrid, D • 'Pearson' (80 days) acid tomato flavor, grow in dry regions, op, D • 'Red Cherry' (65 days) sweet flavor, heirloom, op, SD • 'Red Pear' (75 days) mild flavor, 1 inch diameter, op, ID • 'Sweet 100' (65 days) extremely sweet, hybrid, ID • 'Yellow Pear' (75 days) mild, sweet flavor, op, ID **Salsa tomatoes** (plump, meaty, for chopping): • 'Big Boy' (78 days) meaty flesh, great flavor, hybrid, ID • 'Druzba' (80 days) sweet-tart flavor, Bulgarian heirloom, op, ID • 'Green Zebra' (80 days) green flesh, mild flavor, op, ID • 'Stupice' (52 days) sweet, early to harvest, Czechoslovakian heirloom, op, ID **Sandwich-slicing tomatoes** (big, meaty beefsteak tomato for slicing): • 'Arkansas Traveler' (80 days) sweet-tart flavor, op, ID • 'Aunt Ruby's German Giant' (85 days) fruity sweet green beefsteak, op, ID • 'Beefsteak' ('Red Ponderosa') (90 days) sweet flavor, thick flesh, op, ID • 'Box Car Willie' (80 days) delicious tomato flavor, American heirloom, op, ID • 'Celebrity' (70 days) firm, excellent flavor, AAS selection, hybrid, SD • 'Cherokee Purple' (80 days) sweet, rich, Tennessee heirloom, op, ID • 'Hillbilly' (85 days) sweet, fruity flavor, West Virginia heirloom, op, ID • 'Lemon Boy' (72 days) yellow, mild flavor, hybrid, ID • 'Mortgage Lifter' (85 days) sweet, meaty, West Virginia heirloom, op ID • 'Oxheart' (85 days) heart-shaped, solid flesh, few seeds, op, ID • 'Pineapple' (90 days) red, yellow stripes, meaty, op, ID • 'Tappy's Finest' (77 days) large, pink , meaty, op, ID • Tigerella (56 days) reddish-orange-yellow stripes, op, ID • 'White Wonder' (85 days) creamy white flesh, sweet, firm, op, ID **Sauce tomatoes** (balance between flesh and juice): • 'Juliet' (60 days) full tomato flavor, AAS selection, hybrid, ID • 'San Marzano' (80 days) meaty texture. Italian heirloom, op, ID 'Roma' (80 days) classic sauce tomato, op, D **Soup tomatoes** (ripe and deep flavor): • 'Principe Borghese' (75 days) meaty, little juice, few seeds, op, D • 'San Marzano' (80 days) mild flavor, meaty texture, op, ID • 'Rutgers' (80 days) created by Campbell's Soup Company, op, D

Crop	Favorites ("op" following variety name denotes open-pollinated plant)
Turnip	• 'Hakurei' (38 days) tender, white root, flavorful, eat raw, hybrid • 'Purple Top White Globe' (57 days) long-time favorite, flavorful, op • 'Seven Top' (45 days, greens) grown for its greens, a favorite, op • 'White Egg' (50 days) white root, excellent flavor, op
Watermelon	• 'Allsweet' (95 days) oblong, 18 inches, fir, sweet, op • 'Black Diamond' (90 days) large oval to 50 pounds, tender, sweet, op • 'Charleston Gray' (85 days) cylindrical to 35 pounds, crisp, op • 'Crimson Sweet' (85 days) slightly elongated to 30 pounds, very sweet, op • 'Golden Midget' (70 days) golden skin, bright red flesh, very sweet, op • 'Moon and Stars' (100 days) sweet red flesh, op • 'Sugar Baby' (76 days) small, 10 pounds, good in cool regions, op

Vegetable Varieties for Container Growing:

Artichoke: 'Green Globe', 'Imperial Star', 'Violetto'; choose a pot 24″ deep.

Beans, Lima: 'Bush Baby', 'Bush Lima', 'Fordhook', 'Fordhook 242'; choose a container 12″ wide × 8-10″ deep.

Beans, Snap: 'Bush Blue Lake', 'Bush Romano', 'Contender', 'Provider', 'Rushmore', 'Tendercrop Stringless'; choose a container 1″ wide × 1″ deep.

Beets: 'Baby Canning', 'Burpee Golden', 'Little Ball', 'Red Ace Hybrid', 'Ruby Queen'; choose a container 6″ wide × 6-12″ deep.

Broccoli: 'Arcadia', 'Green Comet', 'Munchkin', 'Small Miracle'; choose a container 8-12″ wide × 20″ deep.

Brussels sprouts: 'Jade Cross', 'Oliver', 'Rubine'; choose a container 12″ wide × 18-20″ deep.

Cabbage: 'Baby Head', 'Morden Midget', 'Earliball', 'Fast Ball', 'Flash', 'Minicole'; choose a container 8-12″ wide × 1″ deep.

Carrots: 'Amini', 'Baby Fingers Nantes', 'Baby Spike', 'Best of the Bunch', 'Danver's Half Long', 'Early Horn', 'Gold Nugget', 'Kinko', 'Nantes Half Long', 'Little Finger', 'Round Baby', 'Short & Sweet', 'Thumbelina', 'Tiny Sweet'; choose a container 10″ wide × 10″ deep.

Cauliflower: 'Snow Cross', 'Violet Queen'; choose a container 18″ wide × 2-3″ deep.

Celery: 'Conquistador', 'Early Snowball', 'Redventure', 'Ventura'; choose a container 8-10″ wide × 10″ deep.

Chard: 'Bright Lights', 'Fordhook', 'Fordhook Giant', 'Lucullus', 'Ruby Red'; choose a container 12-18″ wide × 1″ deep.

Chinese cabbage: 'Bok Choy', 'Michihli', 'Wong Bok'; choose a container 1″ wide × 20″ deep.

Collards: any variety; choose a container 12″ deep.

Corn: 'F-M Cross', 'Golden Bantam', 'Kandy Korn', 'Luther Hill', 'Precocious'; choose a container 3″ wide × 1″ deep; 3 per container to insure pollination,

Cress: 'Curly Cress', 'Upland Cress'; choose a container 8″ wide × 6-8″ deep,

Cucumber: 'Burpee Hybrid II', 'Burpee Pickler', 'Bush Baby', 'Bush Champion', 'Bush Crop', 'Bush Pickle', 'Fanfare', 'Patio Pik', 'Pickalot', 'Picklebush', 'Pot Luck', 'Salad Bush', 'Spacemaster'. Pickling: 'Lucky Strike'; choose a container 1″ wide × 16″ deep.

Edible Flowers: bachelor's button, calendula, dianthus, marigold, nasturtium, sunflower, violas; choose a container 8-10″ deep.

Eggplant: 'Bambino', 'Black Beauty', 'Dusky', 'Easter Egg', 'Florida Market', 'Long Tom', 'Millionaire', 'Morden Midget'; choose a container 16″ deep × 18″ deep,

Endive, Escarole: 'Bianca Riccia', 'Nataly', 'Neos'; choose a container 8″ wide × 6-8″ deep.

Garlic: 'German Extra Hardy'; choose a container 10-12″ deep.

Herbs: basil, borage, chamomile, chives, cilantro, dill, fennel, hyssop, lemongrass, lemon verbena, marjoram, mint, oregano, rosemary, sage, savory, shiso, tarragon, thyme; choose a container 8-10″ deep.

Horseradish: 'Maliner Kren'; choose a container 5 gallons or larger.

Kale: any variety; choose a container 8″ wide × 8″ deep.

Kohlrabi: 'Grand Duke'; choose a container 12″ deep.

Leeks: 'King Richard', 'Lincoln'; choose a container 10-12″ deep.

Lettuce: 'Black-Seeded Simpson', 'Buttercrunch', 'Cos', 'Green Ice, Green Looseleaf', 'Little Gem', 'Mignonette', 'Oakleaf Red Sails', 'Red Fire', 'Red Looseleaf', 'Salad Bowl', 'Tom Thumb'; choose a container 8″ wide × 6-8″ deep,

Mustard: 'Green Wave', 'Osaka Purple', 'Red Giant'; choose a container 8-12″ deep,

Onion: Bunching types: 'Beltsville Bunching', 'Crystal Wad Pickling', 'Japanese Bunching', 'White Bunching', 'White Pearl'. Standards: 'Copra', 'Early Yellow Globe', 'South Redport'; choose a container 10-12″ deep,

Parsley: 'Dark Moss Curled', 'Paramount'; choose a container 8″ deep.

Peas: 'Burpee's Blue Bantam', 'Early Patio', 'Laxton's Progress', 'Little Marvel', 'Melting Sugar', 'Snowbird', 'Sugar Ann', 'Sugar Bon', 'Sugar Daddy', 'Sugar Mel', 'Sugar Rae'. Snow Peas: 'Little Sweetie'; choose a container 1″ deep × 1″ wide.

Peppers: All varieties: 'Canapé', 'Jalapeno', 'Jingle Bells', 'Keystone', 'Peppery Pot', 'Pimento', 'Resistant Giant', 'Red Cherry', 'Yolo Wonder'; choose a container 16″ deep × 18″ deep.

Potatoes: 'Charlotte', 'Cobbler', 'Irish', 'Epicure', 'Kennebec', 'Red Pontiac', 'Rose Finn Apple', 'Russian Banana', 'Yukon Gold'; choose a container at least 20 gallons.

Pumpkins: 'Autumn Gold Hybrid', 'Baby Boo', 'Baby Bear', 'Bushkin', 'Jack Be Little', 'Small Sugar', 'Sweetie Pie'; choose a container 5 gallon tub – 3″ deep.

Radicchio: 'Chioggia Red Preco', 'Fiero', 'Indigo', 'Pall de Fuoco Rossa'; Daikon; choose a container 8″ wide × 6-8″ deep.

Radish: 'Burpee White', 'Champion', 'Cherry Belle', 'Comet', 'Icicle', 'Early Scarlet Globe', 'French Breakfast', 'Red Boy', 'Sparkler'; choose a container 5″ wide × 4-6 inches deep.

Spinach: Any variety: 'American Viking', 'Long Standing Bloomsdale', 'Melody'; choose a container 6-8″ wide × 4-6″ deep.

Squash, summer: 'Crookneck', 'Early Yellow Summer', 'Eightball', 'Gold Rush', 'Goldberg', 'Park's Creamy Hybrid', 'Peter Pan Scalloping', 'Pic-N-Pic Hybrid', 'Richgreen Hybrid', 'Straightneck', 'Sunburst', 'Zephyr'; choose a container 24″ deep.

Squash, winter: 'Butterbush', 'Bush Acorn', 'Bush Delicata', 'Bush Table', 'Cream of the Crop', 'Table King', 'Queen Heart of Gold'; choose a container 24″ deep.

Strawberries: 'Alpine', 'Sarian', 'Tristar'; choose a container 8-12″ deep.

Sweet Potato: 'Beauregard', 'Georgia Jet', 'Vardaman'; choose a container 20 gallons or larger.

Tomatoes: 'Basket Pak', 'Container Choice', 'Gardener's Delight', 'Husky Gold', 'Husky Red', 'Lunch Box', 'Micro Tom', 'Patio VF', 'Pixie', 'Red Cherry', 'Rutgers', 'Saladette', 'Small Fry VFN', 'Spring Giant', 'Sundrop', 'Super Bush', 'Sweet 100', 'Tiny Tim', 'Toy Boy', 'Tumbling Tom', 'Yellow Canary', 'Yellow Pear', 'Whippersnapper'; Dwarf cultivars: 6-8″ wide × 1″ deep. Standard cultivars: choose a container 2″ wide × 2-3″ deep.

Turnips: 'Hakurei', 'Purple Top White Globe'; choose a container 10-12″ wide × 12″ deep.

Vegetable Varieties for Winter Growing:

Asian Greens: 'Green in Snow Mustard', 'Joi Choi', 'South China Earliest', 'Pak Choi', 'Lei Choi'

Beets: 'Detroit Dark Red', 'Early Wonder', 'Little Ball', 'Ruby King'

Broccoli: 'Bonanza Hybrid', 'Calabrese', 'Emperor', 'Purple Sprouting', 'Romanesco', 'White Sprouting'

Cabbage: 'Apex', 'Danish Roundhead', 'Perfect Ball', 'Safekeeper', 'Savory Ace', 'Superior Danish'

Carrots: 'Baby Spike', 'Minicor', 'Orbit', 'Parmex', 'Sparton Bonus'

Chinese Cabbage: 'Blues', 'MIchihli', 'Salad King', 'Two Season', 'Wintertime', 'Wong Bok'

Collards: 'Georgia Blue Stem', 'Vates'

Corn Salad: 'Verte de Cambrai'

Endive and Escarole: 'Cornet D'Anjou' (escarole), 'Fine Curled', 'Full Heat Batavian', 'Nuvol' (escarole), 'President', 'Salad King', 'Sugarloaf'

Kale: 'Blue Surf', 'Dwarf Blue-Curled Scotch', 'Vates', 'Winerbor'

Lettuce: 'Arctic King', 'Black-Seeded Simpson', 'Brune d'Hiver', 'Merveille des Quatres Saisons', 'North Pole', 'Red Montpelier', 'Red Sails', 'Salad Bowl', 'Sangria', 'Winter Density', 'Winter Marvel'

Mustard: 'Fordhook', 'Green Wave', 'Karashina', 'MIzuna', 'Tatsoi', 'Tendergreen'

Radicchio: 'Angusto', 'Early Treviso', 'Medusa', 'Red Verona'

Radishes: 'Champion', 'Cherry Belle', 'Early Scarlet Globe', 'Easter Egg', 'Round Black Spanish' 'Sparkler', 'Tokinashi' (daikon), 'White Icicle'

Spinach: 'Avon', 'Giant Nobel', 'Giant Winter', 'Melody Hybrid', 'Sputnik', 'Tyee', 'Virginia Blight Resistant', 'Winter Bloomsdale'

Turnips: 'Amber Globe', 'Gilfeather', 'Hybrid Tokyo Cross', 'Purple Top White Globe', 'White Egg'

Index

About the Author

Stephen Albert is a horticulturist, master gardener, and University of California instructor. His go-to encyclopedic reference books *The Vegetable Garden Grower's Guide* and *The Kitchen Garden Grower's Guide* are used by vegetable gardeners around the world. Every year more than 10 million vegetable gardeners visit his how-to vegetable garden website HarvesttoTable.com.

Made in the
USA
Monee, IL